STROLLING
PLAYER

STROLLING PLAYER

THE LIFE AND CAREER OF
ALBERT FINNEY

GABRIEL HERSHMAN

First published 2017

The History Press
The Mill, Brimscombe Port
Stroud, Gloucestershire, GL5 2QG
www.thehistorypress.co.uk

British Library Cataloguing in Publication Data.
A catalogue record for this book is available from the British Library.

ISBN 978 0 7509 7886 6

Typesetting and origination by The History Press
Printed in Great Britain by TJ International Ltd, Padstow, Cornwall

CONTENTS

ACKNOWLEDGEMENTS

'Is the Albert Hall named after Albert Finney?' asked my young son, David, one day as I showed him a pop-up book of London's attractions. Such a question, which came during a period of intensive foraging for Finney films and features, reminds an author that writing a book can be an isolating, even obsessional, undertaking. So it's as well to salute one's family for their patience and understanding. Thanks for your Finneybearance.

Albert Finney has always been publicity shy. When another biographer approached him in 1992, Finney replied that his past had a 'hard top on it' and that he had no wish to 'drill it up to go over it all again'. I was therefore not surprised when Finney's lawyer, Nigel Bennett, informed me that his client's attitude had not changed. Indeed, Finney has apparently resisted many offers to co-operate on an authorised biography or write an autobiography.

Perhaps, I hope, Finney would have co-operated if he had known that my primary purpose was to pay him tribute. Those like me, who were fortunate enough to have seen his outstanding stage performances in *The Biko Inquest*, *Orphans*, *Another Time* and *Art*, will never forget them. (And this, naturally, excludes Finney's triumphs in productions that predate me considerably.) These were also important theatrical events that demand to be commemorated, likewise his great screen work spanning more than five decades.

I am therefore particularly grateful to the following individuals for their assistance: Karen Allen, Peter Allis, Michael Attenborough, Graham Benson, Jon Blair, Nan Cibula-Jenkins, Jeannine Dominy, Mike Figgis, Julia Goodman, Bernard Hepton, Agnieszka Holland, Lyle Kessler, Suri Krishnamma, Annabel Leventon, Maureen Lipman, Peter Medak, Priscilla Morgan, John Quested, Kevin Rigdon, Ellen Ross, Robert Sallin, Carolyn Seymour, Jill Townsend and Amanda Waring as well as certain other people who preferred to remain anonymous.

I have also quoted from various newspaper articles and books that are cited in the text.

And, to answer your question, young David – of course it is!

INTRODUCTION

In the early sixties, Finney was the original 'angry young man', mentioned in dispatches alongside actors Richard Harris and Peter O'Toole and playwright John Osborne.

It all began with Arthur Seaton. His bitter, brawling, boozy factory worker from *Saturday Night and Sunday Morning* was seen as *the* anti-hero of the 'new wave'. So convincing was Finney as Arthur, with his beefy build and scowling good looks, that he could have carved out a lucrative career playing rebels. Yet he baulked at the association, resented pigeonholing and trod his own path.

By the nineties, Finney was playing, in quick succession, and equally convincingly, an ineffectual schoolteacher and a repressed gay virgin. The transformations came easily to a performer more deserving of the label 'natural-born actor' than most. Yet they also reveal how Finney perceives his craft. He was always a character man, a versatile dramatic actor who considered the stage his real home. Hence he rejected a golden handcuffs movie contract that would have tied him down.

Finney didn't want to be a conventional movie star or a 'symbol' of any kind. His role in *Tom Jones* bored him, he later said. But the film made him a dollar millionaire at 27 and gave him freedom to choose challenging roles. 'Life is more important than art,' he'd say, hence long sabbaticals, enabling self-appraisal and, yes, a bloody good time. He never felt guilty about having fun.

Yet Finney always worked hard when the mood took him, undertaking gruelling titanic parts at the National Theatre in the seventies – *Hamlet, Tamburlaine* and *Macbeth* – to sometimes grudging reviews. Some felt that classical verse was not his forte. Finney, however, brought a dynamism and masculine authority to these roles. He even played Shakespeare with a northern accent. In so doing, he paved the way for other regional actors to go to drama school and stand tall.

Finney could have succeeded Olivier as director of the National. Yet he wanted to be a strolling player. Hence he also spurned the popcorn-type movies, ones that would have given him even fatter pay cheques, for gritty character roles.

In the eighties, he gave several outstanding performances in *Under the Volcano*, *Miller's Crossing* and, especially, *The Dresser*. And Lyle Kessler's *Orphans* gave Finney his greatest stage performance – indeed one of the finest seen in the West End in recent years.

Finney received four Oscar nominations for leading actor in films: *Tom Jones*, *Murder on the Orient Express*, *The Dresser* and *Under the Volcano*. Capping these successes was a wonderful turn as a careworn, cynical lawyer opposite Julia Roberts in *Erin Brockovich* – and another Oscar nomination for best supporting actor. Yet Finney never cared much for awards. He has also declined a CBE and a knighthood, something that has endeared him to fans even more.

Finney, rather like Daniel Feeld in *Karaoke* screaming 'no biography!' on his deathbed, might not have wanted this book written. Yet Finney's story is a salutary lesson for today's 'stars' in how to keep balanced amid insane temptations. He has proved that it's possible to control your own destiny, preserve your integrity, resist typecasting *and* have a good time without veering into self-destruction. He's also a role model in terms of his behaviour on and off the set and his healthy disregard for others' opinions: 'You should never believe what people say about you – good, bad or indifferent.'

Finney might not have made it, as once seemed likely, into the list of Britain's most bankable stars. But he has created a gallery of unforgettable eccentrics: the psychotic writer in *Shoot the Moon*, the desperate drunk of *Under the Volcano*, the demented policeman of *The Playboys*, the bumptious tyrant of *A Rather English Marriage*, the likeable lush of *My Uncle Silas* and – crowning it all – his endearingly human portrayal of Churchill.

In writing Finney's biography, I was determined to analyse all his major performances. This, it seems to me, is a serious omission from other actors' biographies. They seldom address *acting*. It was especially necessary for a performer like Finney, who has tackled so many demanding transformational parts. I believe that the biographer's task is to analyse the work as well as the man. I have also tried to gauge the success, or otherwise, of the productions themselves. I hope that what follows does not read like some esoteric study of acting. This was far from my aim. But I do believe that biographies of serious artists must analyse art. And with such a relentlessly private individual as Finney – one whose life away from acting is guarded so jealously – my wish is that in some way the work illuminates the man. If this book reminds readers of some great classic productions and performances, featuring Finney and others, then that is a bonus.

The internet has opened up information to the public that was previously inaccessible. It's not my intention here to retread too many known facts but rather to delve beneath them. If, for example, you want to know the population of Salford in the fifties you can find that out fairly easily and I have skimmed over some information that would be readily available elsewhere. Also I have dwelt longer over great plays and films than I have over the mediocre or even dire.

I have been surprised – if only because I was unaware of it beforehand – by Finney's extraordinary personal popularity. Everyone speaks of Finney's warmth, charm, generosity, *joie de vivre* and genuine interest in people. On set, he'd always be early and dead letter perfect. He'd learn the names of all the crew and small-part players. Everyone – cleaners, drivers, bar staff, waitresses and extras – adored him. Indeed, so loved is Finney in the business that an authorised biography would likely have triggered a queue of colleagues seeking to pay tribute. It was clear from everything I have read, and from interviewees' comments, that the respect and affection for Finney is genuine. Merely for the sake of balance, and to avoid this becoming a hagiography that reads as though 'our Albert' is on the dais taking the salute from passing crowds, I have included the acerbic comments of the occasional critic, such as one-time collaborator Lindsay Anderson.

Finney's life is not only the story of a homework-hating bookie's son from Salford who became an international star. It is also about a versatile actor who played the game strictly on his own terms and managed to live as he chose. It is a story and a career that deserves to be reviewed.

Don't let the bastards grind you down!

PROLOGUE

Summer 1965, Chichester. Finney is appearing in several National Theatre productions, including *Much Ado about Nothing*, *Black Comedy* and *Anderson's Last Goodnight*. Canadian actor William B. Davis, now most famous as 'The Smoking Man', a regular fixture on the TV series *The X-Files*, is also in the company.

One night Finney invited Davis and his wife to dinner at Finney's rented house near Chichester. Davis tells the story:

> Rather than give us directions he suggested we follow his car in ours. His car was a chauffeur-driven Rolls-Royce – his insurance would not allow him to drive himself, not that he was a bad driver, he was too valuable an asset – while our car was a 13-year-old Aston Martin DB2 that might or might not last the short trip. When we had arrived the four of us had drinks in the living room – he had his current lady friend with him – before moving to the dining room table which was set for six. Before I could make a fool of myself by asking if there were more guests coming, the four of us were joined at the table by the chauffeur and the cook. The son of a bookie, Albert had not let his money betray his class.[1]

Spring 1986, London. Albert Finney, it is well known, likes to have dinner. Oh yes! It's the night after the enormously successful premiere of Lyle Kessler's new play *Orphans* in which Finney is playing the lead. Sixty people, actors, technicians, cleaners, box office cashiers and marketing assistants – indeed all the employees at London's Hampstead Theatre – pile into a nearby Greek restaurant. The demand is so great that any extra hands are welcome. In the background, a red-faced figure, drenched in sweat and wearing an apron, is bringing plates in from the kitchen and helping to serve the diners. It's our four-time Oscar nominee making sure that everything runs smoothly. This is no act from one of the finest practitioners in the business. Neither is it Finney picking up some tips in preparation for a role. It was behaviour that ran through his whole life. It's just Albert being Albert. In the words of Hampstead Theatre's (then) artistic director, Michael Attenborough, 'He democratised every space he went into.'[2]

The Hampstead Theatre, nestled inconspicuously by Swiss Cottage underground station, was a portable, even quaint, cubbyhole. In those days you went in, arriving straight into the reception and bar, and a few steps took you to an intimate little auditorium that accommodated fewer than 200 bottoms. The foyer housed memorabilia and souvenirs from past productions. A scattering of famous names apart, it was hardly the place you'd expect to find an international star, someone once billed as the successor to Olivier.

I walked up from Regent's Park, excited at the prospect of seeing one of my favourite actors so close to home. As I reached the theatre there was more activity than usual. The box office looked besieged. Suddenly a posh-looking car pulled up outside. A burly middle-aged man, clad in a suit, staggered out and started to stride or, rather, totter, up the pathway towards the back of the building. He clearly knew where he was going but he seemed so pissed I wondered if he would make it. I looked at the man more closely. Oh my God! It's Finney!! And he's drunk before a performance. Repeat – drunk. Triple exclamation mark.

I enter the theatre with trepidation. *Orphans* opens with Finney – as gangster/kidnap victim Harold – drunkenly recounting stories from his childhood. It was just as well that Finney was playing a drunk, I thought. So no one will notice that he really is out of it! I swear I could almost smell the booze on him from where I sat near the front row. It wasn't that his speech was slurred as such. It was more the look of wide-eyed hysteria on his face as he told the kids about his time in the orphanage.

The next scene … it's morning in the house in Philadelphia. Finney is gagged. He convinces Kevin Anderson, playing Phillip, to remove it. Suddenly Harold – alias Finney – is obviously, totally, completely sober. How is this possible? The man I had seen just a few minutes earlier, both outside the theatre and even in the early scenes, was paralytic. How could he sober up? Suddenly it all fell into place. I'd just been taken in by one of the greatest actors in the world … and something of a prankster.

FINDING HIS VOICE

I thought people from my background didn't become actors. I thought actors were bred in special places – a stud farm in Mayfair.

Albert Finney.

When Finney celebrated his 9th birthday, his home city of Salford, within the metropolitan borough of Manchester, was ablaze with bonfires and fireworks. The festivities were not to commemorate his birthday. Even Finney was not so precocious as to be feted at the age of 9 – although given his subsequent achievements nothing would surprise me! It was, of course, to mark VE Day, the end of the Second World War, 8 May 1945, which fell the day before his birthday.

Finney recalled:

I've always found light magical and still find fireworks magical because it seems to me that in many ways they're a bit like lives, about existence because the energy takes it somewhere and then it's gone. I think in some ways our lives are like that. There's hopefully a burst of something or an ascent in some way and, then, it's over. That had a big effect on my life.

Such a major event would have had a major impact on a young boy. And of course, so would the image of Churchill – whom Finney would portray so memorably more than half a century later – giving the crowds in London a victory salute. For Finney, the war years in Salford were sometimes scary and bleak and the blaze of colour that day proved unforgettable.

Yet Finney, unlike many other stars from the provinces, never lamented those days. He has said he always viewed his childhood in Salford with great affection. And Finney is very much a Salford lad, *not* a Mancunian, a distinction he and other Salfordians are always keen to stress.

Perhaps the most famous Old Salfordian was the painter L.S. Lowry (1887–1976), who lived and worked in Pendlebury for over forty years. Others include playwright Shelagh Delaney[1] who wrote *A Taste of Honey* and the screenplay for Finney's later film *Charlie Bubbles*. Actors Ben Kingsley and Robert Powell[2] were also born in the area, as was music hall star Pat Kirkwood (1921–2007).

Seven decades have passed since Finney's childhood. But he still counts several of his schoolmates – including artist Harold Riley and Derek Jackson – among his friends today. And he always loves going back. 'It's just part of you. It's in the blood really,' he'd say. Speaking in 1977, on one of his many visits home, he said his bond with Salford was still strong:

> I didn't feel a sense that I wanted to get away from Salford at all. And I've never felt that I've got away. I've never got waylaid in my profession or lost in it because I've felt very connected to the area … there's something very practical and realistic about living in the area which is of great value.

The only reason he didn't live in Salford at that time, said Finney, was that his work dictated that he spent more time in London.

Albert Finney was born on 9 May 1936, the son of Albert and Alice Finney (née Hobson). His two elder sisters, Marie and Rose, were ten and five years older than him, respectively. The family home was at 53 Romney Street, Pendleton, a two-up, two-down red-bricked terraced house in an insalubrious, highly industrialised area about 2 miles from Manchester city centre.

Albert's father was a bookmaker. Although this was not, strictly speaking, legal, it was a nonetheless tolerated profession. Finney always referred to him as a 'commission agent'. Before betting was officially made legal at the turn of the sixties, bets and transactions were made in someone's house.

It would be safe to assume that Albert Senior was never really short of money. 'But there is a slight false illusion about bookmakers,' Finney said in 1962. 'They're not all tremendously wealthy and own great yachts … which my father doesn't do.' But the excitement of betting intoxicated Finney. Later, he even installed a 'blower' – a phone link with betting information and racing commentaries – at his home.

His father's occupation was a constant theme for interviewers and tabloid hacks. It was almost as though it had some unsavoury connotation. He'd joke that even as a child he, Albert Junior, had acquired the sobriquet of 'Honest Albert'. And Finney, although careful in major business dealings, has always been quick to put his hand in his pocket throughout his life.

The Finney home was damaged by German bombs in 1941 while 5-year-old Albert lay in an air-raid shelter. The family then moved to 5 Gore Crescent, Weaste, a semi-detached house with a garden in an altogether more upmarket part of Salford. Today, the street looks much as it probably did back in 1941. Albert would watch rugby league at the Willows ground. He went to Manchester United's Old Trafford Stadium to see Salford Schoolboys play and became a lifelong United fan.

Finney later described his background to John Freeman, 'I suppose [it was] a lower middle-class home. We were always comfortable … I had a marvellous childhood. I was always very happy. I remember it with great joy.' Finney attended Tootal Drive Primary School. By the age of 9 he was appearing in school plays, starring in such memorable productions as *Belle the Cat*, in which he played the Mayor of Ratville. The young Albert also appeared in puppet shows. 'I didn't do the puppets, I did the voices – and I discovered I had an ability to mimic rather well,' he later recalled. Even at the age of 5, Finney once told Melvyn Bragg, he had developed a gift for mimicry – imitating his teacher as he arrived home for tea.

When he was just 10, Alice even took Albert to a BBC audition in Manchester. In 1947, Albert passed the 11-plus exam[3] to attend Salford Grammar School, the school now known as Buile Hill High School. Yet he was too lazy to do well academically:

I was in the top grade when I went to the grammar school but that didn't last because I wouldn't work. I hated homework. I thought it was an imposition on my childhood. I didn't like school very much and wasn't particularly interested. Much of my energy was spent trying to avoid schoolwork rather than doing it. And I also found myself doing school plays.

At 16, Albert took the minimum of five subjects and failed all but geography. He only passed geography because many of the questions were about Australia, where England's cricket and rugby teams often competed. He was kept back to repeat the classes. The next year he failed them again – and physics as well! In the meantime he had played Henry IV and Falstaff in school plays as well as Emperor Jones in the Eugene O'Neill play of the same name.

His other main interest at school seemed to be sport. Albert proved a fine athlete, an excellent rugby player and cricketer. And Finney loved going to the cinema. A particular favourite, he recalled, was the Stanley Donen classic *On the Town* with Frank Sinatra and Gene Kelly. 'I saw it four times in three days. I really wanted to believe you could sing in the streets of New York and not be told to keep off the grass.'

Though he failed all but one of his O level exams two years running, the talent Finney had shown acting in school plays caused headmaster Eric Simm to recommend he go to RADA. 'There was no burning ambition to be an actor,' Finney recalled. 'I thought, this is fine, I enjoy it.' But Finney later credited Simm with helping him to find his calling.[4]

So, warned by his father that 'if anyone stops you on the street, say no', 17-year-old Albert Finney left home for London. RADA,[5] in London's Bloomsbury, is the country's most acclaimed drama school, so much so that even the least 'arty' of folk have heard of it. Recently, there has been a trend to address this venerable institution by its more (technically) correct title of *the* RADA to preserve its distinction. Not all RADA's intake become stars. Yet a fair number become, if not stars, then at least minor household names. Once you gain a place you may not be guaranteed success, but you will be sufficiently respected to be considered a lifelong 'luvvie'.

The year 1953, however, was Coronation year and the Finneys had trouble finding a room in London as Albert prepared for his audition. Mr Finney was leafing through a guidebook when he stumbled on a hotel called the Dorchester. They reckoned they could just about afford a few days there. Mrs Finney, who had come up with £37 – £10 of that in shillings rolled up in paper – sent Albert to ask what the rooms cost. It was £6.75 a night. So for dinner they sat in the lounge making do with crisps and nuts. By the third night the waiters had cottoned on and kept refilling the bowls for them. The Dorchester was, and still is, one of the grandest hotels in London, and was a home from home for the likes of Burton and Taylor. Two decades later, Finney, who liked to have dinner there, even moved in for a time when his second marriage to Anouk Aimée failed.

When Finney did his audition he managed to land the Lawrence Scholarship, one of a handful offered by RADA, which was then under the stewardship of Sir Kenneth Barnes. Two years into Finney's course Sir Kenneth was succeeded by John Fernald. The aspiring actor who walked through the door at Bloomsbury was an ungainly 17-year-old with a broad Salford accent and a crew cut, emulating, he recalled, the American tennis player Vic Seixas, who had won Wimbledon that year. Most of the students at RADA were older than Finney, some by several years; many had already completed their national service.

No group of youngsters feels more insecure than first-day drama students. It's not like freshers at university, preparing to knuckle down to a three-year English degree. For them it's merely their knowledge under scrutiny. Acting, on the other hand, is uniquely holistic. You as a person are indivisible from your skill. Everything about you – your voice, face, posture, poise, presence, authority, forcefulness and sensitivity – is fair target. It's no wonder that actors take rejection personally.

So we have young Albert Finney, just 17, away from home for the first time, in an atmosphere where acting was no longer just something to amuse himself and avoid homework but something requiring self-discipline and application. Finney had been a bit work-shy up to now, and young men tend to like playing around. If acting is just a way to attract attention and impress a few girls, it's fun; but now he had to learn his craft seriously.

Finney's time there was a vintage one. Some writers tend to overstate the star intake. Richard Harris was *not* at RADA, contrary to the opinion of certain biographers. But some of the greatest stars of British cinema of the sixties were. Peter O'Toole, four years older, was in the same class as Finney throughout and became a lifelong friend. He was the only one to outgun Finney in the fame stakes. O'Toole has said of this period:

> Harris and Burton and Finney and all that mob, all my friends, we were disaffected by authority. There were too many people around with badges, and we were all determined to take life by the scruff of the bloody neck and live it … There was just this tremendous release of energy, this explosion of inhibited talent.

Frank Finlay, a decade older than Finney, and later a versatile Shakespearean actor and a well-known face on television, was also in the same class. So was Alan Bates, another 'angry young man' associated with the new wave, a performer of great range and sensitivity. John Stride was also there, a likeable face on the box and supporting player in films, with a personality similar to Finney: charming, forceful, authoritative but friendly (so much so that when I saw Stride as Alun Weaver in Kingsley Amis's *The Old Devils*, I thought it could have been a great part for Finney). Roy Kinnear was another student, usually confined to playing, by his own admission, 'short, fat, sweaty types', but a gifted comic actor of rare timing.

RADA students Ronald Fraser and James Villiers, although not exact contemporaries of Finney, became legends in their own lunchtime. Both were particularly friendly with O'Toole and formed a trio known for their carousing. Villiers carved out a little niche for himself as upper-class buffoons. He was one of the first to call other actors 'luvvie'. So perhaps we can blame him for the over-effusiveness that later became so lampooned.

Among Finney's other contemporaries, John Vernon played villains in *Point Blank* and *Brannigan*. Derren Nesbitt, who arrived in 1955, often stole films from under leading men's noses, usually as a sadist. (Nesbitt also won the coveted Kendal and Forbes-Robertson Shakespearean awards.) James Booth, most famous for playing Hookie in *Zulu*, was also there and should have had a glitzier career; he ended up writing screenplays and taking bit parts.

Peter Bowles was a friend of Finney's who became a household name on British TV in *To the Manor Born*. Richard Briers[6] also became better known on the small screen, especially in *The Good Life*. He had a gentle, soothing, lightly pitched upper-class bark, vaguely reminiscent of his cousin Terry-Thomas. Briers was also close to O'Toole; in old age they could be seen helping each other up the stairs of the Garrick.

Bryan Pringle,[7] who looked at least ten years older than Finney when he appeared with him in *Saturday Night and Sunday Morning*, was also there, as were distinguished stage actors Brian Bedford, Keith Baxter and Gary Raymond. Even Ronald Allen, forever known as the suave David Hunter in the long-running British soap *Crossroads*, hit pay dirt. So did Nicholas Smith, a regular on the amusing comedy series *Are You Being Served?* Patrick Newell was another familiar face, in particular as roly-poly 'mother' in *The Avengers*.

Among the ladies were Virginia Maskell, who died in tragic circumstances in 1968,[8] Gillian Martell, Valerie Singleton and Rosemary Leach. Fewer of the actresses became household names. Another student, Roy Maxwell, also from Salford Grammar School, believes some of them weren't especially serious anyway: 'Many of the younger Roedean College type females had no intention of going into the professional theatre but mummy and daddy thought they would benefit from the experience of RADA as a finishing school.'[9] He then adds, somewhat mischievously, that 'a fair number of them got a lot more experience than they had bargained for'. By 1955, however, some more famous ladies were making their entrance, notably Diana Rigg, Glenda Jackson and Siân Phillips and, the following year, Susannah York.

Such a great crop of actors fostered a competitive spirit. '[This] was quite good training, although not really what drama schools are meant to be about,' Alan Bates said. 'It got you quite used to the rat race of trying to get into the public show and trying to get jobs. I was the only one who was unemployed afterwards.'[10]

Finney, by his own account, started tentatively at RADA (Brian Bedford, in particular, recalled Finney's 'very flat north country accent'), yet he relished his independence, being let loose in London and responsible for himself. He had a fiver in his pocket and soon several girls were vying for his attention; they outnumbered boys by two to one.

In his first term, Finney said he felt 'very unsophisticated, ungainly and clumsy and a bit uncouth'. Although he'd done plays at school, and been a keen cinemagoer, the nuts and bolt of stagecraft proved a hard grind. But he was always a keen observer. He later remembered being directed by an old Shakespearean actor named Ernest Milton. Finney recalled seeing Milton chase a tram, somewhat breathlessly, calling out, 'Stop! Stop! You're killing a genius!' (Finney later used this incident for the famous train-stopping scene in *The Dresser*.)

It was only later in the first year that Finney started to feel comfortable:

In my third term it suddenly clicked, thanks to Wilfred Walter who was direct-ing *Twelfth Night*. I was playing Toby Belch and when I asked him where I should stand he told me to stand wherever I liked as long as I felt relaxed. He didn't mind untidy productions as long as his students were exploring the stage for themselves, and that gave me a tremendous release, a sense of being myself on the stage … you tend to be told how many steps to take by some of the teachers there. You'd got to control your breathing and use the pitch of your voice. But at the beginning of the third term it changed. I remember thinking almost deliberately. 'I'm not going to go on at rehearsals saying the rest of the class is laughing at me. I'm going to say they're learning from me.' It was almost as deliberate a conceit as that. I realised that I had to take a positive step from feeling self-conscious with my classmates.[11]

By the end of the first year Finney was attracting positive attention. Peter O'Toole thought that Finney was special. He noted that his friend 'buzzed with a confident energy' when playing a scene from *As You Like It*.

Richard Briers described Finney and O'Toole as the undisputed stars of the intake. 'I was in the same class with Peter O'Toole and Albert Finney, who didn't need any lessons at all. I was painstakingly slow in my progress in comparison with them and as a result was always trying too hard,' he recalled.

Elizabeth Rees-Williams, who later married Richard Harris, said, 'when Peter or Albie were doing anything, we'd all go and watch', and theatre director William Gaskill recalled that Finney and O'Toole had made a little name for themselves in the theatre world long before they graduated. But maybe some of this is with the benefit of hindsight, certainly John Stride and, later, Derren Nesbitt, received just as much recognition.

Perhaps we are not only talking of star quality and raw talent, although these were striking in both O'Toole and Finney, but also of sheer confidence, the kind of self-belief that says not only 'I know where I'm going' but 'I'm going to make sure I'm noticed'. This was the key to Finney's success.

And here the person best placed to observe Finney was his friend Peter Bowles with whom he shared a one-bedroom flat in London's Hornsey Rise. There were three beds – one double, one single and a single folding one, Bowles recalled. 'The agreement was that should either of us have a girl with us for the night, then that person would have the double bed and the other would unfold the zedbed and sleep in the kitchen.' Bowles appreciated Finney's no-nonsense attitude. One night they were discussing how to tackle *Macbeth*. Bowles started talking about motivation and demeanour:

> 'How would you approach it, Albert?' I asked.
> 'I'd learn the fucking lines and walk on,' said Finney.
> That's confidence – and from a boy of 18. You can't beat it.

The lesson, concluded Bowles, was simple: 'I realised many years later, after I'd acquired a certain amount of it, that confidence is almost 80 per cent of what's needed for star quality, plus a bit of talent, of course.'[12]

Finney's nonconformity showed in another incident recounted by Bowles:

> My first experience of television casting was, in fact, at RADA … We had been asked by the Principal to come to RADA on this particular day in our 'best' clothes, with hair brushed and shoes shining, because the bosses of a new independent television company (Rediffusion, I think) were coming to cast the first closed-circuit TV play [ITV had not started at this time]. I think they may have used students from other drama schools, but we would play the leading parts; after all, we were the Royal Academy of Dramatic Arts.
>
> 'Bollocks,' said Albert that morning as he put on his usual holed jumper. 'Fuck 'em,' as he ran his fingers through his tousled hair. Albert never washed his hair as he believed nature's oils cleaned it 'like a dog's', he said. Albert still has a magnificent head of thick hair, whilst my once magnificent head of thick, wavy, well-washed hair has all but disappeared! I got togged up as best I could, as I was on that best behaviour scholarship. No 'bollocks' or 'fuck 'ems' allowed.
>
> The bosses of the new TV company, who all seemed to be ex-Royal navy commanders, were to watch us enact scenes from *As You Like It* and I was playing Jaques. Poor Albert was only playing 'a forester'. No wonder he said 'fuck 'em,' I thought. The scenes were to be played in a large rehearsal room and the distinguished guests sat on a raised stage at one end of the room.
>
> The scenes ended.
>
> 'Gather round, boys and girls,' said the Principal. 'Sit cross-legged here in front of our guests whilst they decide who they would like to cast in their play.'
>
> It was to be *She Stoops to Conquer*. We were all very excited and I knew I had done the 'All the world's a stage' speech rather well.
>
> 'We would like to have that boy for a start,' said one of the men, pointing towards a figure who had not joined us cross-legged, but had gone into a corner at the far end of the room, and was standing in the position of a dunce with his back towards us.

'Albert, come here at once. What are you playing at?'

'No, leave him where he is,' said the ex-Naval Commander. 'We want him to play the lead.'

I didn't get a part of any kind. Well, that's the mystique of star quality in an 18-year-old young man, who I think only had one line.

Bowles was a lifelong friend. And Finney was always generous to his pals. When Peter married in April 1961, Finney and Jimmy Villiers were the ushers. (Bryan Pringle was best man.) Finney gave Bowles a cheque for £250, equivalent to about £3,500 today. Bowles later said it served him in good stead because he had several months' unemployment after his marriage. Finney, who was starring in *Billy Liar* at the time, arrived late to the wedding. The reception proved so enjoyable that Finney decided to feign illness and cancel his matinee, giving his understudy Trevor Bannister, later famous for *Are You Being Served?*, his break.

RADA students learnt movement, fencing and ballet but voice control and diction were pivotal. Staff could be carping. Keith Baxter recalled being told by voice teacher Mary Duff that his voice was 'ugly' and that he sounded 'as if your mother dug coal with her fingernails'. Finney later told Roy Maxwell that the academy seemed to employ a deliberate 'good cop, bad cop routine', almost operating teachers alternately.

The students' general impression, however, was that the academy had not moved on. Brian Bedford recalled:

We felt that RADA was a very old-fashioned organisation. It was tired and out of sync with the times. Maybe theatre was out of sync with the times. It wasn't until Osborne wrote *Look Back in Anger* that working-class people were viewed as interesting theatrical subjects. And at the school we were taught that if we wanted to play leading men, we had to be six feet tall, aristocratic-looking and speak with an Oxford accent!

Yet Bedford also remembered that he and his fellow students were surprisingly self-assured. '[We were] all hell-bent on having the best possible time. We had this amazing confidence and I have no idea where it came from.'[13]

Gillian Martell noticed a brazen attitude from Finney – not arrogance as such, but an imposing swagger. 'He did that great moody thing and would wander around with his head down. I remember asking him about it and he explained, "I go downstage with my head down, then I look up and give the audience my eyes."'

That sounds rather Brandoesque. And indeed it would have been surprising if Dean and Brando were not role models for the students. Brian Bedford recalled seeing *On the Waterfront* several times with Finney. 'To this day I still see the influence that Brando had on Albert in every performance,' he said.

Finney also charmed the ladies. Yet much of it was just larking around. Valerie Singleton remembered a fun evening with Finney at a party in Chelsea. 'He was quite boisterous but we didn't make love,' she recalled. 'We just kissed passionately while rolling from side to side. We were on a pull-down sofa bed worryingly close to a fire, and I remember fearing that we might be set alight.' (Strangely, or perhaps not given the passage of time, although Singleton later lived near Finney in Chelsea and they sometimes met in the newsagents, Finney would always introduce himself. He had clearly forgotten about the incident.)[14] A bit of a lad, our Albert.

He was developing a reputation as a maverick, someone who could buck the system. Back then, all Brits did two years' national service (the draft ended in 1960). All Finney's contemporaries were conscripted; but not Albert. Rumour had it that he cleverly dodged it by feigning madness. It was probably an easy feat for someone of his talent. Apparently, he took to sitting on one of the rafters in a Nissen hut. He refused to eat anything and from time to time he fainted. Finney was duly discharged, avoiding the nuisance of a two-year stint away from the important things in life, like drinking and chasing girls, as well as acting.

It was a time of a great many parties. While at RADA, Olivelli's Italianate café was a favourite, along with a local pub called the Gower Arms. Finney, later in life, acquired a reputation for enjoying what Brits call a 'booze-up'. And so he did. But attempts to bracket Finney as a hellraiser, in the O'Toole/Harris vein, won't wash. He was never as self-destructive. I can find no record of him throwing books at teachers or climbing down chimneys, let alone thumping people. It seems that Finney was a drinker, yes, but when he got drunk he did so in a civilised fashion.

Another key difference between Finney and O'Toole was in accent. O'Toole eradicated any trace of a regional background whereas Finney's slightly flat northern accent stayed. It was to become his trademark. Clifford Turner, who later wrote a classic book on voice, taught Finney, O'Toole and Bates. Peter Bowles later recalled that his Nottinghamshire accent was knocked out of him at RADA. 'When I came out, I didn't know who I was,' he says. 'That, if anything, hampered my acting.'

Frank Finlay also recalled the irony of having to eradicate his local accent:

It was still the time when the reps were doing *Who's for Tennis?* plays. So we spent days losing our north country accents. Yet within two years of my leaving they had a full-time voice coach teaching the students how to sound as if they came from up north.[15]

Meanwhile, Finney's reputation was permeating around Bloomsbury. A young man from Hull named Tom Courtenay was studying English at University College London (UCL). Courtenay was interested in acting. He realised that UCL was near enough to RADA to keep an eye on the actors' exploits. He also performed with the dramatics society. One evening, a RADA student came to see Courtenay in what he described as an 'awful play', *The Duchess of Malfi*:

> Our director, Anita, had a friend who was a RADA student, name of Bill, who came to see her production. He was tall, handsome and laid back, with a soft Scottish accent, and he had a lot of authority because he didn't gush. I was very pleased when he told me I would have no difficulty getting into RADA, even though he thought there would be plenty for the teachers to work on. I didn't in the least mind being raw material. No point in going there otherwise. He went on: 'There's a wonderful boy at RADA at the moment. He's very charismatic. Strangely enough, you have something in common with him. You're not at all like him temperamentally and I can't really say why you remind me of him. But you do. I suppose you could be his younger brother.' Intrigued, I asked his name.
> 'Finney. Albert Finney.'[16]

In February 1956, Finney appeared at the Vanbrugh Theatre in the first of a series of plays to be staged by RADA students as part of their training for professional productions. Fernald chose Ian Dallas's *The Face of Love*, a modern-dress version of *Troilus and Cressida*. Finney played Troilus, Susan Westerby was Cressida, Peter Bowles was Hector and Keith Baxter was Philo. *The Times* said:

> Mr Albert Finney and Miss Susan Westerby handle the parting of the lovers with a sincerity which draws out almost all that there is to be drawn from a beautifully written scene. Her voice control is surest in the softer passages, but Mr Finney is able to let himself go and still keep the tension unbroken.

Kenneth Tynan, then *the* up-and-coming theatre critic, exalted Finney, writing in the *Observer* that he was a 'smouldering young Spencer Tracy ... an actor who will soon disturb the dreams of Messrs. Burton and Scofield'.

Finney had one final commitment before he left. RADA staged a final, show-piece production, a matinee, before agents, friends, families, critics and judges.[17] Finney and his peers gave their show at Her Majesty's Theatre on 27 March 1956. Sitting in judgement were the playwright Clemence Dane and actors Margaret Leighton, Laurence Naismith and Eric Portman.

Students performed excerpts from various plays. Finney, as Petruchio, did scenes from *The Taming of the Shrew* opposite Liz Yeeles. Finney and Peter Bowles also appeared as longshore men in Eugene O'Neill's *The Long Voyage Home*, in which Keith Baxter had the lead as a Swedish sailor. Students then reassembled at RADA to be told what prizes, if any, they had won.

Gillian Martell won the gold medal. Richard Briers was awarded the silver medal for what was described as an excellent comic performance in Moliere's *Sganarelle* and Chekhov's *The Proposal*. Briers also won the prize for best diction. Keith Baxter was awarded the bronze. Finney won the Emile Littler Award, for the student who had shown outstanding talent and aptitude for the professional theatre, for which he was given the princely sum of 25 guineas.

While still at RADA, Finney and Peter Bowles received letters from Philip Pearman at the Musical Corporation of America (MCA) inviting them to an interview at the talent agency's offices in Piccadilly. Bowles tells what happened when the agent addressed Finney:

> 'My dear,' said Mr Pearman, the nicest of men. 'First think for a moment of the poster: "Albert Finney as Hamlet." It sounds as though a footballer is trying his foot at acting.' [There was a famous footballer named Tom Finney playing at the time.] 'I really think you ought to change your name, Albert,' he said.

Finney, who nevertheless became one of Pearman's clients, did no such thing. Later, Sam Spiegel, producer of *Lawrence of Arabia*, would urge the same. No way.

By the time of *The Face of Love*, Finney had already been wooed by Binkie Beaumont from London theatrical management company H.M. Tennent as well as by the Rank Organisation, the latter offering him a seven-year contract starting at £1,500 a year, rising to £10,000. What did Finney do? Why, he rejected both, in favour of £10 a week at a repertory company where he could perfect his craft. As always, Finney went his own way.

What did Finney want from acting? We have already noted his confidence. Did that mean he wanted to be a big star? Both he and O'Toole had the purpose and commitment necessary to be stars. Finney also had a huge advantage over his peers; he simply loved acting. Several years later, after the release of *Saturday Night and Sunday Morning*, Finney was still disclaiming ambition:

> I don't give a damn whether I'm a star or not. It's splendid to have money because then you needn't think about it, and that's a great advantage. But I just want to have a go … to act, and to mean what I say, whether it's said jokingly or seriously. If I should incidentally become a star – well, all right, I'll be a star as well.[18]

Although unemployment among actors is commonplace, most RADA gradu-
ates found work when they left, thanks to Britain's many repertory companies.
O'Toole went to the Bristol Old Vic and Finney headed to the famous
Birmingham Rep, whose alumni included Laurence Olivier, Ralph Richardson,
Peggy Ashcroft, Stewart Granger, Paul Scofield, Cedric Hardwicke and Edith
Evans. It was at the Rep that Finney, still only 20, first played big parts. The
young Finney would give performances that theatregoers still talk about sixty
years later.

THE YOUNG GREAT WHITE HOPE

And there was this one young man who came, and he was completely different from anybody else.

Pamela Howard.

Pamela Howard worked as a scenographer at Birmingham Rep. She said Finney was the first person she had met who wore jeans and a T-shirt and said 'fuck'. She also noted that you couldn't take your eyes off him even when he was a spear carrier. That's star quality.

Bernard Hepton, later the director of Birmingham Rep, became the pivotal figure in Finney's professional life. You wouldn't notice Hepton in a crowd. He was like the late Fulton Mackay, an incisive player able to get under a character's skin – an actor of unobtrusive brilliance. On-screen he is best known for playing Albert Foiret, the brave and austere hero of *Secret Army*, the series mercilessly parodied years later in *'Allo 'Allo!* Hepton was ideal for the role. He always looked like he harboured a secret. He usually played second fiddle to the leading man, but what a tune he struck, whether as a cowardly villain in *Get Carter* or one of the more sensitive-looking ne'er-do-wells in Kingsley Amis's *The Old Devils*.

Hepton had arrived at Birmingham in 1952 to take minor parts in *Henry VI Part III*. He was overjoyed:

I went and did these two little parts and I thought, 'I'm here at last, and it is wonderful.' It was a lovely little theatre. They called it 'the little brown box' in those days, and all the upholstery was brown leatherette. It was just delightful.

Such is the fame of Birmingham Rep – a building then based in Station Street, one now occupied by amateur companies – that it attracts visitors from all over the world who just want to savour the atmosphere. Sir Barry Jackson was the wealthy impresario behind Birmingham Rep. He used the fortune inherited from his father's provisions firm to build a 440-seat auditorium, which opened officially in 1913. It was under Jackson's stewardship that it acquired a reputation as a regional cultural capital, producing plays by Aristophanes, Shakespeare, Jonson, Wycherley, Goldsmith, Shaw and Schnitzler. It was a place where actors could hone their craft.

Professor Claire Cochrane, senior drama lecturer at Worcester University, has described Sir Barry as one of the most important theatrical entrepreneurs of the thirties and forties: 'He was a shy man, and people described him as the quintessential English gentleman. He was highly educated, spoke several languages and he was very, very loyal to the avant-garde theatre.'

Jackson was also gay – hardly worth mentioning now, yet he had to be discreet about his conduct at a time when homosexuality was illegal. He, rather like Charles Laughton and Lindsay Anderson, probably had an eye for young male beauty that passed his way. Hepton offers his own take on Sir Barry:

> It was his theatre. He built it himself out of his own pocket and it was his pride and joy. He was a gentleman, he was a scholar and he was a very talented man. I had never met anyone like him. To meet him, he was like a ramrod, very, very straight and he was always smoking cigarettes through these extraordinary holders that he used to make out of paper himself … he used to come to the theatre probably once a week, twice a month, not very often, but he was the reason why we were all there.

Hepton remembers that the theatre was:

> Very sparse … the bottom foyer was not decorated at all, it was a place of work. I went back to unveil plaques to Sir Barry, and I went into the theatre, the first time I had walked in that place for an awful long time, and it was like a palace! There was carpet on the floor, concealed lighting, there was a bar. I thought, 'Good Lord, if it had only been like this!' But it wouldn't have been the same.

Sir Barry might have been in overall charge, yet he gave his directors total autonomy. He never addressed actors about their performance. Hepton recalls Sir Barry passing a note to another director producing a play about Lincoln.

Hepton was playing a southern gentleman. 'Trousers on Hepton are too short!' said the note.

The company, said Hepton, was very close:

> We were all great, great friends and I've never known a company like that either before or since. That all traces back to Sir Barry and the great influence of this man. It is very hard to actually pin it down, what his influence was, but it was there and it was actually in the theatre.

Birmingham Rep had one distinct advantage over other similar companies; it was a monthly rep. Actor Paul Williamson said:

> You had plenty of time to rehearse properly, to take a play apart and put it back together again. Whereas with weekly rep you just got the bloody thing on, in fortnightly rep sometimes you fell between the two stools because you just had time to take the play apart but not time to put it together again. Monthly rep was a luxury.

It was Hepton's predecessor as director of productions, Douglas Seale, who had actually accepted Hepton into the company on Fernald's recommendation. Hepton took over in 1957, although Seale continued to oversee the occasional play. And Hepton directed Finney's first role in *Julius Caesar*. Birmingham Rep had a policy of putting on new plays alongside the classics. So Hepton was busy not only staging and directing plays but reading fresh material.

When Finney reached Birmingham, the rest of the company, which included Geoffrey Bayldon, were intrigued to see the newcomer whom Tynan had heralded. It was an inauspicious entrance. Finney was an hour late, looking distinctly nervous and wearing an old duffel coat. Yet the group's verdict, on breaking for lunch, was unanimous. Finney was *special*. Before Finney's arrival they had joked that he would have to change his surname. Now Hepton knew he was in the presence of no ordinary actor. 'It was the only time that I saw someone cold and knew that he was going to be a star,' he recalled.

Not all Finney's roles were prominent, obviously, but, rather like Richard Burton, Finney compelled attention. Coincidentally, one of Finney's early small roles was as the orphaned clerk Richard in *The Lady's Not for Burning*, a part in which Burton had excelled. Finney had not only a handsome, forceful face but also hypnotic blue eyes. Even when he was scrubbing the floor, when he had his face to the audience one's gaze fell on him.

In another play, a piece of Irish whimsy called *Happy as Larry*, Finney caught the notice of Michael Billington, later a distinguished theatre critic: 'He was one of a chorus of dancing tailors, and there was something about this stocky, square-shouldered figure that instantly drew the eye. He was a 19-year-old fresh out of RADA. It was fascinating to see him mature with every production.'

Billington also remembers walking past Finney near the city's train station:

> What struck me was the confidence with which he held himself. It was that certain set of the shoulders. He didn't so much as walk as swagger in a curious kind of way – call it, perhaps, saunter aggressively – as if he knew exactly who he was and was very, very sure of himself.

It helped that everyone liked 'Albie'. Finney, with Hepton's help, had moved from the rather downmarket Balsall Heath to Pakenham Road, Edgbaston, into the home of Winnie Banks, a housekeeper to a hostess known for her theatrical digs. Finney became friendly with Winnie and continued to visit long after he had become a major star. Coincidentally, or perhaps not, both Finney's immediate successors as 'juvenile lead' at Birmingham Rep, first Ian Richardson and then Derek Jacobi, also stayed with Winnie. Jacobi later recalled that Finney had decorated his bedroom, 'At one point I asked the landlady if I could change the wallpaper in the bedroom. She said, "No, no, no – Albert put that up".'

Finney had also met the actress who was to become his first wife, Jane Wenham, at a party in Stratford-upon-Avon. Wenham, nine years older than Finney, had joined the Old Vic at the age of 17. She had won excellent notices in *Grab Me a Gondola* and was appearing in three important roles during the 1957 Stratford season – as Celia in *As You Like It*, as Calpurnia in *Julius Caesar* and as Iris in *The Tempest*. Finney soon moved into her flat in West Street, Stratford.

Meanwhile, Finney's roles continued. *The Lizard on the Rock* ran for a month in the summer of 1957. Set in the Australian desert, it tells of a successful man reassessing the value of wealth and power. A critic wrote, 'Albert Finney, Geoffrey Taylor and Colin George clearly differentiate the senator's three sons.'

Douglas Seale was still officially the director at Birmingham when he cast Finney as Henry V. Seale had built his reputation on Shakespeare's histories, notably the cycle of the three parts of *Henry VI* and *Richard III*. He was now trying his luck with *Henry V*. The production also featured a young Michael Blakemore, who was hoping to be cast as a member of the French court – the dauphin or the constable. Instead he played Exeter. He recalled that Finney's appearance as Henry V was the first time he had seen an actor playing the part without make-up. Hepton was also in the chorus.

Henry V marked Finney's breakthrough at Birmingham. Audrey Nightingale, in *The Times*, said he reminded her of Burton: 'Always intelligent, moving after

Agincourt, he [Finney] takes the stage with an engaging charm of youth ... sturdy rather than royal ... in the Burton tradition rather than the Olivier.'

In retrospect, Nightingale said, it was Finney's performance in *Be Good Sweet Maid*, as a hardheaded young entrepreneur, that impressed her even more. Nightingale, writing in 1963, said, 'Here was a hint of his future as Arthur Seaton, an incisive piece of work in which the charm was used deliberately as a veneer for a cool and egoistic calculation.'

Critic J.C. Trewin also liked Finney's Henry V. Trewin said that Finney 'failed in the Harfleur speech, a passage that demands the fullest drive', but otherwise he was impressed:

Often in the theatre, Henry has been arrogant, self-righteous, the star of England shining like a gas jet. But Finney could remind us of a cricket captain able to keep our spirits up on a tricky third day. He might not have been a greyhound in the slips; he would have been an uncommonly safe cover-point. This Henry knew his people, and he had enough of the old Hal in him to turn to rough jesting in that moment of relief, the battle over.

The roles continued. In 2013, to mark the centenary of the Rep's founding, audiences were asked to reminisce about the old theatre. Someone mentioned *The Alchemist*. One fan wrote:

We will never forget the young Albert Finney in Ben Jonson's *The Alchemist*, probably late fifties, at the Old Rep in Station Street with the gas lighting on the stairs to the upper level. Newly arrived in Birmingham, it was one of our first visits.

It was during the run of *The Alchemist* that Finney married Jane Wenham – on 1 November 1957 at Holy Trinity Church in Stratford. Since Jane, like Finney, was due on stage that night, in her case in *As You Like It*, any honeymoon plans had to be postponed.

Finney's biggest role at Birmingham was in *Macbeth*. Hepton took a gamble in offering the part to someone as young as Finney, but it paid off. It helped that Hepton had a clear idea about the play: 'I took the witches to be the embodiment of that influence, so when they say to Macbeth, "you will be king", it starts a process of evil.' An announcement in *The Times* on 6 February 1958 stated, 'Albert Finney, a young British actor whose playing of Henry V a year ago was highly praised, is to act the name part in *Macbeth* on February 11.'

June Brown, now forever associated with dear Dot Cotton in *EastEnders* and easily the best performer in the soap's three-decades-long history, was then just 30. Brown only played one season at Birmingham. She remembered the production well: 'Unfortunately, my performance was dire for the first three weeks. Then I caught an awful cold and the part came alive for me. Doctor Greasepaint!'

A photograph of the production shows a young Finney, hair luxuriant and bouffant, with a sharp, pointed beard, chiselled features and an enviable profile. June Brown also looked alluring. She remembers:

> Albie Finney was very young, only about 21. He was a very nice person and actor. A few years later I was at the Royal Court and he came to see me in my dressing room. He said 'Do you remember me?' I said 'Don't be so daft!' as by this time he was very famous.[2]

Finney's Macbeth won mostly rave reviews. 'He now proves that his Henry V last season was no mere flash in the pan. His Macbeth has an authority truly astonishing in someone of only 21,' said the *New Chronicle*. J.C. Trewin thought that Finney's Macbeth 'could suggest soldiership and high scholarship' and that his interpretation was refreshing in its avoidance of excess. Yet it was his impression, and this may give pause for consideration in light of Finney's future efforts, that Finney was a good dramatic actor rather than a speaker of verse: 'On Finney's lips Shakespeare's verse seemed to lack modulation and variety.' To be fair, Finney, who seldom read critiques, would probably have agreed. He later said, speaking in 1963, that he was having 'a bash at parts that are really impossible at 21'.

Audrey Williamson was impressed by the young actor's attitude and self-insight:

> Finney's Macbeth was by no means lacking in weight; his robust build helped him here, and though the full macabre poetry and imagination were lacking, it was a characterisation well thought out, intellectually and technically an enhancement in his powers. By now I knew him well enough to discuss it with him offstage, and was surprised at the grasp he showed of problems raised by the character, and the methods he had taken to solve them onstage. He was too young to have seen any other great actors in the part; he had to build from his own instincts and his own reasoning. Both the instincts and the reasoning were those of a born actor.

Other actors at the Rep were also impressed. Mark Kingston, just a couple of years older than Finney, played Fleance in *Macbeth*:

Seeing this 18-year-old boy walk on and start to do his bit you knew there was something there you'd never have. You just knew that this was a really special talent and quality of sound ... He's gone on to become one of the most distinguished actors in British theatre, one who had the sense to turn down a knighthood![3]

Colin George remembered Finney as 'very much a Manchester lad, he did the lower class, but wonderful person, Albie. I've met him since many times.'[4] And Brian Hanbury remembered that Finney combined a heavyweight physical presence, unusual in a young actor, with an impish sense of humour.

It wasn't just Finney's star quality that other actors noticed. Pamela Howard was an apprentice scene painter at Birmingham Rep. She was struck by Finney's egalitarian attitude:

I can only say that to us workers in the dark bowels of the Old Rep in Station Street, we never imagined an actor would actually talk to us. It was still the period where everyone called each other 'Mr' or 'Miss', and he was the new generation and a breath of fresh air. He got to know us. He was the first actor I think we had ever known.[5]

One distinguished visitor to Birmingham was veteran star Charles Laughton, celebrated for his magnificent portrayals of Captain Bligh[6] and Henry VIII. Reportedly, Laughton saw Finney's Macbeth and said to him, 'You were bloody awful but what can you expect at your age?' before whisking him off for scotch and steak at a nearby pub.

Laughton meant no such thing. What he really meant was, 'You show great promise and it just has to be nurtured and to that end I'm going to poach you away from Birmingham.' Actors have a strange code language. And that's exactly what he did. Laughton and his wife, Elsa Lanchester, who had not appeared on the London stage since 1936, invited Finney to join them in a new Jane Arden play called *The Party*, along with Joyce Redman and Ann Lynn. Laughton would also direct. *The Times* noted Finney's addition, mentioning that the actor, still only 22, 'has done very well for himself at Birmingham Repertory, particularly as Henry V and as Macbeth'.

The West End beckoned. And was Finney intimidated by Laughton? – What do you think?

SEIZING THE MOMENT

Imagine what it was like to be in my dressing room when I heard you all groan.
Albert Finney.

It was several nights into *The Party* with the venerable Charles Laughton, a huge star in more ways than one. During several performances at London's New Theatre Finney had become irritated that, during his big speech towards the end, Laughton's concentration was drifting. The old man would be scratching his nose or bottom or making funny sounds. So much so that Finney told producer Harry Saltzman, 'Tell Mr Laughton that I'll kick him into the orchestra pit if he fucking does that again.'

'Oh will he?' chuckled Laughton.

'He will,' replied Saltzman matter-of-factly.

It was this certain 'I don't give a damn' quality that endeared people to Finney. He treated everyone the same. But he wouldn't take rudeness from *anyone*. He'd tell big stars or theatregoers to shut up if he felt they were out of line. Roger Moore later summed up his friend's appeal, 'That's what I love about Albie – he is completely independent and speaks his mind without fear of upsetting anybody.'

The Party had some themes that were risqué for the time, notably a subtext involving possible incest between father and daughter. Overriding all this was the alcoholism of the father (Laughton) who had been away recuperating in a clinic. He then returns home unexpectedly to interrupt a party given for his daughter, Ettie, played by Ann Lynn.

Arden's play failed, however, to make the impact of Osborne's *Look Back in Anger*. And Finney's part, which marked his official West End debut, was small. 'Joyce Redman and Albert Finney complete a group of accomplished performances which are directed with a somewhat loose hand,' said *The Times* on the play's opening in June 1958.

According to Simon Callow, '[Laughton] felt a huge paternal warmth towards this northern lad, direct, unactorish, of the real world.'

'Actors are useful people,' Laughton wrote later. 'You can tell a lot about what England is like today through Albert Finney.' Ann Rogers, Laughton's personal assistant, thought they were like Falstaff and Hal together. Kenneth Tynan wrote, 'Mr Finney shares the play's best scene with Mr Laughton, who rises like a salmon to the occasion; few young actors have ever got a better performance out of their directors.'[1]

Laughton was past his best, fat and occasionally a little unsteady on his feet. But Finney, according to a young Sheridan Morley, who remembered the production well, seemed to be quietly studying the older actor:

During *The Party* you got the sense that Finney was shadowing Laughton, rather in the same way that, much, much later, Edward Fox did when playing with the by then octogenarian Rex Harrison in *The Admirable Crichton*. You saw Rex handing on the torch to Fox – literally, there on stage. With the extraordinary affinity between Laughton and Finney, something then was clearly being handed on too.

The Party gave rise to another celebration at home. Jane had become pregnant during the run of *Macbeth* and on 16 September she gave birth to a son, Simon, at St Mary's Hospital. Audrey Williamson described the infant as a 'laughing red-blonde Albert in miniature'.

Finney, Jane and Simon rented a flat in Bayswater, west London. Photographs show Finney smoking in a makeshift kitchen, surrounded by pots and pans, dressed casually and wearing a cloth cap, perhaps consciously, or unconsciously, aping Laughton's style of dress.

Finney looked mature for his years. By the age of 21 he was married and a father and had made a West End debut. Many of his peers had barely started drama school. Finney had also appeared in four episodes of *Emergency Ward 10*, the medical soap opera which gave young actors such as Ian Hendry and Glyn Owen (the latter accompanied Finney on his New York run of *Luther*) their first parts on television. He and Jane had also appeared together in a radio play, *The Larford Lad*.

Meanwhile, a young up-and-coming director, Lindsay Anderson, saw *The Party* and delighted in what he called, 'a kind of truthfulness and directness about the way Finney played which, in fact, was not in the least typical of the people of his generation'. Anderson was asked by producer Oscar Lewenstein to direct a production by Willis Hall called *The Discipline of War*. The play was about a group of British soldiers in Malaya during the Second World War. The title was eventually changed to *The Long and the Short and the Tall*. Anderson wanted to cast Finney as the belligerent central character, Bamforth. Finney agreed.

On the second day, however, Finney arrived looking ill. A doctor examined him and told him he had anything but appendicitis which turned out to be precisely the diagnosis. Finney was taken to hospital for an emergency appendectomy. Anderson was still determined to cast Finney in the lead role until it became clear that his recovery would take too long. Peter O'Toole, whose career would dovetail Finney's, replaced him.

Laughton invited Finney to Stratford after he had recovered. The veteran actor was to play Lear, and also Bottom in *A Midsummer Night's Dream*. He wanted Finney in the company. Finney had little choice but to follow his mentor. Finney's period at Stratford, however, was not happy. One of the problems was that at drama school, and then at Birmingham, Finney had been feted as the great young leading man. At Stratford, however, Finney found himself surrounded by seasoned players – and he was still only 23.

The stars, besides Laughton, were Paul Robeson as Othello and Laurence Olivier as Coriolanus. Other veteran performers included Harry Andrews, whom Kenneth Tynan had described as 'the backbone of British theatre'. Also there were Angela Baddeley and Edith Evans – the latter, Finney always said, his favourite leading lady. If only cameras had captured what must have been an extraordinary season. Of these performances, only *A Midsummer Night's Dream* was filmed for posterity.

Zoe Caldwell recorded the magnificent impression made by Robeson:

> We all nervously awaited the arrival of Paul Robeson from Russia.[2] Paul was, in so many ways, a giant of a man. All his life he had excelled – as an athlete, a scholar, and a singer – and because he seemed to have no fear he spoke out against injustice wherever he found it. I think envy had a great deal to do with his being driven from his own country. He was a Gulliver among us Lilliputians. He spoke to everyone in the same voice, no matter how grand the person, no matter how small. And he never mentioned his race.[3]

Meanwhile, Finney, playing Edgar, watched as Laughton, then pushing 60, wrestled with Lear. An air of sadness surrounded the production. For forty years, Laughton had studied the role of Lear. Intellectually and emotionally he was ready, but physically he was not. He walked unsteadily, occasionally veering to the side. According to Caldwell, who played Cordelia:

> He was grossly overweight and standing was a chore. He loved to sit on a chair at the centre of a circle surrounded by young people sitting or kneeling,

listening to his wisdom … Charles had left out the large ingredient for the big roles, stamina.

Caldwell, acutely aware of Laughton's debility, took laxatives the night before each performance, hoping to make herself as light as possible. But still Laughton struggled. Finney watched the older man closely. It was a lesson he never forgot. Many years later, when he was about 60, Finney was asked whether he would ever play Lear. Finney, referencing Laughton's lack of stamina at a similar age, intimated that the moment had passed.

Zoe Caldwell believed that Laughton, who, we should remember, died just three years later, had taken on Finney as a young protégé and was projecting on him his thwarted ambitions:

> I think Charles felt, somewhat vicariously, that he could play roles that he had never played – Romeo, Hamlet, Henry V, through Albert. This is something older actors sometimes do and it does not help either the younger or the older actor. There was a danger in Albert on the stage but like all young actors he had to make his own mistakes, his way, in order to develop his own talent.

Reviewers hardly mentioned Finney's Edgar in *King Lear*, his Cassio in *Othello* or his Lysander in *A Midsummer Night's Dream*. But why should they? The star parts belonged to Olivier, Laughton and Robeson. Priscilla Morgan, playing Hermia in *A Midsummer Night's Dream*, remembers the contrast with the exceptionally tall Vanessa Redgrave (as Helena) with whom she shared a dressing room. When, in the play, she called Redgrave 'a painted maypole', she really meant it!

Morgan thought that the play's young director, 28-year-old Peter Hall,[4] was all wrong for the production:

> I'm not a great admirer of his. He didn't have a great sense of humour and, after all, it was supposed to be a comedy. He'd always say to us – 'show me what you're going to do' – but I was looking for something more from him. I never worked with him again.

She found Laughton's performance to be 'heavy and slow', but she blames Hall. 'He was just so star-struck.' She was surprised to hear that Laughton was only 60 at the time of the Stratford Festival, believing that he was at least 70.

Priscilla married her boyfriend, Clive Dunn, later famous for *Dad's Army*, during the Festival. She remembers Finney rushing over on a matinee day with a box of fruit and vegetables. Vanessa Redgrave helped to wash up after the lady in charge of the kitchen had an allergic reaction to an alcoholic drink. Priscilla says of Finney, 'He was an absolute dear and it was clear that he was going to be a big star.'[5] She didn't see him for another twelve years until Finney produced the stage version of Peter Nichols's *Forget-Me-Not-Lane* in London in 1971. (Finney later starred in a television version in 1975.) She found Finney totally unaffected by stardom.

In Stratford, Finney would leave the theatre unnoticed, riding off on his bike, wearing a mucky-looking beige raincoat. Yet, years later, when audiences reflected on this extraordinary season, it was clear that Finney had won many female admirers. One visitor remembered:

> We also saw *King Lear*, wherein Charles Laughton was Lear, Robert Hardy was Edmund, Ian Holm the Fool and, I think, Albert Finney was Edgar. Our girls' school travelled by train from Bury St Edmunds and both plays made a huge impression on us. We also saw a dazzling young Derek Jacobi as Henry IV at Cambridge Arts Theatre. I think Albert Finney won the heart-throb stakes, but it was a close-run thing.

Yet, heart-throb or not, Finney was unhappy:

> I don't know what was wrong with my work at Stratford. It was more wrong than it's ever been before or since. I was aware of it being wrong. It was one of those times when you feel you're in a tunnel and there's nothing you can do to get out of it. My work was awful, just vile. Every time I went on stage I thought – 'get off, get off, what are you doing?' It was just terrible.[6]

Finney's marriage to Jane was also in trouble. He had settled down too young and couldn't cope with domestic responsibilities and curbs on his freedom. Later, talking to John Freeman on *Face to Face*, he blamed himself full-square for the failure. And Finney, who was still only 23, remembers a rare show of unprofessionalism on his part during a performance of *Othello*, directed by Tony Richardson:

> I did a matinee under the influence and vowed I'd never do it again. I felt so appalled and scared. I was kind of going through a difficult time and I thought 'to hell with it'. I had a sword-fight sequence and I didn't know what I was doing and it got a little dangerous. After that I thought – 'I'm not in control and I may hurt somebody'. After that scene I got in the shower and did my best to sober up.[7]

While appearing in *Othello*, Finney began seeing Australian actress Zoe Caldwell, three years his senior. Caldwell, in her memoir, tells of staying up all night with Finney to help him with his lines when he had to replace Olivier in *Coriolanus*. Curiously, she then admits to an affair but does not name Finney. 'I did, however, break one of my rules during that season. I had an explosive affair with an actor in the company, causing a lot of havoc and pain for which I apologise,' she wrote.

Finney walked out on his wife and young son that summer. For a while he stayed at Robert Hardy's house. It was an acrimonious time (Julia Goodman remembers that Wenham was still complaining about Finney's behaviour when they co-starred in an episode of *Inspector Morse* in 1992).

The attention showered on Stratford's starrier performers only made Finney feel worse. Vanessa Redgrave, much to her subsequent embarrassment, was hailed as a great actress from birth. Harry Andrews had a kind of rock-like presence on stage. (When I saw Finney thirty years later in *JJ Farr* there was something about his granite portrayal that reminded me of Andrews.) Even performers like Robert Hardy and Ian Holm had more experience than Finney.

Hardy shared a dressing room with Finney. The older actor said that Finney, for all his problems, reminded him of Burton, 'He made one think of the bull-fight critic in Ibáñez's *Blood and Sand* who talks excitedly about the man having a quantity of salt. There was a great deal of salt in the air with Finney.'

Yet Finney found it difficult to make his acting come alive. Even in *A Midsummer Night's Dream* the reviews for the supporting players were not great. 'Hard as they and their partners, Albert Finney and Edward de Souza, work to be funny, we are left with the impression that a more graceful dance of misunderstanding would suit the scenes a great deal better,' said *The Times*.

When he dined with Hepton that summer, Finney confided that he was even wondering if he was in the right job. Hepton said:

> He'd been cushioned for two years and allowed to develop week by week. At Stratford he got quite the opposite feeling. Albert said that when he first went to Stratford he sensed that directors didn't seem to give a damn for what he did. It was somehow a great slap in the face for him.

Tony Richardson also recalled Finney's frustration, 'He was just reaching the height of his powers, and he didn't have the right parts. Finney was like a young stallion chomping at the bit, wanting that big, enormous role, because he could really act his head off.'

Everything seemed to be going wrong for Finney at Stratford. Eileen Atkins, in the audience for *King Lear*, recalls that Finney had botched his choice of dress:

> Everybody else, because they couldn't afford it, was in felt costumes. But because Albert Finney was Albert Finney, they gave him real leather. When I sat in the audience, his costume looked lousy and all the felt ones looked great. The felt ones looked like leather, and his looked like plastic.[8]

In the autumn, Finney started to play First Roman Citizen in *Coriolanus*, which starred the 52-year-old Olivier, then at the height of his powers. As well as triumphing in *Hamlet, Henry V* and *Richard III* and as Malvolio in *Twelfth Night*, Olivier had recently starred as Archie Rice in *The Entertainer*, John Osborne's new play at the Royal Court.

Coriolanus, the brave soldier who has to woo the masses despite his disdain for them, was a great part. And Olivier was determined to exploit every possibility. Sir Laurence had played Coriolanus before, in 1938, in a production directed by Lewis Casson in which he had performed a spectacular death fall. Twenty-one years later, Olivier was attempting the same athleticism. His son, Tarquin, recalled the derring-do in a biography of his father:

> Coriolanus stood back stage on a platform 12 feet high, bleeding from many stab wounds and determined in one final dying lunge to drive his sword through Aufidius. To reach him, he had to leap upwards and far out across to stand a chance. So he seemed to literally fly up towards the dress circle; we thought he was going to land in our laps, to be grabbed by strong men grabbing his ankles, gripping him and letting him swing down. But that on its own would have ended with his rump towards us. So he had to spin round in mid-air, with the retainers changing hands on his ankles, so that when dangling upside down it would be his face we saw, arms swinging in utter defeat. It was difficult, dangerous, and a crowning reminder of the physical risks of his career.[9]

Milton Shulman remarked that 'knighthood and middle-age have by no means reduced Olivier's acrobatic daring.'

Finney, as First Citizen, equipped himself well, according to critic Michael Wells:

> Finney, a big, brawny, barrel chested man, played the First Citizen with natural authority combined with a mutinously hang-dog look, a man with a chip on his shoulder who attracted sympathy all the same. Like other actors of his generation he retained a local accent even when playing classical parts.

Finney was still in a trough. Yet watching and acting alongside Olivier was worth all the years at RADA or Birmingham Rep. Elijah Moshinsky, later to direct Finney in several productions, recalled Finney's subsequent comments:

> He always said that he learnt everything about acting from understudying Olivier as Coriolanus. He said that no matter where you went with your voice, you could never be higher or louder than Olivier and you could never be as soft and sweet. He felt in his presence that the range of things – the spectrum of acting – was before you.[10]

Finney noted Olivier's extraordinary vocal range, one moment soothing, the next rousing. 'What was interesting is how a great actor can take the peaks and valleys of a character as written and push them even further apart. He makes the climaxes higher and he makes the depths lower than you can feel is possible in the text,' said Finney.

Finney was also getting a lesson in screen acting from Olivier. Finney had a small part as Archie Rice's soldier son in *The Entertainer*, which Olivier was filming by day in Morecambe. Finney appears briefly at the beginning. His part, as a happy-go-lucky beer-drinking lad about to be dispatched to Suez, never to return, took just a couple of days to shoot. It was a heroic feat on Olivier's part to do Coriolanus and Archie Rice simultaneously.

Perhaps this time Olivier had overstretched himself. Some sources say it was his acrobatics during *Coriolanus* that twisted a cartilage in his knee. Others believe that the whole thing was a ruse to give Finney his big chance. But Zoe Caldwell's version seems definitive. She remembered she was watching Laughton in *A Midsummer Night's Dream* when Finney, white-faced, stricken with a cold, approached her. '"Larry's done his knee in, tap-dancing as Archie, he's off tomorrow's matinee and I have to play. Will you help me learn the lines?" Although it may seem strange that an understudy wouldn't know the lines, we must remember that Olivier was notorious for never missing a performance.'

According to Caldwell, Finney went without sleep as he got to grips with the part:

> I first put Albert's head over a steaming bowl of eucalyptus. And covered him with a towel to get rid of his cold and clear his brain. We stayed up all night and morning, learning lines until he had to go to the theatre for costume fittings and rehearsal.

Such was Olivier's fame that *The Times*, on 9 October, reported on his injury and replacement by Finney. He was not the only one indisposed; Edith Evans was back after a car accident two weeks before.

Especially in those days, when the British theatre was dominated by the great triumvirate of Olivier, Gielgud and Richardson, a trip to see Olivier was a huge event. So when people flocked to the theatre, the auditorium buzzing with expectancy, to hear of the great actor's absence was a colossal disappointment. For Finney it was a classic make or break episode. Actress Sue Johnston, then just 16, was in the audience that afternoon. (Forty years later she appeared with Finney in *My Uncle Silas*.) She remembered:

> I went with the school to a matinee at Stratford to see Olivier in *Coriolanus*. But he'd broken his leg so they announced, to groans from the audience, that the understudy would be playing the role. Well, it was Albert and after two scenes we were mesmerised. I told Albert this and he remembered the occasion, saying 'I had to listen to those groans on the tannoy before going on.'[11]

Actress Pamela Coleman, also in the audience, tells a similar story about learning that Olivier was indisposed: 'We all groaned. Then out came Albert Finney and we all fell in love with him.'

Finney went on, knowing he had nothing to lose. A more diffident performer might have flunked it. But he gave himself a little pep talk beforehand:

> When I went on for Sir Laurence all the difficulties I was going through just left me because, first of all, they expect you to come on with flannels and a book. And I came on and I had the costume on and so they immediately think I'm talented because I've got into the clothes and they can't see the book and I got through it without drying. When you go on as an understudy the card you've got in your hand is that they think you might not get through it at all. And if you can get through it with any degree of nous at all, they think you're very good and I felt – I'm getting there … I don't think it was a very good Coriolanus and also when you hear Sir Laurence's tones ringing in your ears for the number of performances it's very difficult not to be similar because you're working on his blueprint.

Observers didn't share Finney's self-deprecation. Olivier congratulated him effusively.[12] Poet and playwright Louis MacNeice described it as 'a good production with an understudy standing in very well for Olivier.'[13] Zoe Caldwell thought that 'the boyish ring in Albert Finney's make-up, now troubled by adult growing pains, made him a successful Coriolanus.'

Finney suddenly felt liberated. 'I was in a very bad state as regards acting and it was marvellous to play Coriolanus. Somehow just having to go on freed me but that was because the rest of the season was rather black.'

Coriolanus is one of Shakespeare's most moving plays. In particular, the scene in which his mother (played by Edith Evans) confronts her battle-hardened son and pleads with him not to burn Rome is heart-rending. Finney later said he had no need to feign tears; they just ran down freely. Olivier's 'baby of an understudy', as the great man called him, had truly broken through. Finney's period at Stratford had been difficult, but he felt he had learnt a lot:

> A classical training is very important. I was at Stratford for nine months doing Shakespeare. I was very uncomfortable. I found that for the first time I didn't really enjoy acting. But the whole way one responds to a Shakespearean text, to the costumes and the size and conception, is quite different from the way one responds to a modern or a Restoration play.

Now all he needed was a great movie role to make him a household name. *Angry Young Man* beckoned.

ARTHUR

That's someone we all know.

Melvyn Bragg on Arthur Seaton.

Joe Lampton, Frank Machin, Billy Fisher and, especially, Arthur Seaton – these were the new breed of anti-heroes who revolutionised British cinema and sent Noël Coward stocking up on Yardley's shaving soap in a bunker below the Royal Court. The early sixties were to mark a decisive break from the strangulated English, Brylcreemed hair and 'steady number one' barking tones of Kenneth More or Jack Hawkins. Films were being made about working-class people, examining their feelings and lives without condescension or poking fun.

Saturday Night and Sunday Morning holds up better than all the other films of this period. It's worth surveying the competition – especially movies about young men. Tony Richardson's film of John Osborne's *Look Back in Anger* was somehow too obviously a film of a play. Richard Burton's Jimmy Porter was too old and perhaps too grand, a diminished hero rather than an embattled ordinary man. And, as so often with Osborne, one always suspected that he was more destroyer than reformer.

Room at the Top was also among the first of the new wave but now looks hopelessly dated. The open derision of the working class, the ridiculous way that Lampton is forced to stick up for himself, now makes it risible. 'Let me tell you I *am* working class and proud of it,' says Lampton at one point. Laurence Harvey's turn as a northerner was simply unconvincing.

The Loneliness of the Long Distance Runner was better, but too obviously a 'them and us' story designed to tap sympathy for delinquents. Courtenay's Colin Smith didn't have much wherewithal to fight the system, other than 'throwing' the cross-country race at the finale.

Better still was *This Sporting Life*, a strong star vehicle for Richard Harris and well directed by Lindsay Anderson. Frank Machin, however, is a coarse beast and a man of primitive instincts. He's just, in his landlady's words, 'a great ape'. Billy Liar, as played by Tom Courtenay in the film (and on stage, following Finney's stint) was a fantasist and no threat to anyone.

Finney's Arthur Seaton is different because he's bright. He's not articulate in the sense that polite society would ever accept him, yet he's sharp-witted and outspoken. He can hold his own in an argument and, in his own rebellious way, he's a tuned-in guy. Perhaps some of Finney's innate intelligence permeates the character. Seaton has more natural nous than Porter, Machin or Lampton. He knows when to keep quiet or when to vent his spleen. If he were in the army, he'd be good at dodging bullets. His canny appraisal of those around him, though cruel and crude, is usually right.

Those who claim that Seaton is a class warrior should think again. He's trapped by routine and drudgery. He knows that menial work and a drab existence are his lot. The system won't change, he was born into it and will die in it. He'll remain a factory worker until retirement, perhaps rising to foreman if he can keep his trap shut. He can play around a bit but he'll end up marrying a girl from down the street. They'll end up in one of those back-to-back terraced houses, just like everyone else.

It's not his class background that he resents so much as predictability. And it would be, if Seaton were working on a construction site or in a super-market, post office or hotel. Seaton, as played by Finney, is a natural rebel. He's accused of being a communist – 'a red', and the sympathies of writer Alan Sillitoe lay with the Left at this time. But Seaton, perhaps, rather like Finney, is not a political animal. He just wants a good time, 'All the rest is propaganda'. In other words, cut out the ideological bullshit and show me some fun.

Of course, there was an element of socialism in the new wave. The message is bold and clear. Look at the wasted opportunities of young men trapped in menial work who could have done better. But we shouldn't forget that it cuts both ways. Years later, people spoke of these jobs as giving people security. The downside of that was that you knew your place in 'the order of things'.

Peter O'Toole was originally set to play Seaton. But Finney was a better choice than the slightly patrician-looking O'Toole. Finney could belong on a factory floor. His background meant that he knew Arthur very well. He might have even had a menial future, just like Seaton, if fate hadn't intervened.

Finney recalled how he came to be cast:

Karel Reisz came to see me while I was in Stratford. I was in tights at the time. He told me about the project and gave me the book and the script. And I did a bit of filming on *The Entertainer* and that was a kind of living screen test for *Saturday Night and Sunday Morning* because it was the same company, Woodfall Films,[1] making the two.

Finney quickly learnt how to use a lathe:

> I really had to concentrate on the machinery otherwise it could have blown up. I went into the Raleigh bicycle factory [in Nottingham's Radford area] and I was taught how to use one. I was shaping the spindle that goes through the hub cap. So perhaps there are people riding around on bikes that I built who came off them because I didn't do it very well. It's a wonderful thing to be able to concentrate on that reality; it takes the weight off the acting.[2]

Karel Reisz directed as realistically as possible. The camera moves around, not dictating events but rather capturing them. Filmed in the autumn of 1959, with some interiors shot at Twickenham Studios, *Saturday Night and Sunday Morning* has the air of a docudrama, decades before those all-pervasive fly-on-the-wall programmes.

Finney later coined the term 'naturalistic minimalism' to describe his acting style. 'You hope the camera will come in and catch what you're doing.' That did *not* mean that it would have been better to film in a real factory and let the characters speak for themselves. You needed actors to bring the complex emotions alive. Yet in the sense that the camera captures ordinary people's thoughts, without it all seeming staged, it's before its time.

Finney looks handsome but brittle. The other actors also look gritty and older than their age. Finney's voice is deep, harsh and grinding. Insults fly from his lips ten-a-minute – his fat neighbour is an 'old bag', her husband is 'rat face'. A drunk who throws a brick at a funeral parlour is 'a spineless bastard' for not running off. Arthur describes his parents as 'dead from the neck up'. All the women, whether it's Brenda (Rachel Roberts), the wife of the co-worker with whom he dallies, or the girl he ends up with, Doreen (Shirley Anne Field), are 'ducks'.

Arthur resists all attempts to define him. 'Whatever people say I am, that's what I'm not.' He hates the thought that his whole life is planned out for him. 'You see people settle down and before you know what, they've hit the bucket.' 'You've got to be as cunning as them bastards,' he says, referring to his bosses. He doesn't even soften when Brenda tells him she's pregnant. 'I'll go and see Aunt Ada. She's had fourteen kids of her own and that's not counting the ones she got rid of,' he tells her.

His only fun comes from sex and booze or getting his own back on a nosey neighbour by shooting her with an air gun, or putting a rat on a work

colleague's bench. When he takes a beating from some squaddies, set on him
by his cuckolded workmate, he even accepts it philosophically.

Everything is relentlessly downbeat. Reisz captures the factories, the smoke,
the narrow back alleys, the washing lines and the sense of being trapped in a
ghetto. Almost sixty years later and factories are not so commonplace. Yet, in
the workplace, we're still told what to do. Circumstances might have changed,
yet, for many, the script remains the same.

Saturday Night and Sunday Morning marked the first film in which an ordinary
working man's life is viewed realistically. We don't exactly like Arthur Seaton.
He's a bit too crude and brash. But working-class cinemagoers saw someone
with whom they could identify. Finney was the guy you saw downing six pints
on a Friday night, heading to the chippie or to the riverbank. He's mouthy,
sweaty and uncouth, someone you hope your nice daughter would *not* meet in
the pub. Yet, as Melvyn Bragg once said, interviewing Finney in 1996, Seaton
was 'someone we all knew'.

The film was also a milestone, not just to the 'ordinary' cinema-going public
but also to future actors from modest backgrounds. If Finney could portray
a working-class guy and become so famous, there was hope for them. Years
later, the likes of Ray Winstone, Malcolm McDowell and Pete Postlethwaite[3]
mentioned the impact of *Saturday Night and Sunday Morning*.[4] Similar 'rebels'
followed, notably Michael Caine in *Alfie*, as well as movies like *Up the Junction*
depicting the divide between posh and poor London. But *Saturday Night and
Sunday Morning* was the original – much imitated, even parodied, but never
bettered. Finney never sets a foot wrong. Seaton, for all his failings, was someone
to be reckoned with. He is a survivor, if nothing else.

The Times caught the film's appeal, 'There is much to dislike in Arthur but
Albert Finney and Mr Sillitoe never allow him to become negative; he stands
for something, however vague and vulgar it may be, and is prepared to fight for
it.' The reviewer noted the social change afoot, 'Here, as in *Look Back in Anger*
and *Room at the Top*, is evidence of the desire to move away from the normal
run of screen heroes and show the man at the lathe in his attempts to come to
terms with contemporary society.' Moving away indeed!

Shooting on *Saturday Night and Sunday Morning*, which had a modest budget
of £120,000 of which £2,000 went to Finney, came in on schedule. For Finney,
carrying his first big film, the load was enormous. He would sometimes throw
up in the mornings. Yet what appeared on film was seamless, aided by an evocative Johnny Dankworth score.

The producers originally wanted Diana Dors to play Brenda but Britain's
'blonde bombshell' allegedly withdrew because Brenda has an abortion, a
storyline that reminded Dors of her own past. As for Shirley Anne Field, in

retrospect she felt that her role in *The Entertainer*, in which she co-starred as one of Archie Rice's conquests, was a screen test.

Filming in Nottingham was a joy, Field recalled during a visit to the city in 2012 for a photographic exhibition inspired by the movie:

> We got straight off our train and checked into a hotel called The Court, which was very comfortable. The director, Karel Reisz, sat us down and we all had tea and poached eggs on toast. We were full of optimism because we felt we were breaking the mould with Alan Sillitoe's story – making something special of working-class people; making them and their accents sexy. When you think about it, British working-class people were always portrayed in a rather patronising way.[5]

Shirley and Finney had already met when they were doing *The Entertainer* and had begun rehearsals for Lindsay Anderson's *The Lily White Boys* when filming started. She thought Arthur Seaton was a terrific character:

> I think what he did was so marvellous. You could see that his parents had been beaten down by the system, but he wasn't going to be, and neither was she going to be. Remember the last scene where he throws the stone and Doreen asks him 'why did you do that'? And he says: 'it won't be the last one I throw'?

Filming wrapped at the end of 1959 under a veil of secrecy. The idea was to release it quickly, without fanfare, and get tills ringing and critics' tongues wagging. But even Reisz was unprepared for the sensational opening at Leicester Square's Warner Cinema. 'It got its money back after two weeks which scared the shit out of us,' he recalled.

By the time the film came out, Finney was well into his run of *Billy Liar*. In February 1961, the Variety Club of Great Britain voted him most promising newcomer of 1960.

Bosley Crowther in the *New York Times* said that Arthur was portrayed fascinatingly by Finney. Crowther saw Seaton's character, perhaps overlooking his startling nonconformity, as a macho youth. He described him as 'a comforting relief from the devious, self-pitying rogues and weaklings we have seen in a lot of modern-day films'. Seaton is a:

> … tough, robust, cheeky factory worker [who] gripes about his low pay and harsh foreman and spends his Saturday night drinking beer in the pub. Sure, he is sceptical and surly, sarcastic and rebellious towards certain things [but]

he has confidence and a quiet determination. He can stand on his own two feet in the world.

Stanley Kauffmann was perhaps slightly closer to the truth when he wrote that *Saturday Night and Sunday Morning* was 'one of the best [films] of the movement, the only one that faces certain emotional implications for the present-day working-class'.

Kauffmann then put his own political spin on the character:

Better factory conditions and full employment and the National Health Service have given him armour against poverty and the threat of discharge but he is shrewd enough to see that these benefits have sapped the dynamism of the working class, made them relatively resigned and, in a sense, put gilded locks on the class barriers. Naturally he is not against the improvement per se; he is against the implicit attitude, on the part of both workers and bosses, that now they ought to be content with their lot.

If you see Seaton through a political paradigm – and I don't think we should – Kauffmann implied that Seaton was wise enough to see that the social benefits that came hand in hand with exploitation were designed to keep the working class in line. *The Times*, perhaps unsurprisingly, thought that attempts to label Seaton a communist were also misplaced: 'Anyone less of a communist than Arthur it's difficult to imagine – he stands for individual protest, for the right to rebel against laws.'

Seaton was probably misappropriated for serial causes. He would have been a rebel under any system. He was a perennial mischief-maker, looking after number one. What would he do if he won the pools? 'I'd see the family was taken care of. Then I'd make a bonfire of begging letters,' he says at one point.

Finney recalled that the film meant that 'working-class subjects were taken seriously which wasn't a very strong British cinematic tradition and I was aware of that to some extent'. That was the key breakthrough. Also controversial was the movie's graphic depiction of extramarital sex. Finney, speaking in 1982, recalled the upset:

A lot of people were outraged when the film came out. They thought it went too far. They thought the world was going to end because I'd been to bed with a married woman who was not my wife. There was a lot of trouble over it. And Karel got an enormous number of letters saying how disgusting it was. And, in terms of the sex, the law then was that you had to have one foot on the floor, like in snooker. I think that *Room at the Top*, which came out a couple of years earlier, was the first film that kind of intimated that two consenting adults have actually done something in bed together. There was a great discussion about whether I should keep my vest on, my ringlet, or whether Rachel Roberts's slip should be seen. I can't remember the results. It was 1960 and these great debates were taking place.

Finney also remembered:

I was totally engrossed in the film and I really enjoyed working with Karel. I also found film acting very interesting. It took ten weeks plus two weeks of second unit work. I found that it really does take over and that you're obsessed with it. I quite enjoyed that. In film you try to get a breath of life.

He intimated that it was easier to do that on-screen than in theatre.

The movie was a smash hit. The only downer was that people could not differentiate between the actor and the character of Arthur Seaton. Finney said he was different:

I don't think I'm like that [Seaton] at all. I feel that I'm much more inhibited and quieter. If a person like Arthur stood next to me in a bar and I overheard the scene like when he picks up the girl in the film, I'd feel a bit embarrassed. And I'd move away and let him get on with it because I'd feel – oh, men do that, do they? This is how they behave. I'm much quieter, much shyer. I don't drink very much. I can't take it … I was attracted to play someone like that because I'm not like that.

To which we might respond, 'Nice try, Albert!' Perhaps he doth protest too much. He might not have been Arthur Seaton, but he was no introvert either.

In 1960, Finney told Robert Robinson that he always believed that the character should stand in front of him, not the other way around:

They've seen my performance in *Saturday Night and Sunday Morning* and they think that's me – that's my personality. I feel very strongly that audiences should realise that what you're presenting to them is sort of like the work of a potter. You're showing the way, illustrating the way you make the pottery and revealing it to the audience through the marriage of instinct and emotions.

In 1962, he told John Freeman that 'something in me hates the selling of an image to the public, that to sell a product you say this is what he does: he gets drunk, he shoots guns at fat ladies. I felt imprisoned by the feeling of being seen as a north country youth'.

But Finney had difficulties fighting public perception. In 1961, after the film's release, *Time* profiled the 25-year-old. The magazine implied that, if Finney wasn't a dead ringer for Arthur, he was certainly a restless nonconformist. It began by comparing him to Olivier. 'Like Olivier, Finney is immensely versatile. But he has none of the smooth gloss of the classic acting tradition. He is relentlessly naturalistic, and his technique seldom shows on the surface.' The focus then shifted to the private man. 'He seldom spends more than two nights in the same flat, chain smokes, sometimes has kippers and champagne for breakfast.'

So Finney now had two tags to contend with, both with their pitfalls: the 'new Olivier' and the reprobate Arthur Seaton. It made him more determined to always go his own way.

LIFE CHOICES

Eager and pliant and marvellously sensitive with all his toughness and vitality.

Lindsay Anderson on Albert Finney.

Finney was still keen to work with Lindsay Anderson, the new wave director from whose play, *The Long, the Short and the Tall* he had left because of illness.

Their first joint venture was Harry Cookson's *The Lily White Boys*. Class conflict was at the core. Finney, Monty Landis and Philip Locke played juvenile delinquents, while Georgia Brown, Ann Lynn and Finney's co-star from *Saturday Night*, Shirley Anne Field, played their girlfriends. Various 'respectable citizens', all depicted as corrupt, litter the background.

It was Finney's first musical and he later said he thought he had uncovered 'a respectable baritone' while belting out Christopher Logue's lyrics at the Royal Court. A decade later, and the memory of Finney's singing helped him secure the lead, and an eventual Golden Globe, in *Scrooge*.

Ann Lynn thought that *The Lily White Boys* had a strong left-wing message, 'It was like a crusade, very socialist in content, decrying materialism and showing how most people fall into the trap of greed, which tends to happen on the backs of less fortunate people'. Anderson, like most other new wave directors, was someone of strong radical convictions. He adored Finney at this point. In rehearsals, early in January 1960, he noted:

Albert is a joy to work with, and without a talent as outstanding as his the show would be impossible. He is young, though, and in certain ways crystallised, too apt to 'turn in' and get away with it by brilliant naturalism. But he knows this – he is very intelligent about himself, and about theatre and he learns astonishingly fast.

As the rehearsals progressed, and they tackled some difficult numbers, Anderson's opinion of Finney soared:

> Pressing on with numbers; the quartet, Albie is getting it, though this is the most difficult one for him and gives rise to interesting speculations as to whether one needs to be a socialist in order to play this kind of satire satisfactorily. Certainly Albie is coming on tremendously – I mean developing his ideas and his self-confidence. He is so charming and pleasant to work with. Never a trace of egotism or refractoriness. Eager and pliant and marvellously sensitive with all his toughness and vitality.

But when the play opened, on 27 January 1960, the reviews were not ecstatic. 'Its satire rests on the naïve assumption that all business men are crooks and that no business can be done without bribery, that all lawyers are thieves and so on,' noted *The Times*. The reviewer went on to say, however, that Finney, Landis and Locke provided 'vigorous and well contrasted' performances.

Perhaps that is why *Saturday Night and Sunday Morning*, still awaiting release, would be so successful. It just illuminated the lives of ordinary people. Inevitably, in some similar productions, the upper classes become caricatures. With hindsight, it was easy to lampoon prime ministers like Harold Macmillan and Alec Douglas-Home on programmes like *That Was the Week That Was*.

The Lily White Boys ran for just forty-five performances. Yet the muted reception did not dent Anderson's admiration for Finney. Looking back, the play was a dry run for what was to be their most famous collaboration – *Billy Liar*, a three-act play by Keith Waterhouse and Willis Hall.

Theatregoers in the eighties would know Waterhouse as the writer behind the staging of the hilarious drunken misadventures of Soho scribe Jeffrey Bernard. When *Jeffrey Bernard is Unwell* came out in 1989, Bernard was an obscure figure. Thanks to Waterhouse's skill, this sad old sot, whose jottings were described as a suicide note in installments, became an unlikely hero.

Thirty years separate *Billy Liar* from *Jeffrey Bernard is Unwell*, and the two plays were very different. But the style is somehow similar. In Bernard's feverish storytelling we can see some of Billy Fisher's wild fantasies. Billy was a terminally bored undertaker's clerk. Any suggestion triggers endless daydreaming; he becomes a war hero, a fop and a successful businessman.

Billy was another working-class anti-hero but not nearly as belligerent as Seaton; he was diffident and introverted. After all, the extrovert seldom has recourse to a life of vivid fantasies. Both, it's true, were northerners seeking escape. But whereas in *Saturday Night and Sunday Morning* Finney had to project an unnatural aggression, *Billy Liar* called for him to downsize, to capitulate to a rollercoaster imagination.

In July 1960, Finney, Willis Hall and Lindsay Anderson did a little recce to Leeds as part of investigations for *Billy Liar*. Anderson described it as 'two northerners, no-nonsense and colloquially rough spoken, and one upper-class southerner, intellectual type'. Anderson gives an intriguing behind-the-scenes glimpse into Finney 'regressing' into his down-to-earth Yorkshire persona – doing rather than analysing – leaving his intellectual director feeling excluded.

Finney was still anonymous at this stage. All that would change when *Saturday Night and Sunday Morning* opened. But, in the summer of 1960, Finney could still enter a pub or fish and chip shop unnoticed. He was not yet a star or, put another way, he *was* a star but the world hadn't found out yet. This is Anderson's account:

> We went for a drink; first in one pub, then another. Mr Hall [Willis's father] – fiftyish, round faced, spectacled, was almost as chatty as his son – pleasant enough but not exactly forthcoming. Willis and Albert talked about Yorkshire. The second pub was a small, ugly little room crammed with tired-looking, ugly little men swilling beer. I drank light ale. Willis bought half a dozen bottles and borrowed a pack of cards. When we got back Willis and Albert went off to buy fish and chips, while Mr Hall brewed tea. We ate. Then the cards came out. Did I play pontoon? I said no. No effort of course was made to initiate me. They started to play. It was about eleven o'clock I suppose.
>
> I could have forecast the rest of the night … they just played … of course, fate would plan just the kind of situation for me that I am least able to cope with. A situation of exclusion. Stranded in a world I had no relationship with … rather aggressively male … with no time to spare for the sentimentalisms of relationships, for the arts or speculation or conversation, or for politeness, hospitality or charm.

In other words, sensitive southern intellectual feels out of place among the people whose causes he espouses, but also, perhaps significantly, the young Finney, on the crest of major stardom, pulled between two worlds. Few northerners would sit down and analyse their feelings, or articulate in any way 'the entrapment of the working class'. These were for directors like Anderson to explore.

Billy Liar opened on 13 September 1960 at the Cambridge Theatre. It was an immediate critical and box office success. It played for nearly 600 performances, including Finney and – subsequently – Courtenay's appearances. It also spawned a film (making stars out of Courtenay and Julie Christie), a stage musical and a TV series. *The Times* raved about the play:

> Albert Finney keeps us constantly interested in both the outer and inner workings of the hero's mind … In a little scene in a night garden Finney

crowns his performance with an extraordinary deft series of imaginings, beginning with the struttings of a drum major and ending with an impressive rendering of the Last Post.

Saturday Night and Sunday Morning opened during the run. The press caught the whiff of double success before the premiere and interviewed Finney while he was appearing in *Billy Liar*. Finney did not attend the film's premiere. 'It's rather marvellous that I've got the play to do tonight. It's all come in a lump. I don't like first nights at all. I don't like the feeling that it's not yours anymore,' he said.

Overnight, Finney became a star. The producer quickly put his name above the title outside the theatre. One Saturday, shortly after Finney's double success, his parents travelled down to London from Salford to see the play. It had to be a matinee because his father – who we will remember was also called Albert – needed to be home by evening to wrap accounts in the betting shop. Finney recalled the visit:

> I met them at the station and we took a cab to the stage door, where they left their bits and pieces, then we went off for a spot of lunch. We went up the side of the Cambridge Theatre, crossed Seven Dials, and when we got across the road I said, 'Look'. And there it was, 'Albert Finney in Billy Liar'. I said, 'Right, come on, let's go and get some lunch', and my mother and I strolled on, but my father just stood there, looking up. I went back and said, 'Come on Dad, I haven't got much time.' But he just stayed there, gazing. 'I never thought I'd ever see my name in lights,' he said.[1]

Keith Waterhouse also became famous and the play's success triggered a long and fruitful collaboration with Willis Hall. Together they wrote a dozen West End plays, as well as many film scripts. But Finney, as the star of the show, naturally drew the applause. Waterhouse, writing in 2009, recalled:

> Soon there was a regular procession of visiting celebrities through Albert Finney's dressing room. Princess Margaret came. So did Noël Coward who, as he records in his diaries, loathed the play and everything about it – exquisitely polite at the time, he later penned a famously bad-tempered attack on the whole 'kitchen-sink' theatre.[2]

Yet not all 'the old guard' were dismissive. Gielgud wrote in his diaries, 'I saw him [Finney] last week in a funny play called *Billy Liar* in which he is superb'.

Meanwhile, it looked like Finney was getting locked into an even bigger and far more lucrative part. In October 1960, the press reported that he seemed a shoo-in for the lead in *Lawrence of Arabia*. According to producer Sam Spiegel, Finney had been given an exhaustive, and successful, screen test. 'Contracts are now being discussed,' said Spiegel at a press conference at Columbia Pictures, 'with Cary Grant to play General Allenby; with Kirk Douglas to play the part of an American newsman; with Horst Buchholz as Sheik Ali and with Jack Hawkins as Colonel Newcombe'.[3]

Director David Lean, assistant director Gerry O'Hara, editor Ann Coates and Spiegel had all attended Finney's screen test in Borehamwood, shot over four days. Pictures show Finney with dyed brown hair and a full headdress. Coates, reportedly, was ecstatic. Lean's on-the-spot verdict was not recorded. But his subsequent reaction, according to his biographer, Kevin Brownlow, was that Finney:

> was rather too young for it … but the tests weren't half bad. When we saw them on-screen Sam Spiegel said 'what do you feel about him? Will you take him on?' I said – 'Sam, to tell you the truth, I think I can just about drag him through it but I can't say more than that'.

Perhaps on that occasion or a short time afterwards, at a meeting in Shepperton, Spiegel offered Finney, then 24, a £10,000 fee for the film and a contract worth £125,000 over the next five years. Yet the encounter, from Finney's point of view, was unsettling. He claimed that Spiegel had sat opposite him, blowing smoke in his face throughout their conversation. His official reason for declining, and probably the key obstacle, was being tied down to a five-year contract. 'Plenty of people have been ruined by Hollywood. I want to be an actor, not a marketable property like a detergent.'

When it became clear that Finney had officially declined the part, Lean visited him:

> I went to Albert and asked him why he was doing this. Why waste four days?
> He said, 'I think this may make me into a star and I don't want to become a star.'
> 'Why?'
> 'Because I'm frightened of what it will do to me as a person.'

The Finney tests are preserved at the National Film Archive. They reveal Finney well into character, with a solemn, serious delivery, certainly with the presence of O'Toole but perhaps without, yet, the older actor's hypnotically charismatic quality.

Finney's real reason for declining the part was not the film itself as such but what would have ensued – commitment. He hated it. He later elaborated in an interview in 1960, his comments revealing great insight in someone so young:

I do feel strongly about actors being committed too much. I think it's very bad. I'm young. I'm only 24 and I feel that if I'm signed up for five years for big international pictures and if one is a success in the first then one becomes an investment. And then in your next picture, and it's a bit like being a race-horse, the people that own you, they make sure you're sellable and they can confine your acting in order to reproduce what they thought was successful in the first film.

In 1996, outside London's L'Escargot restaurant, the camera caught an exchange between Finney and his interviewer Melvyn Bragg in which Finney said, 'There was something cold about Mr Lean's approach to performance.' Perhaps they simply didn't hit it off.

Finney became a big star anyway as soon as *Saturday Night and Sunday Morning* was released, and especially on the release of *Tom Jones*. But Finney, to his credit, had resisted the big pay cheque. This was something that earned him respect in the business. Gielgud, for example, said he 'greatly admired' Finney for spurning the offer.

Finney could decline a contract, that was his decision. But public recognition, in light of his superb performances, was another thing entirely. That he could not control, and his growing fame made life hard for those around him. Finney was still seeing Zoe Caldwell. On New Year's Day 1961, however, during the run of *Billy Liar*, Lindsay Anderson went round to their flat to be told by Zoe that she and Finney were splitting up. Anderson's diary tells us it was her decision: 'It does seem a shame … now that the room is so nice, and they seem so domesticated and comfortable – but this time, it appears, it's Zoe who has decided that she can't be sufficiently herself in the shadow of Albert.'

Finney was still reluctant to put down roots. 'I don't find the idea of running a flat, or organising or of collecting things. I don't find this very attractive. I don't want to feel that the place I live in is mine for life.' Anderson visited Finney to discuss the role of Frank Machin in *This Sporting Life*. Finney eventually declined it, feeling that the part was too similar to Arthur Seaton. That provoked an irrevocable rupture with Anderson. The director became cool and, later, critical of Finney. But Finney was determined not to be typecast; he wanted to surprise his audience:

Although I don't yet know what my next film will be, I do know that I want the character I play to be someone very different from Arthur Seaton in *Saturday Night*. I don't want to cash in on what Arthur's done for me, whether audiences have hated him or loved him … I hate that kind of idolising of a performance because it seems to stand for certain things, so I want those

people who're going to idolise me for the wrong reasons to get a surprise …
I suppose, in a way, I could go on playing Arthur Seatons for ten years – I'd
go mad!

Finney had now worked with Karel Reisz and Lindsay Anderson, both key
figures in the new wave. Now it was the turn of director Tony Richardson and
playwright John Osborne, the explosive, permanently hard-boiled writer whose
play *Luther* had won plaudits from theatre critics everywhere. (Finney would
also fall out with Osborne but that was years away.)

   Luther charts the life of sixteenth-century German Protestant reformer
Martin Luther, starting with his acceptance into the Augustinian order of
monks. It then traces his opposition to the Church's moral code through to the
Protestant reformation and Luther's eventual rejection of the Pope's authority.

   Finney left the run of *Billy Liar* in June 1961, leaving the role of Billy to
another rising star, Tom Courtenay.[4] [5]Finney took *Luther* first to Paris – at the
Théâtre Sarah-Bernhardt – then, after some regional openings, on to the Royal
Court, the Edinburgh Festival and the Phoenix Theatre in the West End.

   The first performance in Britain was at the Theatre Royal, Nottingham, on
26 June 1961. Some theatregoers had travelled all way up from London for
the opening. Such was the anticipation surrounding Osborne's new play that
Time magazine had even reviewed the script. The final ovation was rapturous.
Tony Richardson, who had feared that the audience might expect a variation
of Finney's Arthur Seaton, believed that Finney played Luther with a passion
unrivalled before or since.

   Finney's Luther evolved as he toured different venues, becoming more feted
by the time he reached London. 'Osborne brings the empirical man to life, and
gives the actor the opportunity to intensify that life on the stage, an opportunity
which Finney seizes masterfully,' said one critic. At the Phoenix a reviewer
said, 'Finney's performance takes on added authority in a larger theatre than
the Royal Court; his delivery of the first sermon being outstanding in its
hammering-in of the play's main theme'.

   Ever the perfectionist, Finney, for a scene where Luther had to throw a convincing epileptic fit, consulted a neurologist about symptoms. Kenneth Tynan
was full of praise:

> No finer Luther could be imagined than the clod, the lump, the infinitely
> vulnerable everyman presented by Albert Finney, who looks, in his moments
> of pallor and lip-gnawing doubt, like a reincarnation of the young Irving,
> fattened up for any cannibal feast.

Eric Shorter in the *Daily Telegraph* wrote of Finney 'clutching at both his stomach and his conscience'.

Osborne, in the second volume of his autobiography, recorded his excitement at seeing his play at the Royal Court, 'My head buzzed with the physical demonstration of my rehabilitated imagination'.[6] Richardson described it as one of those theatrical moments when everything just came together beautifully:

> *Luther* was one of those extraordinary moments of hard-hat type theatre where the crew – John and I, Jocelyn as designer, Jock as Gregorian chant-master, Albert and George in the cast, and other old friends like Peter Bull and John Moffatt – were united in drilling and hammering the blocks of theatrical masonry together.[7]

Finney once explained to Melvyn Bragg (who told Finney that *Luther* seemed like an extended monologue) his way of tackling long speeches, 'With big speeches the question is: what is the driving force behind it? Don't act the punctuation. When it's performed, it's aided by inflexion.'

Michael Parkinson remembers Finney's parents coming to see him, just as they had done when he starred in *Billy Liar*, when *Luther* opened in Manchester:

> On opening night he took a 10-minute standing ovation and we witnessed the burgeoning of a great new talent. The day after Albert Finney's triumph I interviewed his mother. I asked her what emotions she felt as her son received the rapture of that first-night audience. She said, 'I was very proud of our Albert. On the other hand, I kept looking at him on stage and thinking, "Oh, Albert, lad, I don't like your haircut".'[8]

Finney's run in *Luther* in London ended at the Phoenix on 31 March 1962 after 239 performances because of his commitment to start filming *Tom Jones* for Woodfall films.

By now Finney was greatly in demand – not only for roles but for interviews. Everyone wanted to find out more about this young Salford lad. Finney had a colourful private life, yet there was a certain contradiction. You could call him a private extrovert. In interviews he was seldom evasive, yet he seldom granted them. That's why Finney's exchanges with John Freeman were so illuminating. He would reveal more of himself than he had ever done. Sadly, more than fifty years on, it's the only episode unavailable for commercial viewing. Fortunately, the BBC rescreened the encounter in 1988. Let battle begin …

6

TOMFOOLERY

He wanted something where he could rage and tear things in tatters, emote and be a big tragic actor.

Tony Richardson on Albert Finney's attitude to *Tom Jones.*

John Freeman's *Face to Face* is seen as a landmark series. The former Labour Cabinet minister was known for his tough interrogation. His interview with Gilbert Harding, in which the prickly *What's My Line?* panellist was reduced to tears, was seen as a momentous television event. Freeman's badgering of Tony Hancock, although unremarkable by today's standards, also raised eyebrows.

Finney was still only 25 when he submitted to the Freeman treatment. He had appeared in an acclaimed film and two hit plays and been hailed as 'the next Olivier'. Finney's contemporaries, those who became international stars during this period, had not made it so young. O'Toole became world-famous past 30, likewise Harris and Connery. Michael Caine was 32 before *Alfie* secured him name-above-the-title fame. Finney was still *very* young. And so there was a danger that Freeman would uncover a certain immaturity in Finney. How many of today's 'celebrities' could explain their craft coolly and competently at such an age?

Finney's aversion to interviews grew with time. By the seventies or eighties, there was no way that he would ever agree to subject himself to the kind of interrogation meted out by Freeman. He later said he believed in preserving an air of mystery. He thought that this helped him to convince the audience of the character he was playing. He likes to do the work and go home. It was therefore surprising that he agreed to follow in the steps of Martin Luther King, John Huston and Edith Sitwell. Of all Freeman's interviewees, only Adam Faith, just 20, had been younger.

Freeman's style was calm but forensic. Something about the format and presentation seemed to put the subject in the dock. Freeman's face was never shown. All you saw was the back of his head. The camera homed in on the inter-viewee, capturing every grimace (in Hancock's case) or tear (or perspiration) in Harding's; it could detect evasiveness, anxiety, recalcitrance or discomfort. Neurotic personalities became withdrawn and guarded. That Finney agreed to it was, with hindsight, amazing. It was his most comprehensive television interview to date.

It turns out, Freeman's interview with Finney was seen as one of his weakest.[1] Perhaps he liked Finney too much to probe deeply. By Freeman's standards it was a tepid affair. No talk of death or psychological trauma. Yet much of the credit must go to Finney who managed to steer it away from the usual actor's angst. Finney, clad in a roller-neck sweater and smoking a lot, spoke affectionately of his parents. He 'admitted' his background was far from uncomfortable and portrayed himself as a happy-go-lucky youth, enjoying school plays and sport. With this picture of wholesome extroversion and domestic security, Freeman couldn't go for the jugular. Freeman flattered his subject by saying he'd heard that Finney's mother was 'a remarkable woman'. 'Oh thank you very much,' said Finney, who soon lapsed into the habit of calling his interviewer 'John'.

Freeman did draw some telling revelations. Finney blamed himself for the failure of his marriage (but) then added – 'I don't feel anything's a mistake, John, if you come through the other side of it.' He also said that, if he had a crisis in his life, he would handle it himself. Finney is relaxed throughout, although occasionally he wriggles in the chair, squirms his neck and purses his lips. The accent is purely Received Pronunciation – compare, for example, his interview with Clive Goodwin just four years later when he allows some Mancunian vowels to shine through – and the performance perhaps a little too studied.

Yet Finney is remarkably grounded for someone so young. He is, he says, wary of being surrounded only by 'servile waiters' (most modern 'celebrities' would wonder – what's wrong with that?) but Finney's bullshit detector always kept him from going off the rails.

The most illuminating moment comes when Freeman tackles him on the actor's eternal dilemma. Any performer needs publicity. Yet, when they hit it big, they tend to shun it. Or, put another way, a young unknown actor is flattered when he's recognised, but when he's accosted in the street it becomes a nuisance. Finney does not relish the spotlight. Freeman possibly senses this private side of Finney. 'Do you regard your job as done when the curtain comes down? Or do you subscribe to the old-fashioned view that the actor is a servant of the people?' asks Freeman.

'I think that the actor only owes the audience good work in the theatre. I don't feel an actor's private life has anything to do with it whatsoever,' replies Finney, articulating the word 'private' like a quintessential luvvie.

'But do you think that's completely consistent with the business you have to get into, whether you like it or not, of selling your personality – that on the one hand you enjoy the limelight but, on the other, you back out of it as fast as possible as soon as you're off the stage? Is there a temperamental inconsistency there?' follows up Freeman.

'No, because I'm an actor,' says Finney.

Acting was Finney's trade. He considered it done when the show ended. Finney always referred to acting as 'working'. 'I'm working on the stage,' he'd say. (It was around this time, during a performance of *Luther*, that Finney halted a performance to berate a noisy theatregoer. 'I'm up here working, so if you won't shut up, go home. And if you won't, I'm going home.')[2]

Face to Face was a success for Finney. It was not, however, an entirely unselfconscious performance. He came across as someone who was (perhaps understandably) concerned about image. He didn't want the public, who so far only knew him from *Saturday Night and Sunday Morning* and *Billy Liar*, to view him as a kind of north country hooligan. If there was a false note in the interview it was his assertion that he was 'a slow maturer' – pull the other one! *The Times* saluted Finney's self-possession in the duel with Freeman but commented, 'his manner was constantly alternating between urbane pontification befitting his present circumstances and his inheritance of rasping bluntness'.

Up until now Finney had acted in some heavy parts. *Luther* and *Billy Liar* required meticulous preparation and Finney later said that he sometimes felt he was taking himself a bit too seriously. So he and Tony Richardson thought it would be fun to do something completely lightweight and 'without social significance'. This from the man who had directed *Look Back in Anger*, *A Taste of Honey* and *The Loneliness of the Long Distance Runner*!

Tom Jones, the bawdy adventures of an eighteenth-century bastard who rises to become a country squire, became Finney's most famous movie. It was certainly a big money earner, not only for Finney and Richardson but also for John Osborne, who wrote the screenplay. Ironically, it was shot at breakneck pace and wrapped on a tight budget in ten weeks. 'The idea of spending, say, six months shooting a film would appall me,' said Richardson later. Filming started at the end of June 1962 and had ended by mid-September.

Yet, more than half a century on, *Tom Jones* has fared less well than *Saturday Night and Sunday Morning*. Once a film has been mercilessly satirised, people tend to forget its original appeal. Great comedy has been milked out of, for example, the famous eating scene with Joyce Redman (much of it apparently improvised) in which a gluttonous feast serves as extravagant sexual foreplay (comedian Dave Allen had a hilarious skit on this). And the film, one suspects, influenced other filmmakers to make imitative and derivative efforts, notably Stanley Kubrick's *Barry Lyndon*.

Luscious breasts, libidinous characters and rather hammy acting (especially from Wilfred Lawson and Hugh Griffith) all seem a little clichéd to present-day audiences. Likewise the filmmaking technique, replete with handheld camera shots, over-the-top narration (from Micheál Mac Liammóir), silent comedy scenes and long shots of Finney and English rose Susannah York riding through the West Country. But this was 1963. And Finney, with his flowing red locks, *did* look handsome; fantasy fodder for legions of cloistered young girls. And many of his subsequent female co-stars claimed to have developed a crush on him after seeing him in *Tom Jones*.

At the time Finney described the film as a welcome change of pace. He told Clive Goodwin that he needed a lighter role: 'It was good to do *Tom Jones* when instead of walking around the pool and considering what I did, I had to dive in and do things more spontaneously and not mind that the public would see a spontaneous reaction.'

Spontaneity and improvisation were also Richardson's credo. 'Tony was in his element, picking, blending, substituting, rearranging – if a scene took two days to shoot, the odds were he would change it all on the second day,' said Finney. Peter Bull also remembered Richardson telling him to ad-lib, '"Don't think what you are saying now is very funny. Go off darlings and make up something and we'll shoot it!"'.

Later, much later, Finney, although pleased that the film was a box office hit, claimed the whole experience was demeaning. He saw himself as a character actor and felt he was just being used to 'sell' something. 'Albert was bored by Tom Jones,' Richardson later admitted:

> He thought it wasn't an interesting part, it was reactive, and that all he had to use was his personality. And he found that frustrating. He wanted to tear into passion. The part didn't give him the opportunities of *Hamlet* or *Macbeth* … he wanted something where he could rage and tear things in tatters, emote and be a big tragic actor.[3]

Ironically, considering the film would be so successful, Finney took some convincing to accept it. He only agreed after securing the role of associate producer. Later, he traded this for a share of the profits. His first cheque made him a dollar millionaire.

Susannah York was also unenthusiastic, declining the part five times. Tony Richardson and his then wife, Vanessa Redgrave, treated her to two expensive lunches at the Savoy. Yet she kept refusing, claiming that theatre was her real home. The 23-year-old only agreed after she had invited the Richardsons round to her flat for dinner and inadvertently put sugar in the casserole instead of salt. Guilt-stricken, she finally accepted.

Tom Jones was tangibly a feel-good holiday film. *The Times* said as much, but then added a sting in the tail:

> There is, thank heavens, no law which says that 'serious' filmmakers should not make lightweight popular films from time to time. The only complaint one has against this particular example is just that popular though it may be, it just is not a very good film.

Alexander Walker in London's *Evening Standard* was particularly cutting, 'Tony Richardson has proved himself a clever director in the past. It saddens me that this time he shows himself to be merely clever, however.'

Yet none of that mattered. Finney and Richardson could do no wrong. Even *The Times* acknowledged that the film has 'a first-rate star-hero, Mr Albert Finney, who may not have all the acting finesse in the world but slams his personality over with a vigour which is guaranteed to rock the women in the audience and incite the men to emulation'.

Audiences loved the roustabout roaring, bottom pinching and Hogarthian high jinks. It had cost less than half a million pounds to make and went on to gross £25 million. Queues formed around the London Pavilion Cinema. It proved even more popular in the US. The *New York Times* wrote, 'Prepare yourself for what is surely one of the wildest, bawdiest and funniest comedies that a refreshingly agile filmmaker has ever brought to the screen. Mr Richardson gives his film the speed and the character of a keystone comedy.' So popular was it that a magazine cartoon in *The New Yorker* showed a patient moaning to his analyst, 'Doctor, what's my problem? *Tom Jones* depressed me.'

Tom Jones was one of three British films, the others being *Billy Liar* (which had been Finney's original role in the London play) and *The Servant*, shown at the Venice Film Festival in September 1963. In December, *Tom Jones* was voted best film of the year by the American National Board of Review of Motion Pictures. The same month, it won three honours in a ballot of New York film critics: best picture, best actor for Finney and best director for Richardson.

Tom Jones was also one of the biggest money-makers at the British box office in 1963 along with *From Russia with Love*, *Summer Holiday* and *The Great Escape*. Finney came in as the eighth most popular star in Britain after Cliff Richard, Peter Sellers, Elvis Presley, Sean Connery, Hayley Mills, Elizabeth Taylor and Marlon Brando. It was clear that both Finney and the film would be in the running for Oscars.

Before the film's release, Finney, in typical fashion, had decided to 'disappear' by directing some productions at Glasgow Citizens' Theatre – Pinter's *The Birthday Party* and Sheridan's *School for Scandal* – and starring in Pirandello's *Henry IV*. Finney simply wanted to direct but couldn't find any major theatres ready to take him on.

Interest in Glasgow Citizens' Theatre soared. And this was before *Tom Jones* had been released. Finney's *Henry IV* broke all box office records for the month that it played. The critics might not have been effusive – 'What was lacking was a secure mental control of the character,' said one reviewer – but the same critic then saluted Finney's audacity in taking his talent to a relatively unknown theatre, 'It's an event of importance when a success-laden performer such as Albert Finney chooses to resist the haphazard careerism of the London theatre in favour of seeking out the experience he needs, even if it leads into semi-obscurity'.

Perversely, throughout his life Finney sought insecurity. His life journey, at this point, seemed to be the opposite of most people's. His warm, loving childhood had offered too much certainty. So now, in his mid-20s and fiercely independent, he had discarded possessions and permanent digs. Even before *Tom Jones* had appeared, Finney was making good money. Yet his biggest purchase was an inexpensive sports car. He wore turtleneck sweaters, dungarees and sneakers. And all his worldly goods fitted into one trunk and three suitcases.

When Finney had attended a Variety Club dinner in London to collect his award for the most promising newcomer of 1960, he reportedly wore a green corduroy jacket, beige denim trousers and sandals over yellow socks. Other contemporary photographs show him in rumpled shirts, scarves and a flat cap. All actors, and there's no reason to believe that Finney was totally devoid of vanity, make a fashion statement of some kind through their appearance. Finney was projecting, consciously or not, a working-class image.

To say that Finney had footloose connections was an understatement. Even friends, he once said, were something of a 'liability'. But girls were different. They were vital. Finney's regular girlfriend was now Samantha Eggar, a stunningly beautiful actress, then 23, who had been signed for her movie debut in *The Wild and the Willing* by producer Betty Box after she spotted her in *A Midsummer Night's Dream* and *Twelfth Night* at the Royal Court. Eggar remembers that she saw *Luther* almost every night. Then she would rush home to cook dinner at her flat behind the Dorchester in Park Lane.

Finney's divorce from Jane Wenham came through around this time. Wenham was granted custody of their 3-year-old son, Simon. Finney would have little contact with his son over the next few years.

Eggar's role in *The Wild and the Willing* cast her opposite Ian McShane, the son of a Manchester United footballer who followed the trail that Finney had blazed – liberating young working-class talent. McShane was playing another boozy, skirt-chasing character somewhat in the mould of Tom Jones. Finney visited Samantha in Lincoln, bringing her some *fraises du bois* to console her during a freezing shoot. On a whim, Betty Box decided to put Finney in the film. He is seen, uncredited, wearing a college scarf.

Finney and Samantha particularly enjoyed holidaying in Greece, staying at the home of actor Peter Bull on the island of Paxos, just south of Corfu. Paxos, an hour's speedboat or hydrofoil ride away from Corfu, is even now relatively quiet. 'Bully', as he was known to his friends, was a supporting actor and a genuine eccentric who had once written a book about teddy bears. Say no more! Finney enjoyed several trips to his home.

Playwright Emlyn Williams was another early distinguished Corfu coloniser; likewise, Susannah York. In those days the island was undiscovered. Finney would ride into town on a donkey box trap. He enjoyed the anonymity, especially later when he became an international star. One story had Finney greeting locals warmly from his donkey and being unable to understand why they were all laughing at him. It turned out that Finney was saying '*kalamares*' which means squid, instead of '*kali mera*'!

Finney liked Greece so much that he and his second wife Anouk Aimée bought a home on Ipsos. One famous visitor, Tab Hunter, noting the 'sleepy time down south' nature of the place, referred to Finney's entourage as 'the hammock people' because all they ever wanted to do was take turns lying in the hammock, watching the world go by.

By 1963, Finney, who had been working constantly for almost a decade, was getting tired. The hammock was starting to look enticing. But he wanted to make another movie with Karel Reisz. They settled on the story of Ned Kelly, the legendary Australian outlaw. David Storey, who had written the script for Lindsay Anderson's *This Sporting Life* (the film Finney had declined because he feared the character of Frank Machin was too similar to Arthur Seaton) was commissioned to write it. Filming would take place in Australia. Finney and Reisz flew there on a ten-week recce in October 1962.

At a Sydney press conference, Finney seemed enthused. He said he had studied a Royal Commission report on the outlaw and had read ten books about him. 'Ned Kelly was an extremely complex character,' he told the gathering. 'In the film we want to try to show what Ned Kelly did but we do not want to portray him as a hero or a rogue.'

Filming was supposed to start in spring of 1963. But the project fell through because British labour regulations stipulated a British crew. This made the whole project unaffordable.[4]

Instead, well, the publicity for the film they *did* make should tell the whole story. 'The lusty brawling star of *Tom Jones* goes psycho!' screamed the posters. Finney and Reisz settled on a remake of Emlyn Williams's shocker, *Night Must Fall*, about a psychotic axe murderer on the loose in the English countryside. The movie has a particularly memorable scene in which the central character cuts off an elderly woman's head and places it in a hat box.

Reviews were also cutting. Here was *The Times*:

> Producers have followed the modern trend and used this film as a vehicle for examining what goes on in the mind of a homicidal maniac. But it is not easy to explain why anyone, even if he is as glib, persuasive, and unscrupulous as Mr Finney presents him in this new version, should undergo these particular brain storms and then find relief in this particular form of violent exertion.

Reisz believed that the post-*Tom Jones* Finney was starting to view screen acting as dull, especially if all he had to do was project easygoing charm:

> He had begun to feel what many male actors often feel about acting. Is this a proper job for a man – to keep smiling for the big world out there? The result was, I think, that he resisted playing Danny's charm and lightness and instead went for the pain and inwardness of the character.

Finney's fans from *Tom Jones* were disappointed. Reisz remembered showing a preview of the film. Apparently MGM wives laid into him, 'What have you done to this beautiful man, Tom Jones?'

For Finney, who wanted to be seen as a serious actor, it was just the kind of reaction he hated. Perhaps that's why Finney chose to persevere with character leads, taking *Luther* to New York's St James's Theatre in 1963. Finney proved a hit with audiences, critics and the fairer sex. His first taste of Broadway was a rip-roaring success. The *New York Times*'s Howard Taubman hailed *Luther* as a landmark in theatre, 'As drama, it has size and distinction. It is about matters worth thinking and talking about. It makes the theatre 10 feet tall.' Taubman added, 'Whatever your allegiance of faith may be, you owe it to yourself to rediscover the excitement that a vital play can deliver.' Finney was 'superb', he said. *The New York Daily News* described it as a work of power and integrity in which Finney gave 'a thoroughly splendid performance'.

Finney thought that the Broadway production was an improvement on the original. 'From the start, Tony [Richardson] and I admired the play so much and felt it was a holy grail. Now we are able to use it more.'

Finney, still only 27 in 1963, was basking in twin applause for his performances in *Luther* and *Tom Jones*. He had conquered both London and Broadway and was an international star. About twenty national magazines and newspapers were clamouring for profiles by the time of the New York production of *Luther*. The nation's largest weekly magazine asked for a cover portrait, and a leading women's fashion magazine wanted him to be the first man to appear on its cover.

Finney was part of a golden season on Broadway. Other acclaimed shows on at the time included *One Flew Over the Cuckoo's Nest* with Kirk Douglas, *Barefoot in the Park* with Robert Redford, *Oliver!* starring Clive Revill and Georgia Brown, and *The Ballad of the Sad Café*, based on Carson McCullers' novella, which Edward Albee had turned into a play.

Actor Michael Dunn[5] appeared in the Albee play, and he and Finney would swap stories over beer and steak at various actors' hangouts. Finney drank steadily yet seldom seemed drunk. But he knew how to have fun:

> Each Sunday morning a bunch of us would go over to Downey's at eleven – it was before the legal opening, but we had friends – lunch there, go up to Yankee Stadium, see the Giants, have a few drinks from the flask. The trick then was to find some girls to come home and cook dinner, say, while we watched the West Coast game on the television and partied some more.

The following spring, in 1964, Richard Burton would play Hamlet. New York theatregoers were treated to another British acting giant. And Michael Dunn was to have another seasoned drinker to keep him company.

Finney invited his mother and father to New York the week before Thanksgiving in 1963. Early in the afternoon of Friday, 22 November, Finney and his parents climbed to the observation deck on the top of the Empire State Building. Finney had to be back at the theatre by early evening. As they were coming down, around 2 p.m., the elevator man told the party, 'They've shot the president!' It was an enormous shock for everyone, let alone first-time visitors to New York.[6]

Finney later said he was struck by the solemnity and civility of New Yorkers, especially the driver of the Fifth Avenue bus who told him, 'I didn't like JFK's politics, but this is no way to solve the problem.' Rather typically of Finney, he keeps his own feelings close to his chest. Instead, he reports on the comportment of others. He's not naturally effusive in his public comments. He 'liked' his father very much, he said, after he had died in 1975. When his son, Simon, was born, Finney admitted that he 'was rather shocked that the sense of separateness was so strong'. This should not be taken for a lack of feeling. You could describe it as northern reserve or an English reluctance to gush.

Finney, and other stars, were enlisted to pay tribute to President Kennedy. Two days after the assassination (and one day before the funeral), a special live television programme entitled *A Tribute to John F. Kennedy from the Arts* was broadcast by ABC on network television. The screening featured dramatic readings from Finney as well as Christopher Plummer, Sidney Blackmer, Florence Eldridge and Charlton Heston. Plummer and Finney performed Hamlet's dying speech ('I am dead, Horatio …') with Finney taking the role of Horatio. The programme has never been repeated or released commercially.

Luther continued its New York run until early in 1964. By then his performance had evolved. A critic wrote:

> He acknowledges now that in those early days of *Luther* he stood in awe of the great historical figure whom he was impersonating. Both he and his fellow actors seem now to have a fuller comprehension of their difficult roles and to have found the proper moments for irony and passion.

Finney was rewarded with a Tony nomination for best actor. Finney loved New York. And the city's ladies, including some illustrious names, reciprocated. One of his famous girlfriends in 1963 was Shelley Winters. The actress, sixteen years older than Finney, recalled in her autobiography how she and Finney consummated their relationship in a car she had expressly bought for the purpose. She notes:

> It seems ridiculous now, but this was, remember, the pre-sexual-revolution early sixties, and then as now Finney was a very private person. But it was getting dangerous to park by the lake in Central Park and I was amassing parking tickets.[7]

Finney took his womanising seriously. 'I used to deal in bulk. There is nothing wrong with that. Why not? It was a lot of fun. I tended to hunt alone, like a U-boat, going about quietly to operate,' he once said.[8]

Peter Ford, son of Hollywood veteran Glenn Ford, remembers gatecrashing a party at Finney's apartment over Christmas 1963:

> Inside a bacchanal was in progress, awash with beautiful people partying with uninhibited zeal … I can remember bits and pieces of the evening which didn't end until daybreak. Was that Elizabeth Ashley French-kissing me as I sat in Finney's living room? Who were those naked women in Finney's bedroom (with Finney passed out on the bed) singing Christmas carols to him?[9]

Finney may have played the Protestant Luther, but it seems he was a man of Catholic taste. Finney's list of conquests in the sixties was impressive. The relationship with Samantha Eggar proved short-lived and Finney was moving on. There were legions of beautiful women across the high seas. So it was, after the enormous success of *Luther* and *Tom Jones*, Finney decided that a 'sabbatical' was in order, well away from the madness of celebrity, awards and movies. A year of free living followed. Oscars be damned!

SLOW MOTION

I have no regrets about the choices I've made. What I've done is what I should have done.

Albert Finney.

Jack Lemmon hosted the 36th Academy Awards, held on 13 April 1964. Frank Sinatra presented the award for the best picture to *Tom Jones*. Rita Hayworth announced the best director as 'Tony Richards', a faux pas for which she was mortified. And Anne Bancroft presented the Oscar for best actor to … Sidney Poitier for *Lilies of the Field*.

Finney had been favourite to win the Oscar. Yet at that moment he was thousands of miles away. Finney was seriously involved in the hedonism business while the awards rolled. He once told a story to Michael Blakemore that summed up his mood. Blakemore relates the tale:

> When Albert made his million on *Tom Jones* and went on his sabbatical trip around the world, he stopped in Acapulco. One evening he was drinking Dom Pérignon on a balcony with the most beautiful girl in Mexico. He took her into the bathroom and put his cock into her. With every thrust, he said, out loud: 'That's for Dad, that's for Mum, and that's for Uncle Ted, and that's for Cousin Jim, and that's for Auntie Marion …' A whole working-class family shared that fuck.

Back in 1964, it wasn't quite so compulsory for nominees to attend the Oscars as it is today. Nevertheless, Finney had done himself no favours by his absence. Yet this was just the start. Finney did no work for the remainder of 1964 once his run on *Luther* ended in January. His agent, keen to capitalise on his young client's success, was appalled. Finney later reflected:

I remember my then-agent in New York. He said, 'But Albert, they won't remember who you are.' I said, 'They didn't know who I was six months ago in New York, so what's the difference?' What I realised in that eleven months of travel was that I want to get outside the profession now and again … I learnt that lesson in '64, that I need to be able to get away from it for a while and just be without thinking: How is the character I'm trying to learn about? How would he be at this point? You have to remember how YOU are at that point.

And despite grumbling from those who had something to profit from Finney's lucrative period, he never regretted the year off:

People told me to cash in on my success while I was hot. But what I wanted to do then was go around the world. I'd been acting for about eight years and had only had one vacation. So I decided to take a year off after my contract in *Luther* ended. I'd always wanted to travel. Captain Cook had been a hero of mine when I was a kid, and I thought it would be exciting to go to some of the places in the Pacific where he'd been. That's what I did. I have no regrets about the choices I've made. What I've done is what I should have done.[1]

Finney was in Hawaii on Oscar night. He had already visited the islands the year before and had befriended Eddie Sherman, Hawaii's premier journalist. Now he was staying for an indefinite period. As the red carpet was being unfurled at Santa Monica's Civic Auditorium, Finney called Sherman:

He asked me what I was doing on the night of the Oscars. 'Just gonna watch the show', I said.

'Then how about joining me? I've got some birds [girls] I'm taking out on a catamaran.'

I told him I'd only go if I could bring a radio along so I could listen to the Academy Awards. If he wins, I figured, I'll have me a nice scoop.

Finney agreed. He didn't care to see or hear the show. He just wanted to go sailing. I found a nice spot on the tarpaulin above the deck of the catamaran to observe the action and listen to the Academy Awards. Finney was having a great time, tossing down the Polynesian drinks and dancing with his 'birds'.

Finally, 'best actor' was announced. Sidney Poitier was the winner. When I yelled down the information to Finney, he stopped the dancing and asked everybody to raise their glasses in a deserved toast to a great actor: Sidney Poitier. That was class. Then the music started up again, and the dancing and the fun continued.

It was dark by the time we sailed the cat back into Waikiki. A bunch of lights from shore hit the vessel. TV reporters were waiting. Finney asked if I would talk to my contemporaries on his behalf. So I jumped off and said to them, 'No story here. Sidney Poitier won for *Lilies of the Field*.'

But the reporters were persistent and Finney reluctantly talked to them.[2]

Tom Jones had won four Oscars in total, for best film, director, adapted screenplay and music. Finney seemed genuinely underwhelmed. During his Hawaiian sojourn he told Sherman:

> I realise that when one gets famous there is a public responsibility. But I don't quite know how to handle it. Basically, I'm a stage actor and have been earning my living on the stage since I was 19. People don't usually bother stage actors but it's different in films. Right now I just want to travel anywhere in the world I want. I want to see places and people. I don't want to be tied down with commitments. If I knew I had a picture to do, five months from now, I'd be worrying about the part and couldn't enjoy anything else.

And travel Finney did, beginning in Mexico, and exploring Hawaii, Fiji, Australia and Hong Kong. Finney's enthusiastic lovemaking in Acapulco, even more enthusiastically related second-hand by Michael Blakemore, was marred by a nasty incident at sea. Artist Annette Nancarrow[3] recalls the encounter:

> When I met him he was in great pain as he had been scuba diving and had stepped on a sea urchin and the poisonous spines had entered the sole of his foot. I could see he was suffering from a fever. I took his pulse and immediately took him to a doctor friend of mine who applied a primitive remedy known in Acapulco. This doctor lit a pork wax candle and let it drip on the foot where the spines had penetrated the skin. Miraculously, the spines came out. The doctor also put him on antibiotics, and Albert Finney recovered very quickly.

Throughout this period Finney had plenty of time – between navel-gazing, making love to exotic beauties, Tahitian dancing, swimming, sailing and sinking mai tais – to define his philosophy. He wanted to remain (primarily) a stage actor and he wanted to be free to do whatever he wanted. 'I don't want to be a victim of supporting a lifestyle that you have to get huge salaries to support, even if you do things for nothing,' he'd say later.

Sure, there would be some films, but he would choose them carefully. So it was, in ensuing years, he declined the chance to work with Julie Andrews on (ironically) *Hawaii* and on *The Molly Maguires* with Sean Connery.[4] Richard Harris starred in both instead. Finney also opted out of John Huston's *The Bible*.[5]

Finney was away travelling for almost a whole year. By the end of 1964 he felt, as he later admitted, so 'wound down' that he barely had the motivation to open a book. It was time to get home. Predictably, he resisted juicy film offers to tread the boards. Finney was realistic enough to know that he had to ease himself back gently. So he played Don Pedro, a relatively small part, in the National Theatre production of *Much Ado about Nothing* at the Old Vic, directed by Franco Zeffirelli.

It was his first performance for the National. He told Clive Goodwin that he felt he needed to get his breathing equipment into gear again. 'I couldn't quite time when to take my breaths anymore. I felt that it took me about three months of being back in the theatre to feel match fit.' Not that colleagues or audiences thought Finney was out of practice. He seemed as brilliant as ever. Ian McKellen, playing Claudio, remembered, 'I couldn't believe that Albert Finney, such a star, was playing what I took on the page to be the supporting part. I hadn't realised that Don Pedro is probably the best part. Couldn't keep my eyes off Albert, just riveting.'

Derek Jacobi, playing Don John, later inherited the part of Don Pedro from Finney. He found Finney a hard act to follow:

> Albert Finney as Don Pedro was unequivocally marvellous and as part of his performance and throughout the run he smoked cigars – provided free by W.D. & H.O. Wills. At the end of the play there were two banquettes on stage, on either side, and Don Pedro would be left on his tod, puffing thoughtfully on his cigar. Albert would blow a smoke ring and the smoke went curling slowly round, expanding beautifully into the auditorium. He was such a master and it was a lovely moment.
>
> Sometime during the run, which went on for years, the cast changed and Ronnie Pickup took over Don John from me. I took over from Albert the part of Don Pedro. There was a great drawback here because I couldn't blow smoke rings, and also by now they had to buy the cigars for me – no Albert's name on the programme![6]

A more testing role for Finney was as John Armstrong in John Arden's *Armstrong's Last Goodnight*, directed by John Dexter. Among the forty-strong cast were Graham Crowden, Paul Curran, John Hallam, Ian McKellen and Geraldine McEwan. Set in sixteenth-century Scotland, it tells of King James's attempts to establish authority over local barons. It was a complex play with various Scottish dialects to differentiate between the gentry and the common folk.

Native Scot Iain Cuthbertson had played Armstrong to perfection at Glasgow's Citizens'Theatre. *The Guardian*'s Benedict Nightingale preferred Cuthbertson's approach:

> Finney emphasises the sullen, brutish side of the character; he appears to take one line of the play, that he is violent, proud and abominably selfish, entirely literally. He misses the warmth and generosity of heart. At the end, when poor Finney dangles dead from a tree, it's difficult to feel concerned.

Lindsay Anderson, who had been disappointed by Finney's refusal to accept *This Sporting Life*, stayed with Finney in Chichester. The director, it seems, was determined to castigate Finney and everything he appeared in. He described Finney, in his diary entries:

> … boringly constricted in taste and conversation, completely closed. The acting also: closed, technical; uninteresting … I was bored with Armstrong which I find tiresomely affected – all this ridiculous Scottish accent and vocabulary – and atrocious construction.

Anderson, from this point onwards, always painted Finney as a spoiled dilettante, corrupted by money and fame. Newcomers to Finney territory, however, like actor William B. Davis, found him to be the complete opposite: likeable, generous and grounded. Finney was also endearingly honest when a part wasn't working for him. Davis, who was treated to the 'egalitarian' dinner that featured in our prologue, was startled to see Finney interrupt director John Dexter during *Armstrong's Last Goodnight*, before a particularly long speech, to tell him that he (Finney) didn't know how to play it. Davis remembered it was close to a full dress rehearsal. Davis never forgot the lesson:

> What has stuck with me to this day is that there's no point chattering on with a long speech if you don't know what gets you into it. I often tell students to rehearse the start of a monologue – no point rehearsing the rest of it if you don't have the beginning working.[7]

Underlying all Finney's behaviour was a rare humility in such a big star. Take *Armstrong's Last Goodnight*. The *Daily Telegraph* critic W.A Darlington had earlier slammed the Chichester production:

> If your idea of a well-spent evening is to listen to slugs of talks in an ersatz dialect of medieval Scots for more than three hours here is your play. You get

some decapitations thrown in, a bit of murder, some elementary pageantry and a realistic hanging. But speaking quite personally, I don't know why anybody wanted to write it or anybody wanted to put it on.

When Darlington saw the play at the OldVic, however, in a restaging by Finney, he reversed his view completely:

The whole atmosphere of the piece is subtly changed. The action seems closer knit, the dialogue less uncouth, and more easily followed, the characters more human and individual. How much of this startling change is due to the more intimate kind of staging I cannot guess. It is pretty clear, though, that great credit must go to Albert Finney, who re-staged the original Dexter-Gaskill production, for the warmth and humanity the piece now has.

Darlington was surprised to receive a letter from Finney himself, which the critic described as 'reflecting an attractive modesty in the writer'. In the note, Finney disclaimed the credit for the improved production. Instead he paid tribute to Dexter and Gaskill's work and said it was the OldVic itself, with its greater intimacy and the closer concentration of a proscenium theatre, which accounted for the improvement.

Finney, although ever conscientious at the National, still had a healthy work/play balance. Julia Goodman, later to become an actress (best known for *The Brothers*) was a teenage usher at Chichester in 1965. She recalled heading back to the flat of Finney's great friend, Norman Rossington, (who had co-starred with him in *Saturday Night and Sunday Morning*) for an eventful evening in which Finney and Norman were busily proving their manhood. The carnal pleasures, I must hasten to add, did not include Julia. She was busy chasing an enormous moth out of the premises.

Julia's uncle was the racehorse trainer Gordon Smythe;[8] she would subsequently introduce Finney to him. All these years later, she believes that it's clear that 'Albert has never had a full-on acting career. His real love was horses.' Nevertheless, Julia remembers first-hand the impact of his performances. She thought Finney was marvellous in *Armstrong's Last Goodnight* and has a particularly vivid memory of Finney bellowing 'you're nothing but a whore!' in a thick Scottish accent.

For Julia, however, the highlight was Peter Shaffer's *Black Comedy*, performed in a double bill with *Miss Julie*. *Black Comedy*, which opens on a darkened stage, related the misadventures of a young artist, Brindsley Miller (Derek Jacobi), saddled with an idiot fiancée, who has invited a millionaire art collector round to see his work. He smartens up his flat by pilfering furniture from a gay neighbour,

Harold Gorringe, played to the hilt with hand-on-hip hysteria by Finney. Julia remembers 'a distinctly podgy Finney, dressed in a pink shirt, outrageously camp … no one had ever been so funny in the part.'

Derek Jacobi was in awe of Finney and Maggie Smith – the latter cast as his ex-mistress. So Finney, perhaps sensing Jacobi's diffidence, tried to allay his anxiety by inviting him out to dinner. 'You've got the bigger part, so don't you worry about Maggie and me. We can look after ourselves. This is your play and your big part. Get on with it,' Finney told him.

Jacobi remembered Finney's quick-wittedness:

In the play I hide Gorringe's [Finney's] Buddha statue under his raincoat. Gorringe enters in a fury, carrying his lighted candle, sees his raincoat, grabs it, and pulls the statue on to the floor, which then breaks. But one night the business went arse over tit. Albert came on, seized the raincoat, pulled it off the table, the Buddha hit the floor but it didn't smash as expected. Albert went 'Ah', blew out the candle, all with the speed of light, a fantastic moment of inspiration.

Black Comedy was a great success, triggering laughter in surprisingly high places. Shaffer recalled a funny incident on the night of 10 March 1966, just before the curtain rose at the Old Vic. He was leaving the theatre when he saw the Queen arriving. 'I'm so looking forward to this, your farce, because my sister [Princess Margaret] came last week and she almost died laughing,' the monarch told him. Shaffer replied. 'Well, I hope you do too.'[9]

In *Miss Julie*, Strindberg's classic study of a duel between servant and mistress, Finney was praised for his 'subtle compound of materialism and social pretension'.

An interesting encounter during a production of Congreve's *Love for Love*, which starred Laurence Olivier as Tattle, was with Anthony Hopkins, then Colin Blakely's understudy. Hopkins was expected to take over from Blakely when he went away on tour. Finney took the role instead at short notice. But Hopkins remembered his first meeting with Finney because they would rehearse songs together. '"Hello", he said, "I'm Albert Finney. Can yer sing? No? Welsh, aren't yer?"'

It's worth comparing Hopkins to Finney. In the eyes of many, Hopkins became Britain's greatest modern actor. He certainly eclipsed Finney in fame, becoming an Oscar-winning international star. Hopkins is also much less choosy. Hence, although they are both about 80 (Finney being nineteen months older), Hopkins has twice as many screen credits. He is a household name to American audiences in the way that Finney no longer is.

Back in 1965, however, the reverse was the case. Finney was the big name, mature and self-confident in only his late 20s. Hopkins, by contrast, was a late starter. It wasn't until he turned about 35 that he really came into his own. Nowadays the internet occasionally buzzes with the kind of fun-filled comparison that keeps keen movie fans busy. Who was the better actor, Finney or Hopkins? Both are tangibly great modern actors with many acclaimed stage and film parts to their credit. Occasionally they have vied for the same role. Both were considered, for example, for *Under the Volcano* and, at various times, were in the running for *Gandhi*.

Both tackled Shakespeare on stage at the National to middling reviews. Hopkins's *Macbeth* was a fraught production which saw the Welshman storming out of the Old Vic and off to Hollywood. His Lear in 1986, which I saw at the National, was a bit of a one-pitch screamer. Critics compared him to a bantamweight boxer. He reminded me more of one of those talented fighters, punch drunk and past his prime, still belting away but to no great effect. Not that he was too old to play Lear — he was only 48 — but Hopkins simply appeared exhausted, performing, as he was, *King Lear* in tandem with *Antony and Cleopatra*. Around this time he gave sensitive performances in *84 Charing Cross Road* and *The Bounty*. This was just before he started 'expecting an old friend for dinner', eating human liver with Chianti and all that *Hannibal* madness.

Hopkins, when they met at the National during *Love for Love*, was full of admiration for Finney:

> There was a pretty heavy cast in *Love for Love* — Olivier, Geraldine McEwan and so on — and you must remember that he hardly knew the part, so he was having to mug along. As he walked on, the audience went berserk and Finney just stood there, milking the applause. I'd never seen such bravura. Olivier went quite red and even turned a somersault on stage to see if he could steal a scene. They were having a drink afterwards and Olivier said to the assembled, through tight lips, 'Albert's doing so well!' Finney replied quickly, ''cos, I'm a bloody big star.' He was so friendly and accessible; just the sort of four-square, full-frontal actor I admire.

Finney's statement that he was a 'bloody big star' should be taken as tongue-in-cheek, for, in almost every way, Finney and Hopkins are diametrically opposite. Finney wanted to be an actor, *not* a star. He said that, if stardom came, it was merely incidental. On balance, Finney always preferred the stage to screen. He only stopped theatre work when he sensed he was losing his stamina. Hopkins has always expressed dissatisfaction with the stage. Even when he was winning plaudits for fine stage work in *Pravda* or *M. Butterfly*, he never seemed happy. Filming suited him better. 'You do it, it's in the can and you move on to something else,' he'd say.

Many years later, when Hopkins had moved to California, he would reflect on the dreariness of doing a midweek matinee at the Old Vic – the rain lashing down, audiences coughing as they took off their duffel coats. In his mind the London theatre seemed mired in eternal winter. Hopkins also had another reason for disliking the stage. He ached to be a big star. And here a psychologist would doubtless find the roots of ambition in childhood. Hopkins, an extremely solitary only child, was a school dunce and poor at sports. He was, by his own account, hopeless at everything until he turned to acting. At home it was no better. He once said that his father was 'a man of little patience who was always putting me down'.[10]

Hopkins craved attention and adulation. He always said he wanted to be 'loved' by vast numbers of people. He was insecure, neurotic, always chomping at the bit, screaming at directors if he felt that they were treading on his toes. Predictably, perhaps, his drinking spiralled out of control. It all ended in a tequila-fuelled escapade in California. He woke up in a strange place with no recollection of how he got there. Next, he called Alcoholics Anonymous.

Finney was very different. He had a warm background. He was popular at school and a talented sportsman. He did not become an actor to be loved but simply because he enjoyed it. And Finney never moved to Hollywood, preferring to base himself in Chelsea. My point is this – Hopkins was, in many ways, the more typical representative of that screwed-up species known as the late twentieth-century screen actor: angry, ambitious, tortured, neurotic, self-obsessed and insecure. More actors are like Hopkins than Finney. Hopkins envied Finney's poise and aplomb and remembered asking Michael Gambon if he'd ever seen such confidence in a young actor. 'Never,' replied Gambon.

The two actors have contrasting styles. Hopkins's performances are (mostly) marked by quiet understatement – his gentle, lilting voice is perhaps more lyrical than Finney's – with little brushstrokes filling out the character. Finney has always been more liberal with his colours. I am not concluding who was better, merely making a comparison.

Significantly, however, Hopkins always believed in Finney's greatness. Later, he said, 'I think the first British actor who really worked well in cinema was Albert Finney. He was a back-street Marlon Brando. He brought a great wittiness and power to the screen. The best actor we've had.'[11] More than thirty years later, the two great actors met again and Hopkins recalled that he (Hopkins) became quite emotional.

Finney's final turn at the National came in *A Flea in Her Ear*, Feydeau's turn-of-the-century comedy about two almost identical-looking Frenchmen, one an upper-class lawyer, the other a drunken porter in a brothel. Finney did a riotous double act in a revival staged by French actor and film director Jacques Charon.[12] Finney had to perform many quick changes backstage.

John Mortimer had translated it and he, Finney and Olivier pored over every line to ensure that the laughs punctuated the play at appropriate moments. It all worked splendidly. The National's first French farce was such a hit that when it opened at the Old Vic in February 1966 queues formed round the block. Soon the only tickets left were for matinees. Everyone, it seemed, tried to get tickets to *A Flea in Her Ear*, including another of Finney's famous friends, Vidal Sassoon, who claimed to have seen Finney in *Luther* three times. He went to see it with the actress Adrienne Corri:

> The play was a riot. The curtain came down and Adrienne said, 'let's go back-stage and congratulate Albie'.
>
> As Adrienne and I walked into the dressing room, Albert kissed her, turned to me and said, 'Hello, Vid, meet Larry.' I looked up. It was Laurence Olivier. The Laurence Olivier. He looked me over and said, 'Did he call you Vid? What's your real name?'
>
> 'Vidal Sassoon.'
>
> A sigh came from Olivier. 'Ohhh, so you're that barber.'[13]

Fergus Cashin pronounced *A Flea in Her Ear* 'the funniest thing that has ever happened in the theatre'. Michael Billington believed that 'Finney's masterstroke – in a real sign of acting intelligence – was never to exaggerate the difference between the two men so that the confusion of one for the other became totally plausible.' *The Times* merely thought that Finney's turn 'was one good comic performance among others'.

In June 1966, Robert Lang took over the dual roles in *A Flea in Her Ear*. By now Finney's new girlfriend was Edina Ronay, the voluptuous daughter of food critic Egon Ronay, who had appeared as a young girl in *The Pure Hell of St Trinians*. In the mid-sixties, she was Michael Caine's companion. But Caine ditched her after *Alfie*, released in 1966, made him into a huge international star. She went to live with her parents but a week later she bumped into Finney at the opening of an art exhibition. 'Albie was just the right kind of man to be with – warm, friendly, a wonderful companion. I stayed with him a year,' Edina recalled.

The relationship, like all the others, did not last long. The strolling player was off again. Finney was about to make his first film in three years. He had to spend the summer in the Mediterranean with Audrey Hepburn. Somebody had to do it. It was to be a glorious summer of love.

8

AUDREY

She was rather like a blooming flower and then when her husband arrived, the flower closed up and shrivelled.

Albert Finney on Audrey Hepburn.

Such was the tearful description of Albert Finney, not normally someone given to so sentimentalise, for his co-star in *Two for the Road*. More books have been written about Audrey Hepburn since her tragically premature death in 1993 than almost any other female star. There is something untouchable about her. No other actress of her generation had her combination of grace, elegance, dignity, warmth and sensibility.

Take the competition. Elizabeth Taylor, legendary superstar, was a bit of prima donna – 'I don't pretend to be an ordinary housewife' – flirtatious, spoiled, impulsive, brash and hot-tempered. Bardot was *the* sex kitten, voluptuous, sensual and passionate, obsessed with her causes and occasionally driven to destructiveness through them. Deneuve: haughty, icy and slightly aloof. Loren: proud, strong-willed and tigerish. All in their own way were tough, brassy women.

Hepburn, by contrast, was elegant, gentle-voiced and doe-eyed. Above all, Hepburn was a lady – nobody like her. 'Class,' Billy Wilder once marvelled. 'Someone who went to school, can spell, and possibly play the piano … You're really in the presence of somebody when you see that girl.'

You couldn't lose if you paired Hepburn with a handsome on-screen partner: Cary Grant in *Charade*, Rex Harrison in *My Fair Lady* or George Peppard in *Breakfast at Tiffany's*. And at the time, 1966, where better to examine a strained twelve-year marriage? The South of France, naturally – the sophisticates' playground.

Two for the Road is not, I think, fundamentally a problem picture. It may be presented as such, but it's with a wink to the audience. We know the couple's marital problems are not meant to be taken too seriously. And with such an attractive couple, bickering by the bougainvillea, the bitterness is not real. It's Courvoisier or Grand Marnier suffering, offering few accurate reflections on relationships, let alone married life. But it proved perfect fare for cinema-going couples in 1967, a year of innocence just before the terrible year of 1968.

Just as another film from this period, *Guess Who's Coming to Dinner?*, was described as the problem picture that isn't (because the black would-be groom is so eminently attractive), so *Two for the Road* is not marriage guidance stuff. Joanna is so adorable and Mark would be stupid to ditch her. Like many films by Stanley Donen, it's ultra-glossy, smartly packaged, glitzy and, ultimately, insubstantial. But that doesn't make it any the less enjoyable.

Screenwriter Frederic Raphael and his wife had always taken summer holidays in the South of France since they were childhood sweethearts. It was Raphael who first suggested the story of a couple's twelve-year marriage, viewed through various time bands, but played out under the summer holiday sun. Donen liked the idea. After all, what was there *not* to like?

Paul Newman was the original choice to play Mark Wallace, but he declined. Tony Curtis was then considered and rued losing it, 'I was pretty sure that Audrey liked me but later I heard that when my name came up that Audrey's husband, Mel Ferrer, who made those decisions for her, didn't want me in the picture.'[1]

The part was then offered to Finney whose screen persona couldn't be further from Hepburn's. Whereas Hepburn was shy, demure, sweet-natured and vulnerable, Finney conveyed a strong, surly masculinity. Perhaps the contrast was necessary to avoid the picture becoming over-schmaltzy.

Finney was only 30 in *Two for the Road*, but he looks more mature; Audrey was 37 but their being born only a few days apart, Audrey on 4 May, Finney on 9 May, seemed a good omen. Finney was aware that Hepburn was his most famous co-star to date and this was a big international picture. Yet he was determined not to be dazzled; he cultivated an almost blasé, jokey attitude from the start. Finney phoned Donen to warn him that he would be staging a little show for their first meeting in a restaurant.

The Finney who walked in, arm-in-arm with a male companion, was the mincing homosexual from *Black Comedy*. He acted effeminately for a full half an hour, fussing and faffing around over the dining table, his jacket draped over his shoulders, rearranging the cutlery and serviettes. He prefaced every comment with 'we' while holding on to his male friend, 'We really liked your last picture ...'

Hepburn didn't know what to say. She couldn't reconcile the actor before her with the robust factory worker of *Saturday Night and Sunday Morning*, or the skirt-chasing rascal of *Tom Jones*. Not that she had seen either film. Hollywood

stars can be surprisingly cut off from other actors' work. But she knew of
Finney's reputation. She kept quiet, however, and went along with it. Eventually,
Finney could sustain the act no more and broke up. Hepburn then collapsed
into helpless laughter when she realised the charade. From then on, he and
Audrey bonded. She was won over by her co-star's flirtatiousness and, above all,
his down-to-earth attitude.

The production took over the Hôtel du Golf at Beauvallon, near St-Tropez.
While other actors retreated to their camper vans, Finney and Hepburn were
happily swimming and rolling about in the sand. Donen was delighted; it would
make it easier for them to do love scenes. And happy stars make for a great set.
'The Audrey I saw during the making of this film I didn't even know. She was
so free, so happy. I never saw her like that. So young … I guess it was Albie,'
said Donen. Actor Robert Wolders agreed. 'Audrey cared for Albie a great deal,'
he said. 'He represented a whole new freedom and closeness for her. It was the
beginning of a new period in her life.'

Indeed. So much so that writer Irwin Shaw, who visited the set, said:

> They behaved like a brother and sister in their teens. When Mel dropped in
> to watch, Audrey and Albert got rather formal and a little awkward as if they
> now had to behave like grown-ups … she and Albie had this wonderful thing
> together, like a pair of kids with a perfect understanding and a shorthand of
> jokes and references that closed out everything else.

Finney later told of his feelings towards Audrey:

> Audrey and I met in a seductive ambience in the Mediterranean. We got on
> immediately. After the first day's rehearsals I could tell that the relationship
> would work out wonderfully. Either the chemistry is there or it isn't. … that
> happened with Audrey. During a scene with her my mind knew I was acting
> but my heart didn't, and my body certainly didn't. Performing with Audrey
> was quite disturbing, actually … with a woman as sexy as Audrey you some-
> times get to the edge where make-believe and reality are blurred – all that
> staring into each other's eyes. I won't discuss it more because of the degree of
> intimacy involved. The time spent with Audrey is one of the closest I've had.

A love scene, filmed in a closed set in a hotel, was quite nerve-racking for
Hepburn who had a complex about her thinness. According to Alexander Walker,
'all this had to be performed by Audrey naked except for a pair of briefs and a
sheet partially covering her own and Finney's bare torsos. Chris Challis behind
the camera talked her through it, assuring her that it was sexy and proper.'

Finney helped her to feel confident, complimenting her on her beauty and being especially tender with her in a scene that unnerved Hepburn, in which he had to throw her into a pool. They apparently romped together on the deserted beach nearby before the dunking. Finney and Audrey were indeed 'close', as the saying goes. Did something happen? Photographer Terry O'Neill was on set with them. 'I believe they were having an affair,' he said, 'although I never saw any evidence. I never saw any hanky-panky'. But he ventured that he had 'never seen her so happy on a film set', adding that Finney clearly adored her:

> Everyone who met her fell in love with her. You couldn't help it. The girl you saw on-screen? She was that person. She was the most down-to-earth movie star I've ever met. I couldn't take a bad photograph of her.[2]

Another person associated with the film, commented, 'If he and Audrey did make love, they were discreet about it, but no one doubted the warmth between them.'

Finney never elaborated. But one or two (glaring) clues exist along the way. Paul Colby remembers talking to Finney at his nightclub in New York's Greenwich Village:

> I told him that one of my favourite movies was *Two for the Road* with him and Audrey Hepburn. In the film, while trying to work out marital problems, they drive all over Europe in a white Mercedes 230sl. I said, 'Albert, I was so impressed with your performance and the car that I went out and bought one. I got my car from *Two for the Road.*'
>
> 'Yes,' said Finney with a wry smile, 'you may have gotten the car but did you get Audrey Hepburn?'[3]

But by far the most reliable source is Robert Sallin who worked with Finney a couple of years later on *The Picasso Summer*. He revealed that Finney told him, almost teary-eyed, of his affair with Audrey. Sallin said that Finney related he was spellbound by her 'loveliness'. He also recalls Finney telling him – and, yes, I know I'm repeating it but I like it so much that I shall – that 'she was rather like a blooming flower and then when her husband arrived, the flower closed up and shrivelled.'

Audrey was more effusive about Finney than any of her co-stars since William Holden:

> I love Albie. I really do. He's so terribly, terribly funny. He makes me laugh like no one else can. And you can talk to him, really talk. He's serious too,

completely so about acting, and that's wonderful. Albie's just plain wonderful, that's all there is to it.

According to Hepburn's biographer Donald Spoto, Mel Ferrer warned Audrey that if she didn't end her relationship with Finney, he would sue for divorce. Fearing that she would lose custody of their son, Sean, in a court hearing, Audrey stopped seeing Finney.

What appeared on film, ungallant though it may be to say it to its legions of admirers, was marginally less wonderful, although always an enjoyable nostalgic 'ride' on the telly on a wet winter Sunday afternoon in Britain. Mark is rather surly and Finney, just as he does later in *Charlie Bubbles*, seems determined not to give us any real screen charm in the Cary Grant (or even Tony Curtis) mould. Finney looks quite truculent, giving us little clue to the off-screen fun. It's difficult to figure out why. He seems to be reminding the audience of his Britishness at every turn. Perhaps the actor in him thought that to be *seen* to be having a good time, to capitulate too wholeheartedly to this frolicking in the sun, was beneath him.

Maybe Finney deliberately decided to project a slight cynicism and hardness against Hepburn's softness. But it makes the film a bit sour. What, one wonders, did Joanna see in this oaf? Just occasionally, Finney lightens up. Yet he can't help looking a bit bored. The movie offers us idyllic locations but nothing particularly profound about the human condition. Once you accept it on that level, it's a nice escapist entertainment. The dialogue provided pithy comments on marriage:

'What sort of people sit in a restaurant and don't even try to talk to each other?'
'Married people.'

John Russell Taylor in *The Times* noted the disparity between the two performances:

Mr Finney is rather charmless for a character meant to be a charming oddball … the central couple in *Two for the Road*, whose marriage we see through 12 years of sunshine and showers are Hush Puppy sophisticates. They exchange, in winsome moments, strained bits of verbal humour, suggestive of After Eight munchers downing their gallons of black coffee on the terrace of that dream villa … Albert Finney is compelled to play the husband role as though he were a hater of women and a slave driver to boot.

A critic in *New York Village Voice*, on the other hand, noting the chasm between the two performances, concluded that it made the film. 'The disparity in shapes and temperament between the thin, ethereal Hepburn and the chunky, earthy Finney makes the romance more moving and the relationship more challenging.'

Finney and Audrey certainly looked good. Fashion designers enjoyed fitting Hepburn out with a succession of eye-catching outfits. Everything from a psychedelic mini dress with flared sleeves through to what could be described as a kind of Star Trek cocktail party piece made out of acrylic pieces, sewn on thin metal chains. Finney's outfits were apparently supplied by Savile Row tailor Hardy Amies.

For Finney, his slight on-screen surliness notwithstanding, the experience of working with Audrey was one of his happiest. And he was unusually forthcoming about it:

> If I close my eyes, I can still see both of us spending a summer filming in the South of France. I see Audrey in the make-up trailer because it was hot and she had to change her hair, make-up and costumes three times a day. She was remarkable. She worked from five in the morning to late at night ... I've been very lucky to work with pros. And sometimes when I think back, I actually cry about it. These are people who have been capable of going out on a limb in some way. And courage always impresses me.

Yet Finney's next film was a world away from the fun and frolics of *Two for the Road*. He was about to gamble his reputation on directing and starring in a highly personal project that many observers saw as a slice of semi-autobiography. 'If they reject *Charlie Bubbles*, they reject my feelings, attitudes and everything,' he once said.

Finney never directed a film again. Finney, who seemed to be born under a lucky star, was about to experience a rare commercial failure.

9

CHARLIE

That always stayed in my head, that scene …

George Best.

Some images just sum up a mood. A celebrity takes off on his own in a hot air balloon. He has no destination in mind. He could be going anywhere. It seemed right for 1967, a time when the new breed of artists, often from humble backgrounds, struggled with their superstar status and just wanted to escape into the sky …

Salford-born Shelagh Delaney was only 19 when her play *A Taste of Honey* made her a star. Finney heard she was writing a story about the effects of early fame. Finney read what he later described as not so much a script but an outline, a sixty-page document, featuring a young, acclaimed northern writer, now London-based, disorientated by his surroundings and fazed by his success.

Finney said the project chimed with a point in his career when he felt the need to stretch his talent. 'I have a facility for acting,' he told Clive Goodwin[1] in 1967 shortly after *Charlie Bubbles* had wrapped:

> My danger is that I can do it [acting] too easily. I need the neurosis of making my work more complicated and more difficult than it need be in order to avoid this facility – that I'm not just getting away with it. It wasn't that I was looking for a subject to direct. But I responded very much to the character and the situation – and felt I wanted to act it. I felt very strongly about the way it should be treated and that it would be wrong for me to hire a director. So I did both which has been very interesting.

Charlie is a successful but terminally bored author. He's got too much money and can't get his head around his business affairs. He visits his accountant (Richard Pearson) in a private West End club. Pearson, once accurately described by film historian David Quinlan as a 'dead ringer for British Cabinet Minister Geoffrey Howe', advises him on his finances in a monotone mumble. And, here, Finney, as director, cleverly has Pearson address the camera like a politician announcing the budget. Charlie is distracted by a friend in the same club, Smokey (Colin Blakely). They have a spaghetti fight and then adjourn to an old-fashioned drinking den where Smokey gets sloshed. Later, Charlie, with his secretary (Liza Minnelli), drives up north to visit his ex-wife and son.

On first viewing, *Charlie Bubbles* seems tame stuff, simply because our hero is so apathetic. Success has rendered him listless. Put simply, it's the old story of a person for whom fame and fortune have come too early and too easily. What is there to do now? To which, naturally, most people would react that they would like to have his problems. Yet, if the story now feels clichéd, that doesn't invalidate it.

Here we must note the similarity between Finney and Charlie. The actor became a huge star in his mid-20s. None of Finney's talented contemporaries proved so precocious (perhaps, a quarter of a century on, only Kenneth Branagh would be more versatile at such a young age). It's as though Finney's life was on fast-forward. He had escaped national service, propelling him to drama school at just 17, and then had become a hit in his first film at just 24. By 30 he was a major star, producer and then director.

Significantly, Finney looks and plays older than his age in *Two for the Road* and *Charlie Bubbles*. In both films he exudes world-weariness, a jaded disappointment at wealth and opportunity. Charlie is famous but Finney is even more so. So it's easy to see Finney's first directorial effort as a reflection of his own attitude to stardom. The difference is that Charlie is relentlessly dour and unsociable, far removed from Finney. But, in terms of experience, and reaction to the perils of overnight fame, we can see parallels.

Displacement plays a big part in *Charlie Bubbles*. A local boy made good, corrupted by the Big Smoke and all its falsity, goes home. Strangers will be servile. Hangers-on will be eager to share his fame. Friends will rib him about his success. Also, perhaps, some envious souls will be itching to tell him that they no longer recognise the old Charlie. Finney must have felt all this too. It's Burton returning to Wales or Finney returning to Salford.

Finney appears a bit grumpy in *Charlie Bubbles*. His personality is so powerful that his disillusionment fills the screen. It is still the performance of a star, but he is not really likeable. He rarely smiles or interacts much with other people. People approach him and then retreat quickly as if repelled by his defensiveness.

The film has a few laughs. Scribblers will permit themselves a wry smile when a hotel waiter (Old Salfordian Joe Gladwin) asks, 'Do you just do your writing or are you still working?' Other than that, it's all downbeat. 'You seem to forget you've got a son … it's time you grow up and face reality,' his ex-wife, Lottie (Billie Whitelaw), tells him. (Whitelaw and Finney had, in real life, what the actress referred to as a 'mild affair … we'd known each other for donkey's years'.)[2]

When Charlie goes home we see the full failure of his private life. Even his son hides from him as his car pulls into the driveway. They play football but do not communicate. Later, watching a match at Old Trafford, they occupy a secluded box. An old friend (John Ronane) delivers the line that sums up perceptions of Charlie: 'It seems to me you can get bogged down with a lot of false values living in London'. Ho-hum …

Charlie's disconnection is laid bare when his son runs away from the match. He can't even describe the boy to the police. The film ends with Charlie sleeping over at his ex-wife's home. 'No champagne and kippers for breakfast,' she tells him. The following morning, he takes off in a hot air balloon. It's an intriguing end, a charming get-out, or a cop-out, depending on your point of view. Either way, fame and fortune never looked as unappealing as they do in *Charlie Bubbles*.

It would be wrong to assume that Charlie was Finney. But the questions besetting Finney and Bubbles were doubtless similar. Where does this road take me? What does it all mean? Just as in the film Charlie has a young son whom he seldom sees, so in real life Finney had infrequent contact with his son, Simon, who was 8 when he made *Charlie Bubbles*. Because Finney did not have full-time parental responsibilities – and unencumbered by having children at home – he could follow his own path. But was the price tag too high?

The ending resonated with other celebrities, perhaps those like Finney, who dreamed of disappearing from the public gaze. George Best, for example, liked the premise and the final scene:

I knew Finney for a bit in Manchester back in the old days. He was in one of my favourite films, *Charlie Bubbles*, about a writer who can't cope with fame and attention. In the end, he goes up in a balloon and cuts the rope. He sails off into the big blue sky. That always stayed in my head, that scene. Pure escape, turning your back on it all, on the world.[3]

Overall, *Charlie Bubbles* is a film more to admire than like. Technically, it's accomplished but Finney's performance is a bit too in-your-face downbeat. Subsequently, he revealed that, had he been directing another actor, he would have made the performance a little 'less heavy'.

The film is also rather ghoulish because so many of the supporting players died young. Colin Blakely, whose drinking bout with Finney is like a sequel to their encounter in *Saturday Night and Sunday Morning*, was just 56 when he died.[4] On the way up north there are motorway encounters with the doomed Yootha Joyce and the even more doomed Alan Lake. Joyce plays a rich ex-girlfriend of Charlie's, dolled up like a gangster's moll. A fine actress (witness her cameo in *The Pumpkin Eater*) she was swallowed alive by the *George and Mildred* comedy series. Drinking heavily, she died of liver failure in 1980, aged 53. Alan Lake, appearing here before he met Diana Dors, was Finney's stand-in for the film. He also played a besotted fan who hitches a lift. Lake's drunkenness made him difficult to employ. He committed suicide in 1984, several months after Dors's death. Also appearing in *Charlie Bubbles* – but blink and you'll miss her – was Finney's new girlfriend at the time, actress Jean Marsh, most famous for classic television series *Upstairs, Downstairs*. Marsh appears, uncredited, as a waitress in the motorway café.

Delaney's screenplay avoids making the players too clever or articulate, and in this context it's a compliment (Delaney, deservedly, won best British screenplay from the Writers' Guild of Great Britain). Renata Adler, in the *New York Times*, caught this realism in her review, 'The movie, in conversations, in gas stations, in elevators, always tends to stall exactly where life does. Very realistically, just long enough.'

John Russell Taylor in *The Times* noted Finney's surliness:

> As an actor, Finney has nearly all the gifts except charm. He's fine as a rough diamond (*Armstrong's Last Goodnight*), a fanatic (*Luther*) and as a maniac (*Night Must Fall*) but when he is required to appeal directly to audience sympathies, as in parts of *Two for the Road*, there seems to be some sort of block. It is, one might say, not so much that he cannot charm as that he will not. There is a sort of dogged stiff-necked refusal to ask for sympathy which runs through everything he does.

But the same review described *Charlie Bubbles* as 'the most exciting, personal and accomplished feature film debut by a British director since Anderson's *This Sporting Life*'.

Pauline Kael, however, reviewing it in *The New Yorker*, and later a fan of Finney's work in films like *Shoot the Moon*, disliked it:

> The movie is glum. Charlie's life is seen through his eyes, and since he sees people joylessly, with apathy and distaste, much of it consists of close-ups of semi-repulsive faces that look cold and dead. The entire painfully monotonous movie is based on this single, small, unoriginal idea – the kind of idea that could be one element, or good for a short sequence.

Charlie Bubbles did not draw crowds anywhere but fared particularly badly in America. And the movie was very 'British'. The depiction of wealth as an encumbrance, the exposé of the north/south divide – all this is quintessential 'Blighty' social commentary. It's also permeated with homegrown British emotional understatement. Behind Charlie's glumness there lurks someone of deep feeling, most graphically seen when he throws up after 'losing' his son. Yet his behaviour is perhaps too detached to resonate with American audiences. The movie was probably lost on them.

Finney was very much the returning local hero on *Charlie Bubbles*, giving lifts in his Rolls-Royce to commuters. He elaborated on the shooting to Hunter Davies in the *Sunday Times*:

> We had this location which was a slum clearance in Salford, about two miles of it. I got up there about an hour early, at 7.30 a.m., still in the dark, to see how we could do the sequence. It was an area I used to know as a boy, I was walking around it when this copper stopped me, wondering what I was doing. 'Oh it's you, Albert.' He knows I'm filming in the area.

Finney had many responsibilities on *Charlie Bubbles*, not least casting for the film. Kate O'Mara recalled an interview with Finney in which he gave her the (polite) brush-off:

> Finney was charming and we were getting on famously when suddenly the phone rang on his desk. He picked it up and said 'Oh yes, she's here – it's for you,' handing me the phone. I was mortified and apologised profusely. 'It's all right,' said Finney, grinning, 'it's your agent, you'd better see what he wants.' He seemed highly amused at the interruption. Embarrassed, I spoke to my agent as briefly and tersely as I could, with Finney watching me, chuckling all the while. I apologised again as I handed the phone back to him. 'It was just to say I've been offered a TV series, that's all,' I said, trying to make it sound unimportant. 'I think you'd better take it, don't you?' said Finney in his charming flat north country accent. 'Well, you know, just in case you don't get this,' he added kindly, and I realised he was letting me down gently as he didn't think I was right for the part in his movie. 'All right, thank you, I will,' I replied breathlessly. I had seen Finney in *Tom Jones* and thought him devastatingly attractive. He eventually cast Liza Minnelli in the film, so it was quite obvious he thought I was completely wrong for the part. I remembered he had described the character as 'kookie' – I'm a lot of things but 'kookie' is not one of them![5]

Finney never regretted directing *Charlie Bubbles*:

> I suppose I had the most intense sense of creation I've ever had – at least sus-
> tained over a period of time. One of the drawbacks about being an actor is that
> it's a very subjective profession. You go to the studio and look at yourself being
> made up. Then you look at yourself in costume. You rehearse and worry about
> your lines and your character. There's a lot of self in it. Me, me, me. Directing
> is wonderful because you worry about everything and everyone else. It's an
> objective position, and that makes for an extremely refreshing change.[6]

Charlie Bubbles was also the first film Finney had produced under the auspices of
his new production company Memorial Films (a pun on the Albert Memorial
which – of course – is named after him), founded by Michael Medwin and
Finney. Medwin is best known as one of the stars of the television series *The
Army Game* and, later, a regular as radio boss Don Satchley on the delightful
series *Shoestring*, starring Trevor Eve.

Speaking in 1982, Finney explained the genesis of the company:

> We never wanted to threaten Twentieth Century Fox. And indeed we're [he and
> Michael Medwin] both actors, we're both, you know, I suppose, temperamen-
> tally, strolling players normally. We didn't want to sit in offices and go in at seven
> and read scripts and do deals. We kind of felt that now and again we might come
> across something we'd like to get made or like to see made, and that was the
> principle behind it. Which is why we have a rather infrequent record in terms
> of production … We made a film with Julie Christie called *Memoirs of a Survivor*,
> which we made two years ago. But we've not – I think our average since the
> company was founded in 1965 or 6, is something like .42 of a film a year.'

Memorial did, however, produce an iconic movie from this period, Lindsay
Anderson's *If …* starring Malcolm McDowell. The film, which made McDowell
into a star, could be seen as a scathing attack on Britain's public school system or
simply a fable for the times, with its theme of revolution and anti-establishment
fervour. Finney was a hero to McDowell. He also idolised Finney's future girlfriend, Anouk Aimée. McDowell, coincidentally, remembers Anouk stopping
him in the street to praise him on his memorable entrance in *If …* when his
caped schoolboy returns on the first day of term.

Other films produced by Memorial were *O Lucky Man!* starring McDowell
and directed by Lindsay Anderson, and Mike Leigh's first directorial effort, *Bleak
Moments*. Leigh's feature, about a secretary's dull existence, was made for just
£18,500.[7] Although Leigh didn't really become prolific until at least a decade

later, he subsequently said that *Bleak Moments* remains, in some ways, 'the mother of all Mike Leigh films. And I'm very proud of it.'

Perhaps in a bid to publicise *Charlie Bubbles* in America, Finney undertook his second stint on Broadway. He played Bri in *A Day in the Death of Joe Egg*. This was strong stuff, Peter Nichols's harrowing black comedy about a married couple coping with a severely disabled daughter. Finney had first seen Nichols's work at Glasgow's Citizens' Theatre and immediately saw its potential. Memorial then bought the play and took it to London.

A Day in the Death of Joe Egg broke new ground. An appalling tragedy is largely played for laughs, even like some extended farce. And then, suddenly, the mask drops and we see the protagonists, Bri and Sheila, for what they are, a young couple forever living a shaggy dog story in which every emotion can be viewed as selfish or altruistic. If they put the child in an institution, are they abdicating their duty as parents while saving their marriage? If Bri lives out his fantasy of performing a mercy killing, is he a compassionate parent, ending the life of what his wife refers to as 'a living parsnip', or is he a cold-hearted murderer? The parents shun the choice and hide behind absurd, ironic jokes. 'Lovely soft hands, you've got – like silk – they've never done rough work,' says Bri to his daughter. It was, as Irving Wardle said:

> One of the rare occasions in which audiences can feel the earth moving under their feet … it marks the theatrical arrival of a young dramatist capable of the hardest task in his trade: treating an intensely painful taboo subject with absolute truthfulness and yet without alienating the public. Peter Nichols and a dazzling cast have significantly shifted our boundaries of taste.

Bri, as originally played by Joe Melia in Glasgow, and then in London, was a disturbed, beaten down, slightly seedy figure. The *Daily Telegraph*, in its obituary of the actor, who died in 2012, noted, 'with its poignant mix of irony and music hall asides, the play always teetered on the brink of bad taste, but Melia's timing, warmth and theatrical wit as he danced down to the footlights just about pulled it off.'

Finney, by contrast, had a tendency to bring the thunder with him on stage, perhaps not the kind of actor best suited to conveying habitual self-doubt, but he certainly boosted its appeal by bringing it to Broadway. From the beginning, however, Finney insisted he would only play Bri for eleven weeks, opening at New York's Brooke Atkinson Theatre on 1 February. He then handed over to Donal Donnelly. Clive Barnes, reviewing the play for the *New York Times*, said it was 'not a comfortable evening but very much worthwhile'. Finney received a Tony nomination.

A subsequent movie was made of the play, filmed in 1970 but not released until 1972, starring Alan Bates in the title role.[8] Perhaps Bates's air of befuddled eccentricity was a better fit. So was Eddie Izzard who played Bri in a more recent revival. Critic Harold Clurman made a similar point at the time, 'If you should be obliged to see the play after Albert Finney has left it, don't let that worry you. Finney is a splendid actor but I would guess that his part could be rendered just as effective, if not more so, by a less formidable player.'[9]

Finney was perhaps also simply too handsome to play Bri. And in photos around this time he looks at his best, a fine figure of a man with an impressive physique and a face that somehow appealed to men and women. Both *Two for the Road* and *Charlie Bubbles*, although Finney might not like it, had traded on his sex appeal. Finney and Audrey were *the* sixties couple. And Charlie, world-weary and disillusioned though he might have been, was still attractive to women.

The young Amy Irving remembered having a huge crush on Finney after seeing him on stage in *Joe Egg*:

My favourite teenage fantasy is when Albert Finney came to my house and had me on the floor, on the piano, everywhere. I used to have a thing for Albert Finney. After he was in *Joe Egg*, I followed him from the dressing room, stage door to the restaurant, just kind of crying, wanting him. And he wouldn't sign my programme.[10]

Perhaps Finney was too distracted at the time. Jean Marsh had accompanied him to New York in early 1968 to work on *Joe Egg*. But by the time Finney had started work on his next film, *The Picasso Summer*, the oddest movie he was ever involved in, they had broken up. Marsh recalls their time together fondly: 'He was adorable, very sweet.'

The Picasso Summer, which has Finney and Yvette Mimieux crossing Europe to meet the famous painter, could be seen as kind of (botched) sequel to *Two for the Road*. In both movies Finney plays an architect. The film, a real oddity, had a complicated genesis. Word reached Hollywood that Pablo Picasso wanted to contribute towards the animation sequences on the film. This was the bait that got everyone on board. Ray Bradbury was then commissioned to write a script about a young couple, disillusioned with life in San Francisco, who leave home and meet Picasso in the South of France. That is, after some luscious scenery, breathtaking locations and encounters with bulls.

Serge Bourguignon, a French director who had enjoyed some success with a film called *Sundays and Cybele*, started shooting in California and France. Bourguignon, however, behaved highly eccentrically. Not only did he disapprove of the script, but he apparently preferred to direct on horseback. When the producers saw the final cut, they were appalled. And, indeed, it seems that everyone agreed. It was an unmitigated disaster.

Meanwhile, Finney, licking his wounds after his split from Jean Marsh, had retreated to Corfu once filming with Bourguignon had ended. He was staying with a fisherman's family when one of the movie's producers, Roy Silver, flew to the island to convince him to return to the Riviera for more scenes. They decided to re-shoot the movie with Robert Sallin, a talented maker of commercials. Sallin was something of a child prodigy; he'd been producing programmes for NBC Radio from the age of 15. He had previously directed the opening ten-plus minute film sequence of the first Bill Cosby-NBC Special.

Finney, enticed by the prospect of an extra $25,000 a week, agreed to return for three weeks' further filming in the South of France. Sallin, who had ambitions to become a full-time film director, was on $5,000 dollars. And who wouldn't want to spend an additional few weeks in locations such as St-Tropez, Menton and St-Paul-de-Vence? It wasn't such a hard sell.

Yet an air of imminent catastrophe hung over the whole enterprise, and Sallin was nervous at the prospect of working with such a big star:

> It was intimidating but there was nothing to be intimidated about because he couldn't have been more amenable and professional in every way. We had a lot of laughs together. He had an extraordinary mastery of his craft. He was just wonderful. I remember reflecting at the time on how wonderful it was to work with Brits because they have centuries of tradition in their craft. If I'd asked him to climb a vertical wall, he would have done it. In St Paul de Vence there was one scene where Yvette was saying something and I was shooting over her shoulder to catch Albert's reaction. I asked him to pull his reactions back just a little. And it was like working with the most delicate scalpel. It was as though if I'd said, 'can you pull back just 22 per cent?' he could have done so.[11]

But Finney and Sallin still had a problem – how to construct a film out of such a thin plot. Sallin felt that the story meandered to no particular conclusion. 'The whole premise was so weak that it wasn't really worth watching,' he said.

On the eve of shooting (on the Sallin version) he remembered a long chat with Finney in the actor's trailer about the storyline. Sallin had been studying the script and had some definite ideas. Finney, it turned out, had a rather different take on the film. But Sallin, much to his surprise, found Finney willing to listen. Finney and Sallin did the best they could to make the film coherent. The deal was that if *The Picasso Summer* had a theatrical release, Finney would pocket an extra $100,000. It never did, however, reach cinema screens, and perhaps that was just as well.

Sallin, like everyone who worked with Finney, was bowled over by his accessibility and charm: 'He was very much a "what you see is what you get" kind of person. He had no side to him at all.' Finney reminded Sallin a bit of Burton, but 'Albert had greater warmth and humour and an all-round lighter touch than Burton.' He was a little surprised that Finney never achieved more in his career but thinks that he made his own choices and lived on his own terms. Sallin would occasionally meet Finney again in London. They had the same tailor, Douglas Hayward.[12] But, apart from a dinner many years ago in Sun Valley, Idaho, where the Sallins kept a second home, they have never met since.

For Sandra Sallin, her overwhelming memory was of Finney's sex appeal and intelligence: 'Albert is just as bright and handsome as he appears. Quite the hunk. I mean really a hunk.' Robert Sallin remembers that on the last day of shooting, in the exquisite location of St-Jean-Cap-Ferrat, they all had a farewell dinner. Sandra was so sad to say goodbye to Finney that she started crying. Not that Finney had any romantic involvement with Sandra or his co-star Yvette Mimieux, however 'delightful', in Sallin's words, she was. By the end of the film Finney only had eyes for one lady – Anouk Aimée. Enter the second Mrs Finney.

10

ANOUK

When we left the cinema, the entire audience was dancing down the street, we were all so happy.

Annabel Leventon on Scrooge.

Claude Lelouch's *A Man and a Woman* is one of those romantic films that moisten the eyes of art house cinema-goers, especially fans of French new wave cinema. It has evocative Deauville locations, two lovers exchanging meaningful glances as they skid through the wintry countryside, a catchy Francis Lai score and effortless, inexplicable flitting between colour and black-and-white, the latter an ingredient that makes people assume it just *has* to be something special.

The movie won two Oscars in 1967, best foreign language film, and, unusually for a non-Hollywood film, best original screenplay. Lelouch's direction and Anouk Aimée's acting also received Oscar nominations. At the Cannes Film Festival it took top prize and also won the Golden Globe as best foreign-language film.

Aimée, with her air of high-class, darkly sensuous sexuality, radiated charm and warmth but also melancholy. She was easy enough to fall in love with on film. And Finney did so for real. He first spotted her when he was having lunch with Robert and Sandra Sallin in the South of France. She was taking a break from filming the title role in *Justine* alongside Dirk Bogarde. As Finney later told it:

> She was staying at the Colombe d'Or, down in St-Paul-de-Vence with her daughter and her daughter's boyfriend, on a holiday. And I was there with some people for lunch. And I kind of caught her eye, and I said, 'I'll be back'. And I came back for dinner, and we just went on from there.

Robert Sallin remembered that Finney went over after lunch and introduced himself. Soon, according to Sallin, she started to show up regularly. And Finney's attention was shifting – in Sallin's words, 'he wanted to go and play with Anouk.' Hence it was no surprise that Finney was determined that the three-week stint of filming would end as stipulated. He even told Sallin that he 'wanted to teach these boys [the producers] a lesson'. Sallin replied that Finney's withdrawal would make him 'almost a feature director', referring to the unfinished film. According to Sallin:

> I don't know anything about his relationship with the producers, or what might cause his displeasure with them. I can only speculate that Albert's real reason for leaving had to do primarily with his burgeoning romance with Anouk.

Sallin has a particularly vivid memory of a dinner in the hills above old Nice at a restaurant called Le Petit Ferme de Saint Michel. Robert and Sandra Sallin were there as well as Yvette Mimieux and Anouk. By then it was clear: Finney and Anouk were in love.

Anouk Aimée was four years older than Finney. Both her parents were actors; her mother was Geneviève Sorya, her father, Henry Dreyfus (there may be some connection to Captain Alfred Dreyfus, but this has never been proven). A talented child, Aimée studied acting and ballet in Paris, London and Marseilles; her training in dance at the famous Bauer-Therond School prepared her for future roles as a performer in such films as *Lola* and *The Model Shop*.

Aside from *A Man and a Woman*, she was best known for Federico Fellini's acclaimed 'romp in Rome', 1960 comedy drama *La Dolce Vita*. Yet she had made her film debut in 1946 when Finney was just 10. By the late sixties she was catching the eye of Hollywood directors like Sidney Lumet who cast her as a high-class whore in *The Appointment* alongside Omar Sharif, with whom she had a fling. When she met Finney she was married for the third time, to actor Pierre Barouh, whom she had met on the set of *A Man and a Woman*.

By the time Aimée was filming *Justine*, she seemed to be in one of her periodic depressions. Bogarde, who had known her since she was 15, told Eve Arnold of his co-star's loneliness, 'She is never so happy as when she is miserable between love affairs. Somehow, when one thinks of Anouk, it is inevitably a tiny figure alone huddled up and sobbing in the back seat of a Rolls.' Bogarde also described her as 'wan and sad for most of the time, since she had suddenly realised, too late, that her decision to accept *Justine* had most probably been, for one reason or another, a serious error of judgement on her part and was now feeling abandoned'.

Finney and Anouk at first claimed they were just good friends, but that didn't convince. The press got the whiff of something more serious when Finney took her to meet his family in Gore Crescent. Then they holidayed together in Corfu in spring 1969. They made an elegant couple, Anouk often dressed in fur coat and boots, Finney in Savile Row suits and carrying Louis Vuitton bags.

One friend believed that the match between Finney and Aimée was 'a classic fusion of codependency'. Finney, a heavy drinker, was looking for stability and the right lady to keep him grounded. Anouk 'was an insecure, gorgeous creature who also needed to be loved … both were looking for love without loving themselves'. In other words, two people looking to be fixed by each other. The same friend said that it was clear that it would be a difficult union to sustain. 'Albert was a fun-loving, popular guy, and was considered a major catch. He was devastatingly attractive and utterly delightful. And Anouk was *the* dream woman of the time: French, beautiful and mysterious.'

Few of Finney's liaisons had proved long lasting. Up to this point he had had difficulty sustaining any relationship beyond a year. It seemed that Finney couldn't really commit to anyone – not only a strolling player but also a roving lover. Maybe Finney had never really 'lost himself' in another person, the kind of love that went beyond lust or infatuation. He relished company and he adored women, but until now his romances had been fun-filled flings. Perhaps the idea of choosing a lifelong companion unsettled him. But, as men enter their thirties, roving loses its appeal, and so it was that Finney, the hard-drinking philanderer, looked for someone to fix his wayward streak.

They eventually married at Kensington Registry Office on 7 August 1970. Michael Medwin was best man. Anouk wore a simple shift dress, classic of the era, Finney a dark suit with cream-coloured shirt and tie. Somehow his red hair, unusually long and wavy, made him look younger than in *Charlie Bubbles*, filmed three years earlier.

Perhaps Finney was glad to be his real young self again, because before he married Anouk he had appeared as the old miser in Ronald Neame's musical version of Scrooge. (Neame had also directed the 17-year-old Anouk Aimée in an exotic 1950 thriller called *The Golden Salamander*.) Finney was third in line for the part. Richard Harris, who had enjoyed spectacular success with *Camelot* and the hit single *MacArthur Park*, was the original choice. (Harris always denied he could sing, once telling chat show host Michael Aspel that 'if I sang for you now, you wouldn't rush out and buy a record'. To which Aspel, ever the quick wit, replied, 'I *would* rush out!') Harris suddenly became unavailable when he took over as director of *Bloomfield*, in which he also starred.

Rex Harrison was the next choice – and had the off-screen prickliness to make Scrooge credible – but the veteran actor became exhausted and was stricken with pneumonia while appearing in the West End.[1] Suddenly Leslie Bricusse, one of the producers, had a film without a star just as it was about to roll. Bricusse instinctively wanted Finney. He already knew Finney from his stint in *Luther* on Broadway when he and Anthony Newley were in *Stop the World*. Bricusse recounts how he wooed his man:

> It is hardly flattering for any actor to learn that he is not the first, nor indeed the second choice for a role, but a practical actor – and God knows Mr Finney is that – understands the fickle unpredictability of the lunatic lottery called the film industry. Getting the right role is what matters, not how you get it. I called Albert and explained the project, the situation and the urgency. He invited me for dinner the same evening. Anouk cooked a meal as delectable as herself, and the three of us sat and ate and talked way past midnight until I had run out of killer persuasive chitchat. I left Albie with the script and score of *Scrooge* and went home to pray. Happily, God, Albert, Charles Dickens and the department of fate were all listening. Less than 24 hours later, Albie was having his first costume fitting.[2]

Finney, on the set of *Scrooge*, told a visiting journalist for *Line-Up Film Night*:

> I got into it rather quickly and was extremely attracted to the thought of playing the character. When I read the script I liked it very much and the juices started to work inside. I hadn't read a script that had had that effect on me for some time.

Asked about his singing voice, Finney said that the old man 'doesn't have much resonance in his voice and he doesn't have great quantities of breath. So I wanted the singing to be very much in character except at the end of the film when he's changed by his experiences. Then a little more resonance comes back in.'

Finney was probably a better choice than either Harrison – essentially a light comedian – or Harris, who might have played it too broad. But the make-up department had a long haul transforming a handsome 34-year-old (he was twenty-eight years younger than Harrison and six years younger than Harris) into a bent, balding old codger, someone whose appearance matched his reputation as 'the most miserable skinflint who ever walked on earth'. The final result has Finney resembling Wilfrid Brambell in *Steptoe and Son*. And his Scrooge is a truly nasty bit of work, resenting any provision for the poor and even declaring that he's glad the workhouses are still operating. 'If you were in my will, I'd disinherit you,' he tells Cratchit (David Collings). Somehow Finney makes you believe he means it.

Kenneth More, Alec Guinness and Edith Evans provided strong support. The songs, however, were not especially memorable, eclipsed as they were by *Oliver!* the previous year. Nevertheless, the film was a smash. *Scrooge* opened at Radio City Hall in New York the following November, breaking all box office records. Bricusse accepted a Golden Globe on Finney's behalf.

John Russell Taylor in *The Times* admired Finney's approach:

> Albert Finney, on the face of it an unlikely choice for Scrooge, proves in the event to be a very good idea; he really plays the part as an acting role, and when he is required to be a nasty old man does just that, not merely your nice, handsome, kindly star pretending to be.

Actress Annabel Leventon has a more direct memory of *Scrooge* after seeing it at the Dominion in London's Tottenham Court Road: 'When we left the cinema, the entire audience was dancing down the street, we were all so happy.'[3]

Scrooge's director, Ronald Neame, scored an even bigger hit a couple of years later with *The Poseidon Adventure*. Neame enjoyed several large tipples at lunch-time and then again in the evening, long into old age. His doctors told him to cut down. As he liked to tell it, however, they all died before him. He lived to be 99. If he hadn't drunk so much he'd probably have lived longer!

As for Finney, he admitted only that the role prompted him to keep turning off the lights at home. But perhaps he simply had more lights to turn off, because he and Anouk had moved into a house in Brompton Square, Knightsbridge, one of London's most glamorous addresses. Harrods was spitting distance away and so was San Lorenzo in Beauchamp Place, an Italian restaurant which soon became one of their favourites. The owners, Lorenzo and Mara Berni, also became good friends. This was at a time when authentic Italian food was still regarded as a novelty. San Lorenzo became *the* haunt of the stars, first Peter Sellers and Britt Ekland, and then the likes of Jack Nicholson, Princess Margaret and, in the eighties, Princess Diana.

Anouk effectively gave up her career to be with Finney. That did not come easily, especially for someone who had been acting since she was a teenager. Nevertheless she loved living in London and she became a fan of rugby, a good time to like the game, as she later said, because France won all the time.

Anouk and Finney liked watching old movies on the television. One of Finney's favourites was John Huston's classic *The Maltese Falcon*. And Finney had already practised his Bogart accent in *Two for the Road*. No surprise then that he quickly accepted the part of Eddie Ginley, a Liverpool bingo caller who fantasises about becoming a Sam Spade-style sleuth in *Gumshoe*.

Gumshoe was Stephen Frears's first movie and it has that refreshing quality that you find in a debut director. The film is an enjoyable pastiche, rarely shown until its recent release on DVD. Raising money was easy, in spite of *Charlie Bubbles'* commercial failure, because Finney was such a big international star. More of a problem, according to Frears, was a misunderstanding about the story itself.

Frears explains:

> Columbia Pictures, who bought the film, thought Albert Finney was playing a private detective. You'd say – 'no, it's actually a film about a bingo caller who wants to be a private detective'. So it was as though all they could see was a bloke in a trench-coat, but actually what was on offer was a rather more complicated film about a bloke who wanted to be a man who wore a trench-coat. I mean, wearing a trench-coat is easy but being Humphrey Bogart is presumably harder. So there was always that gap.[4]

Apart from Finney, Frears managed to assemble a great cast – Billie Whitelaw, Frank Finlay and Janice Rule. But it was Finney who was the central star and also producer – for Memorial.

Frears said:

> Albert was the first person I came across who used to imitate Bogart. I've seen Belmondo do it since but Albert used to do it too. ... [Albert] was a bloke from Salford. English to his fingertips. Riddled with Englishness. Hopelessly, provincially English. But of course he'd become a big star. And the big star was also the boss of the company making the film. This sometimes got us into difficult situations. For example, Chris [Menges] always wanted to shoot towards windows which means you have to balance the light. If the light drops outside you have to drop the light inside so they're always in relation to each other. Well, that's quite a delicate thing to do particularly in November when we were shooting. Albert would say, 'why don't you just get me up against the wall and shoot me?' ... he couldn't understand why we were interested in things other than just photographing him.

Frears, however, got on well with Finney:

> I guess if he did something that didn't make sense to me I'd ask him why. But it just seemed to me what he was doing was good. If people are being good, what is there to talk about? What was complicated was that Albert had really been taught by Karel and Lindsay too. So, of course, it was rather complicated when I turned up, somehow connected to them. He was always rather suspicious of educated people. I think he thought I was too clever. I probably drove him mad. But he was great.

Maureen Lipman, playing a minor part in *Gumshoe*, was only on set for a couple of days. Up until then her biggest film role had been in *Up the Junction*. She remembers finding the recently married Mr and Mrs Finney lunching together in the canteen. Lipman, then 24, not long out of drama school, joined them. She soon realised she was encroaching. Subsequently, she says she always felt like apologising whenever she spotted Finney at a party. 'He's a lovely man,' Lipman recalled. 'He's very comfortable in his own skin. It's very valuable that, someone who doesn't change.' She said you can't underestimate the influence of figures like Finney and Courtenay on other actors:

> I came out of drama school able to talk in my own accent because of people like them. I started to watch Finney like a fan. I saw him at the Old Vic when I was a junior member in *A Flea in Her Ear* and *Much Ado about Nothing*. He's a great physical presence. He's a colourful actor – and he's like Olivier in that, on occasions, he has a tendency to over colour … but Albert is the only actor I know who has used acting to benefit his life rather than the other way round.[5]

Carolyn Seymour, later best known for her role in the British TV series *Survivors*, also had a small role in *Gumshoe*:

> It goes without saying that I adore the man [Finney]. I knew him quite well, not only working with him, but socially as well. He was going through the 'Anouk' part of his life which meant that we didn't associate too much together after they met. I was never a girlfriend, I hasten to add, although if the situation had presented itself …! He was then, as now, a consummate actor and for me to be in a movie with him, Frank Finlay, Billie Whitelaw and Janice Rule, was absolutely awe-inspiring. The whole experience was amazing and I learnt so much. He is a special man.[6]

Anouk visited the *Gumshoe* set regularly. Dirk Bogarde, in his memoir *Snakes and Ladders*, recalls Anouk's cats being brought to the set of *Justine* in Tunis. According to Bogarde, she fed them on fillet steak, which angered the waiters in their hotel who had to make do with chickpeas. And Carolyn Seymour also remembers that Anouk, whose presence on-screen has, ironically, been described as 'feline', was also enamoured with her dogs: 'Somehow they got smuggled into London to prevent them being quarantined – an excellent feat, I may add, requiring an enormous amount of planning.'

Gumshoe turned out agreeably well, a now dated (with politically incorrect language) but enjoyable send-up of Bogart films. Tom Milne in *The Times* paid tribute:

Given a brilliant script by Neville Smith (his first) and a brilliant cast – apart from the superb Albert Finney and the equally superb Fulton Mackay as a moth-eaten Glaswegian hood, Frears has directed the film with such self-effacing skill that it is likely to be undervalued even by those who enjoy it.

Finney was suddenly on a roll with films. But then a great new play and one of his favourite co-stars brought him back to the Royal Court.

HELL IN SLOANE SQUARE

I spent some considerable time trying to decide whether Richard Burton or John Neville would ultimately inherit the mantle of Olivier. I needn't have bothered: it will be Finney.

Sheridan Morley in 1974.

'A marriage which cannot live yet refuses to die', screamed the poster for the subsequent film adaptation of Ted Whitehead's stage play *Alpha Beta*, starring Albert Finney and Rachel Roberts, first staged at the Royal Court in 1972. Somehow that's an appropriate metaphor for Roberts's marriage to Rex Harrison, a union from which the actress could never move on.

Roberts's suicide in 1980 was shocking. When you see her in *Saturday Night and Sunday Morning* or *This Sporting Life*, or even at the end of her career in minor roles, it's ironic to think that someone who played such forceful characters could end so pitiably. She was a highly emotional woman, a depressive and an alcoholic, prone to the mad mood swings and exhibitionism of those so afflicted. She would get on all fours and bark like a dog or strip off in front of strangers at a whim. In Richard Burton's words, she 'made outrage legitimate'. In her diaries she wrote that 'everyone has not just a story but a scream'. Finney commented, like many on her death, that 'if only he'd known she was that desperate ...'[1]

Strangely, Whitehead's tale of a deadlocked, violent working-class marriage, which marked Finney's return to the London stage after a gap of seven years, never experienced a revival until recently. Michael Billington said of *Alpha Beta*, 'As a portrait of domestic entrapment, it rivals Strindberg's *The Dance of Death*'.

Whitehead's script must have been disturbing for the time. Take Frank's view of unrestrained male sexuality, as articulated in the first act:

The male pokes everything he can get until one day he inadvertently pokes himself into wedlock; after that he stops poking and starts lusting. The morality is rigid because, once married, the male never actually pokes anything and it's depraved because he lusts his life away in masculine obscenities and dirty jokes.

Irving Wardle in *The Times* described the progress of Finney's character in the marriage:

At first a bottled up youth plagued with fears of middle-age, he steadily thickens and coarsens, going through a phase as a clubland buck, putting up a defensive barrage of songs, and finally slumped into booze-sodden middle-aged defeat.

Again Finney, just 35, was playing older than his age. Finney's old friend from Hawaii, Eddie Sherman, in London for a surprise visit in 1972, remembered his impression of the play: 'Finney's character was a slovenly, middle-class [!] British man. Of course, he was just brilliant. As we walked up the theatre aisle after the show we talked about how brilliant he was.'

Later, the play was made into a film and Richard Eder, in the *New York Times*, was ecstatic, 'Rachel Roberts and Albert Finney are so extraordinary as the husband and wife that they make *Alpha Beta*, cinematic or not, a startling and wonderful experience.'

The seventies were marked by Finney doing mostly stage work. In March 1972, Finney accepted an invitation to become Associate Director of the Royal Court. The first piece he chose to stage and direct was Irish playwright Brian Friel's *Freedom of the City*, a thinly disguised depiction of the Bloody Sunday massacre. The play was perceived as an anti-British polemic and a critique of the Heath government's policy.

Actor Stephen Rea, a friend of Friel's, described the play:

Previously his [Friel's] work had been personal rather than directly political. His first hit play, *Philadelphia, Here I Come!* had dealt with private anguish in the context of emigration. But *Freedom of the City* had such urgency that the Court's director, Albert Finney, demanded that the Court alter its schedule to stage it as soon as possible. The play was received in a frost of ignorance.[2]

Friel preferred to let his work speak for itself, but in one interview, a decade after it was staged, he admitted he might have got a bit carried away:

One of the problems with the play was that the experience of Bloody Sunday wasn't adequately distilled in me. I wrote it out of some kind of heat and some kind of immediate passion that I would have wanted to quiet a bit before I did it.

Friel subsequently scored a major hit with his play *Dancing at Lughnasa*, which was made into a film starring Meryl Streep.

While Finney was directing *Freedom of the City* by day, by night he was starring in a play by another distinguished Irish playwright, Samuel Beckett's *Krapp's Last Tape*. The one-act, one-man play was written for – and is forever associated with – Patrick Magee, the character actor known for horror movies and, especially, his collaboration with Stanley Kubrick on *A Clockwork Orange* and *Barry Lyndon*. Magee's voice – metallic, grinding and harsh – had a sinister quality to it, ideally suited to Krapp. Eccentric players were usually the best interpreters of Beckett's masterpiece, notably Max Wall (in a 1975 production directed by Magee) and Harold Pinter in 2006.

Beckett, who seemed to be an uninvited guest at some of Finney's rehearsals, felt that Finney was miscast. His biographer James Knowlson, recorded the playwright's dim view of the proceedings, 'He never believed in Albert Finney as Krapp. And Finney became acutely conscious that he was not satisfying Beckett.'

Yet Irving Wardle in *The Times* praised Finney's original approach:

> What it possesses, besides abundant physical skill, is a steely contrast between the senile figure, hawking and rasping among his treasured lumber, and the recorded voice of Krapp at the midnight of his youth. The sense of erotic desolation comes into merciless focus through this perspective (to Krapp, his spools are his children) and, as before with this masterpiece, the effect is overwhelming.

Finney had not been in a movie since *Scrooge*. And, as he later said, nobody really recognised him in it anyway. Now Finney was about to undergo another huge physical transformation. It was a particularly punishing schedule. By day, he was Hercule Poirot, Belgian super sleuth, at Elstree; by night, he was Phil, a hedonistic architect, in Peter Nichols's *Chez Nous*, a part especially written for Finney.

The double undertaking was a rebuff to those who ever thought Finney lazy. He was in virtually every scene in *Murder on the Orient Express*. Perhaps only Anthony Hopkins worked so hard when he played Frank Doel in *84 Charing Cross Road* by day and Lambert Le Roux in *Pravda* by night.

Producers Richard Goodwin and John Bradbourne signed up Sidney Lumet, who had a reputation as a superb actors' director. Lumet, who had made such classics as *Twelve Angry Men*, *The Hill* and *The Pawnbroker*, was a safe pair of hands who could bring the film in on time within its six-week schedule. 'We had an extremely good script by Paul Dehn and needed a resourceful director to deal with what could easily have become rather flaccid material,' said Goodwin. 'We thought of the film as quite small in scale and felt we could do it inexpensively but still with a good cast.'

It was Lumet who first suggested Finney. This required some makeover. Finney was tall(ish), ginger-haired, very British-looking and only 36. How could he be transformed into a short, stout, middle-aged Belgian? Well, he had become Scrooge, so why not Poirot?

The strain on Finney was overwhelming. The demands of the play, portraying such a loquacious sage during the day, and submitting to hours of make-up every morning, would tire anyone. A solution was found. Finney was woken at 5 a.m., lifted gently out of bed and transported in a limousine, still sleeping, to the studios. Then the make-up team worked on him for a couple of hours. He was given a false nose, padded cheeks and a meticulously trimmed, waxed, liquorice-like period moustache. The jet black hair was a work of art all on its own, attained with a mixture of Cherry Blossom boot polish and Vaseline, set every morning, and requiring half an hour under the dryer – *et voilà!*

Equally important was Finney's gait and posture. He adopted a stooped stance, walking stiffly with his head down, almost buried in his chest. Presumably this was to accentuate the impression that he had a double chin. When he addresses the 'suspects', he appears to look up at them, rather like a child responding to a teacher. His head is cocked to one side, as if he's suffering from a permanent stiff neck, accompanied by abrupt, birdlike jerking movements. Finney sometimes looks awkward in his disguise.

David Suchet, *the* television Poirot of the nineties, agreed. He thought Finney was 'masterful' but then reflected, 'I remember thinking privately that Finney's performance in the 1974 film had struck me as rather tense and stiff – he hardly ever seemed to move his neck – while his accent had been very gruff, almost angry.'[3] Bernard Hepton, who saw the film many years after he had parted company with Finney, thought that Finney's portrayal was 'outrageous' and that he was simply 'overacting'. Hepton even wondered if his old protégé was 'taking the piss' out of the character by going so over the top.

It is interesting to compare Finney to Peter Ustinov several years later in *Death on the Nile*. Ustinov was more natural and less forced, aided by a physique closer to Poirot's. Yet this should not detract from Finney's performance. It is studied, mannered, perhaps too obviously a feat of transformation, acting rather than being, but it's a tour de force nonetheless. Finney's Poirot is more zestful than Ustinov's. And Christie herself thought it the most authentic on-screen depiction, although she was disappointed with Finney's moustache.

Finney enjoyed getting to know the cast:

There were a lot of people I'd never met before and, being a movie buff, I liked talking to them about their films. We all started saying how we should perhaps do one of those films every year, like a glamorous repertory company.

When they did actually ask me a couple of years later if I'd play Poirot again, I wasn't so sure. They said they were going to the Nile this time; it had been quite hot enough for me at Elstree.[4]

Nearly all the action, other than the murder itself, revolved around Poirot with the others responding to his interrogation. Sean Connery was heard to grumble that 'the rest of us are only glorified extras'. And Lauren Bacall, during filming, spoke of the difficulty of such distinguished actors having to keep quiet. 'It was so frustrating. Everything revolves around Albie who talks all the time. We just react. The other day when he left early for his matinee, we all went absolutely bananas and couldn't stop speaking. It was complete chaos.'

The movie itself has a claustrophobic feel, set as it is on a train stalled by a snowstorm (compare it, for example, to *Death on the Nile* in which audiences were taken not only down river but also to the pyramids and even Abu Simbel). The cast is a dream: Connery, Bacall (especially impressive), John Gielgud, Rachel Roberts, Richard Widmark, Ingrid Bergman (mysteriously winning an Oscar for her portrayal of a mousy missionary), Anthony Perkins and Colin Blakely, hilariously billed as 'Colin Blankey' in the credits. Also in the film, making her second appearance alongside Finney, was Jacqueline Bisset as Countess Andrenyi. (Finney, many years later, once confided to a dinner companion that he had 'rather fancied' the beauty who was then at the height of her fame.)

'It's all great insanity and glorious fun. I wanted a name cast to make the movie glamorous. It's going to be done with gaiety and humour and the best of fakery,' said Lumet during production in early 1974, noting that most of the $3 million budget went on stars' salaries.[5] And commenting later, he seemed pleased with the result:

> Although there was quite a lot of chit chat and kidding going on, everyone let him [Finney] have his concentration and, for his part, he generally sat to one side, slightly closed off, thinking of his next scene coming up. From my point of view he had the extraordinary ability to give you absolutely everything you wanted and immediately.

David Robinson in *The Times* gave it a (halfhearted) endorsement, 'No more or less than the book itself, it is a perfectly pleasant entertainment, a couple of hours of nostalgic escape, if you're prepared to go easily with it'.

And 'go with it' the punters did. The film earned more than $20 million in the United States alone. Finney was nominated for best actor at the Oscars but didn't attend. The other nominees were Jack Nicholson in *Chinatown*, Dustin

Hoffman in *Lenny*, Al Pacino in *The Godfather Part 2* and Art Carney who, although the outsider, won for *Harry and Tonto*.

For Finney, who rarely filmed in the seventies, the only problem was that his name became indelibly associated with the part of Poirot. 'People really do think I am 300 pounds with a French accent,' he once said.

After a gruelling day of filming at Elstree, Finney would rush off to the Globe Theatre to act in Peter Nichols's *Chez Nous*. Nichols drew inspiration for the play from time spent at his own family's home in France. Two couples holiday in the Dordogne, Dick and Liz (Denholm Elliott and Pat Heywood) and Phil and Diana (Finney and Geraldine McEwan). It emerges that Dick and Liz's youngest child is actually a grandchild, fathered by none other than Finney's character, Phil, when the daughter was just 14. A difficult storyline but one actually billed as a domestic comedy because Dick has bought the French hideaway thanks to the phenomenal success of his bestseller, *The Nubile Baby*, which extols the merits of free love. Cue a deluge of ... What went wrong with our parenting? What will people think? Yet nobody actually considers the (offstage) teenage girl affected.

Michael Billington thought the denouement was particularly powerful and showed Finney's depth:

> He presses his palms flat against his skull, as if to beat down the awful truth, the colour drains from his big, cratered face, tears prick his eyes. It was like watching a man age twenty years in three seconds. When Finney lets his defences drop he can actually be extraordinarily moving on stage.

Sheridan Morley interviewed Finney a few days before *Chez Nous* opened. Finney told Morley:

> I'd like to do more of Nichols's plays if only he'd write some. He's got a vibrant theatrical sense, a sense of presentation, which I find a little rare elsewhere. This play is quieter, less frenetic, I think, than *Joe Egg* but there's still that sense of rhythm. It's a beat or two tighter and quicker than most.[6]

Pressed about the future, Finney was uncertain but hinted he was ready for big roles:

> I still can't decide whether I'm supposed to be a director/manager or a rogue and vagabond player. I got intense, creative pleasure out of directing *Charlie Bubbles*, and I enjoy my involvement with Memorial and the Royal Court but then again I tell myself that these next fifteen years, from now until I'm

around 50, are the most important for an actor, and that if I'm ever going to buckle down it has to be now. But my main aim is still what it's always been – to be, even if sometimes perversely, in control of my own destiny, and I've needed at least this amount of time to find out what I think I should be doing with my life.

Finney was preparing to take on some of the major classical roles. But before he did he still had one or two engagements for the Royal Court. In summer 1973, he played O'Halloran, one of a pair of Irish labourers, in David Storey's *Cromwell*, directed by Anthony Page. It was a rare foray into historical drama from a playwright associated more with modern realism (Storey wrote the screenplay for *This Sporting Life*). Despite the title, Cromwell never appears at all, nor is he ever named by any of the characters. He is merely a presence, a background figure set against a story depicting the futility of conflict in the seventeenth century.

The play was not well received and closed after just thirty-nine performances. Finney's old director Lindsay Anderson thought Finney was out of kilter:

> The actors are good, though occasionally incomprehensible as a result of an over-naturalistic approach. Albert is the exception: I think he gives a very bad performance, selfish, with mistaken ambitions towards giving a 'great' perfor-mance, artificial and grimacing, vocally affected, and, most disastrously, with no relationship at all to his buddy and sidekick, who is thereby rendered pale and insignificant. I think Brian [Cox] does extremely well, in that impossible part. There is a truthfulness to his acting which is quite absent from Albert's.[7]

Hell hath no fury like a gay director scorned? Anderson would be a repeat critic of Finney.

Finney also directed but did not appear in a production of *Loot*, Joe Orton's brilliant, award-winning dark farce. Finney cast James Aubrey as Dennis after he spotted him in an episode of *Z Cars*. Aubrey, who died in 2010, aged just 62, was subsequently best known for his portrayal of Susan Penhaligon's violent husband in Andrea Newman's kinky saga *Bouquet of Barbed Wire*. Other parts went to Jill Bennett, Philip Stone and David Troughton. Aubrey paid tribute to Finney's skill as a director, in particular his belief that, no matter how farcical the proceedings, everything had to be played completely straight:

> Basically, anything we did was our own creation but with his own absolute confidence in our performances and talent backing us up. If he got a little cross, it was an actor getting cross with another actor. Yes, he had the odd snap

at me. I thought I knew Orton better than he did, and he'd occasionally say, in a slightly sarcastic way, 'oh yeah, you knew him, did you?' He never became authoritarian about it, never, 'this is the way I want it and who's directing this anyway?'[8]

Finney's stint at the Royal Court was ending. Meanwhile, the National Theatre was beginning its gradual, and perpetually delayed, relocation to new premises on the South Bank, the mass of concrete that Finney came, much later, to dislike so much. The National's move coincided with a time when Finney felt ready to tackle a succession of classic roles. In the 1974 interview with Finney, Sheridan Morley had concluded thus:

> When Finney was starting his career at the Birmingham Rep, and I was finishing off my teens by lurking around London theatres, I spent some considerable time trying to decide whether Richard Burton or John Neville would ultimately inherit the mantle of Olivier. I needn't have bothered: it will be Finney.

But did Finney really want it badly enough?

CLASSICS IN CONCRETE

… the right sort of generosity …

Laurence Olivier on Albert Finney.

Laurence Olivier was looking for a successor as director of the National Theatre. Many candidates were mooted. Richard Attenborough (later to triumph with *Gandhi*) was one – a safe pair of hands, close to Olivier, but essentially more devoted to screen work than stage. Richard Burton was another possibility, but unlikely; his drinking and tempestuous on–off relationship with Elizabeth Taylor made him an outsider. Also, Burton had not even been a UK resident, for tax reasons, for many years. Burton, who was on record as saying that one of the real reasons for being an actor was to make money, would have had a substantial pay cut.

Finney was the more obvious choice. In Olivier's words, he was 'a person of the right sort of age, with the right sort of following, the right sort of promise, the right sort of generosity and natural trust with his colleagues'. Finney certainly commanded the respect for such a position. But he had always gone his own way. Everything in his career, from his refusal to play Lawrence and his rejection of the Spiegel contract, indicated wariness of long–term commitment. He would have been good at talent spotting, mentoring and encouraging younger actors and choosing productions. But, rather like Burton, the day-to-day board meetings, and simply the lack of freedom this would have imposed on him, deterred him.[1]

Olivier later wrote, 'I tried to interest Albert in the idea but his own acting prowess was so marketable that he could naturally see little point in vastly increasing his responsibilities and decimating his income.' Finney's own observation of the toll exacted on Olivier deterred him. He remembered seeing Olivier at the Old Vic one night, still blacked up for *Othello*, and exhausted. He'd had a board meeting earlier, then played Othello, and still had another meeting to get through.

In the end, Peter Hall took over in November 1973. Almost immediately Hall and Finney held meetings, not for Finney to assume any role as an actor manager, but to plan Finney's assault on some big classical roles, notably *Hamlet* and *Tamburlaine*.[2] Hall would direct both productions, although Michael Blakemore had been mentioned as a possible director of *Hamlet* at one point. *Hamlet* would open at the Old Vic and later transfer to the Lyttelton Theatre when the new building opened.

Hall was more enthusiastic about *Tamburlaine* than he was about *Hamlet*. But Finney felt the time was right. According to Blakemore, 'his father at the time was far from well and Albert felt that this had given him a particular insight into the part'.[3]

Finney knew his Hamlet would be examined forensically. Doubtless the sharpening of pencils in Fleet Street could be heard in Waterloo Road and, subsequently, in the concrete jungle of the South Bank. Immediately the critics engaged in comparisons, trading memories of former princes, sometimes in a bid to show off their credentials but also in a bid to quash a contender like Finney.

One brilliant contemporary, Nicol Williamson, was giving Finney stiff competition in the classics. His 1969 *Hamlet*, directed by Tony Richardson at the Roundhouse, was acclaimed as one of the greatest of his generation. Williamson was even invited to perform it in front of Richard Nixon at the White House. Nowadays, you often read on the internet that Williamson 'bested Finney in the classics'. Maybe, but Finney proved more durable in film and theatre. (When Williamson died in 2011, his obituary in *The Times* noted that Williamson viewed two close contemporaries, Anthony Hopkins and Ian McKellen, disparagingly. Apparently he described them as 'technicians'.)[4] However, there's no record of Williamson, or indeed Finney, referencing any mutual rivalry. Jill Townsend, Williamson's wife for most of the seventies, said she never recalled Williamson making any derogatory comments about Finney.[5]

Finney, at 39, was perhaps a few years past his prime for Hamlet, as Peter Hall mentioned in his diaries. Exactly forty years later, another 39-year-old, Benedict Cumberbatch, would play Hamlet in a sell-out run. Yet somehow Cumberbatch has a boyish air about him; Finney, on the other hand, looked mature for his age.

Hall decided on an unabridged text, resisting pressures to cut it to keep costs down. Angela Lansbury, although only seven years older than Finney, would play Gertrude and Denis Quilley was Claudius. (Peter Hall had approached Kenneth More but the actor declined, later reflecting that 'there were so many great Shakespearean actors who could have done it better'.)

Finney, sporting a high level of fitness after workouts at the Grosvenor House Hotel (but still smoking and drinking Guinness),[6] portrayed Hamlet as burly, hard-bitten and athletic. And, according to many observers, including Ian McKellen, Finney played it with a northern accent. (McKellen, unlike Finney, had, while at Cambridge, deliberately ditched his Lancashire accent.)

On 3 December 1975, ironically when Finney was rehearsing the scene from *Hamlet* where he witnesses his father's ghost, he was told his father had died. Hall wrote in his diaries that Finney was 'very upset, but extremely brave'. The first preview fell the day after his father's passing. Finney apparently told Hall that he knew if he let his emotion run away with him, he would lose control. 'He therefore had to check it forcibly,' Hall relates. Hall also said that Finney told him a story about his relationship with his father:

> Sometime back he suddenly realised that he had never told his father what he meant to him – how he respected him. His father was in a nursing home, ill, so Albert sat down and wrote him an eight-page letter trying to put into words his feelings. There was no answer. After a time he rang up and asked if he'd received the letter. 'Oh yes,' said his father, 'there's a reply in the post for you.' It read 'Dear Albert, thank you very much for your letter. Love Dad.'

Finney remembered his father fondly, describing him as 'very droll and very dry'. Neither man, it seemed, went in for ostentatious displays of affection but they had always had a good relationship. Finney went home for the funeral. In his absence, the National ran another play in its repertoire.

Domestically, it was not much better. Stanley Kubrick was filming his visually stunning but monumentally long epic *Barry Lyndon*. Anouk met the star of the film, Ryan O'Neal, at a party during shooting. O'Neal, devastatingly handsome, brash and supremely famous, and Anouk were instantly attracted. It was a quick conquest, one echoed several years later when Lee Majors entrusted O'Neal, his best friend, to look after Farrah Fawcett during his absence (according to some observers, O'Neal and Fawcett kissed each other so fiercely that their lips started to bleed).

Marriages between two big stars are never easy. Gene Wilder, who got Finney to speak just one line in his film *The Adventures of Sherlock Holmes' Smarter Brother*, became friendly with Finney and Anouk in the period just before they broke up. He tells the story:

> I had never met Albert Finney but he did me the great favour of acting a tiny part in one scene. He sat as a member of the film audience that was watching a slapstick Italian opera. Albert had one line to say: 'Is this wonderfully brave or just rotten?' After his scene was over we made plans to see each other again. During that summer I became good friends with Albert and his wife, Anouk

Aimée. They were very loving with each other, but Albert is a big talker and Anouk had to fight with him for equal time.[7]

The way Anouk tells it, at the beginning she was happy to be a stay-at-home wife. Then she changed her mind as the marriage failed. As she told *The Times* in 1982:

I really didn't ever plan to act again after we married. I'd been at it a long time, there was no script around that I particularly wanted to make, and I genuinely thought that maybe I should take up painting or writing instead. I even bought an easel, on which the canvas turned slowly from white to yellow as it lay untouched in a corner of the house. While the marriage was good, I saw no point in being an actress; when it began to fail, I went back to work.

A mutual friend believes that Anouk's insecurities ultimately doomed them and that she and Finney were never truly comfortable together:

I don't think he was prepared for her jealousy and possessiveness, which considering his place in the acting world at that time was hard to take. And she couldn't relax with his popularity. She was more 'provincial' than he expected and very private.

Finney, never seemingly distressed by a relationship ending, viewed the break-up philosophically:

It was time for Anouk to move on, and she did so with my blessing. I do believe that when you're together out of habit, I have the right to say, 'It's been grand, but ...' and so does my partner, if she feels pulled towards another man – or woman, for that matter.

Later that year, 1975, Finney moved out of the Brompton Square home and into the Dorchester. He was back into one room again, albeit one with impeccable room service. Perhaps Finney would have bumped into the hotel's regular guest, Richard Burton, who was marking his 50th birthday in London at the time. They certainly met at the *Evening Standard* British Film Awards on 12 November, when Burton handed Finney the best actor award for *Murder on the Orient Express*. Burton, according to his diary entry, praised Finney, 'whom I've never seen' – but whether he meant never met face to face or never seen on-screen is unclear – as 'uniquely remarkable'.

The next day, Burton records, he saw Finney 'for the first time' in *Murder on the Orient Express*. He described it as 'very amusing'. Whichever way you read this, it's rather odd. If Burton meant he had never seen Finney on film, it sounds unbelievable from someone in his position. Was he really so cut off from film-making that he had never seen a performance from an actor as great as Finney? If Burton had never met Finney in person this is also surprising, but perhaps more understandable given the younger actor's path away from mainstream Hollywood. Finney, it should be noted, had also never (formally) met Tom Courtenay before they filmed *The Dresser* or Judi Dench before *Skyfall* in 2011. By 1980, however, Burton was telling an interviewer that 'Albert Finney is the greatest actor in the world. Then Peter O'Toole.'

Finney was now footloose again. Carol White, in her autobiography, recalled that Finney, an 'old friend', started to see her again as she prepared to film *The Squeeze* in 1976:

> Albert was appearing in a season of Shakespeare at the National Theatre and the words he learnt during the day, he rehearsed in his sleep at night. It was strange to wake up and hear him performing a monologue, but he did it so well I started to enjoy it.[8]

Peter Hall seemed optimistic at the beginning of rehearsals for *Hamlet*. He noted that Finney 'looks wonderful with his beard: a powerful, passionate, sexy Hamlet, glowering with resentment. I looked at him and felt cheered.' But an entry from 16 October 1975 shows Hall's mood starting to pall: 'Not a bad day's *Hamlet* rehearsal, though I have a sense I am hanging on by my fingernails.'

Angela Lansbury has since said that she felt she was miscast:

> At times Albert resembled a kind of black-clothed paratrooper, while I felt rather like a rather roughly hewn chess-piece as the queen – chained to the ground. There was no sexuality in the piece at all, which was curious. I was extremely disappointed about that because I felt that one of the reasons that I could be cast in this role effectively was the fact that I had a somewhat shady reputation for play-ing rather incestuous mothers. Yet I didn't have a chance to display any of those qualities in the production. … those [poor] reviews were fair and square. There was no drama. It was the most untheatrical production I've ever been a part of.

Kenneth Hurren in *The Spectator* gave Finney a sharp rebuke:

> Albert Finney's Hamlet is as dreadful as might be imagined of an actor of his unquestionably superior talents. I shall not quarrel greatly with his monotonous

verse-speaking, which is no worse than that of most of the company, for it might imply that I feel he should adopt some special 'poetry voice', whereas my modest requirement is merely that he should convey the sense of the lines (which often he does not).[9]

By the time the production had moved to its new home, the 870-seat Lyttelton Theatre, in March 1976, Hurren had not changed his mind, 'I am grieved to say that neither Albert Finney's aggressively ill-spoken, weather-beaten Hamlet nor the production as a whole has improved in the merest particular'.

Irving Wardle in *The Times* also disapproved:

We have given up looking for princely Hamlets but it is no easy task to say what Finney is offering instead. He cuts out pathos, reflective philosophy and melancholy and bases his performance on energy, bluff comradeship and sardonic derision, the voice rasps as monotonously as a buzz saw, bringing the play scene, for instance, to a climax of insult well before the scene reaches its own climax. Mr Finney has the energy and presence to carry the part physically; but he casts no light on it.

Benedict Nightingale agreed that Finney's Hamlet lacked delicacy. 'Albert Finney's Hamlet was a disorderly dropout from Wittenberg University, a turbulent bull who could hardly enter an anteroom without knocking over the people as well as the china.'

Not all the reviews, however, were so cutting. Bernard Levin noted a few idiosyncrasies, including words out of place. He added, while the production was still at the Old Vic, that he hoped that when he saw it again he would 'hear rather more of Shakespeare's words and less of Finney's'. But, Levin noted, Finney was wrestling with a full, unabridged text. He acknowledged the muted reception, but concluded with a generous tribute:

Albert Finney's Hamlet has not been received with the kind of unanimous acclaim that he has hitherto received for almost every part he has played and not only received but richly deserved, for this great actor brings to mind what Dr Johnson said of Goldsmith: truly Finney touches nothing that he does not adorn.[10]

Overall, however, the reception was disappointing. John Gielgud noted in a diary entry for 1976, 'Have not dared to see the Finney Hamlet. Everyone says the performances are poor all-round.'[11]

Perhaps Wardle's comment on Finney cutting out 'pathos, reflective philosophy and melancholy' is the most telling. One can guess at a simple problem. The
Great Dane is contemplative, tentative, introspective and disillusioned. None of
these characteristics apply to Finney. In Sheridan Morley's words, 'Finney is no
introverted scholar'. To which, you may say – so what? He's an actor, and Finney
subsequently proved his worth in many films where he was acting someone far
removed from himself. Yes, but on stage, it's harder to suppress one's true self,
especially in such a long part as Hamlet. Perhaps Finney's natural ebullience
shone through so that we ended up seeing a more virile Hamlet than intended.
Others wondered if Finney's instinctive style, to give people an up-front, forceful Hamlet, would have clashed with Hall's pedantic approach to the text.

Finney himself was unfazed. In a diary entry for 11 December, Hall noted,
'Albert is still elated; not put down at all by the abuse, which is vociferous here
and there'. On 19 December, Hall dined with Finney at the Dorchester:

> He [Finney] was most complimentary about the *Hamlet* work and about the
> experience of working with me – wants to go on, is determined to tackle
> more big roles, and determined to stay with the National Theatre, with the
> occasional film away … he said he loved playing the part.

Finney later said he felt imbued with energy, even after a colossal part like Hamlet.
It was as though the play, as written, fulfilled a cathartic need in an actor:

> The great difference between stage and screen is that in the theatre, if you're
> playing a demanding part, you can get a physical sense of repletion. At the end
> of the evening you really feel that you've been used and stretched physically,
> mentally, imaginatively, emotionally. Playing Hamlet is extraordinary that way.
> You go through the whole evening talking, talking, talking. And then you get
> to the duel with Laertes, and you feel you've got nothing left. But because
> the playwright asks you to do something physical, it's actually a very energis-
> ing moment in the play. You're using a different part of yourself for five or
> eight minutes after all this 'to be or not to be' stuff. Having been an actor,
> Shakespeare understood how it would work. In movies you don't get that
> physical fulfilment, because you spend a lot of time sitting around waiting for
> just a little burst of energy. You go home mentally tired, but you've not used
> your body. Some days are very frustrating, when you go in full of beans, and
> three-quarters of the day is lost in lighting the scene.[12]

Mediocre, even poor, reviews did not dent Finney's morale. As he milled around
the new South Bank building, at first for rehearsals and then after the play's

transfer to the Lyttelton, he declared he felt at home. 'I want a decade as an actor in the theatre. I shall be here for a long time if the marriage works, and I'm very happy at the moment,' he said. 'It's just like John Neville in the great days at Nottingham in the sixties,' said Vivien Wallace from the National's press office.

Finney proved a great company man at the National, learning the names of many of the building's 500 staff: technicians, cleaners and bar staff. Linda Tolhurst, stage door keeper at the theatre, starting at the Old Vic in 1975 just before the move to the South Bank, recalled Finney's friendliness, 'Albert Finney was the first famous person I ever met. He'd buy everyone drinks at the bar. He said to me, "Don't call me Albert; call me Albie".'[13]

Finney even declared he was happy with the acoustics at the Lyttelton Theatre, saying that he had never found the Old Vic's horseshoe shape ideal. The Olivier, on the other hand, where he took his *Tamburlaine* later in 1976, he described as like performing in 'an aircraft carrier'.

It was impossible to dislike 'Albie', who took to enjoying a cigarette and Guinness with the staff. As ever, Finney was a hero to young actors who remembered his anti-establishment Arthur Seaton. A young Ray Winstone, then working in the wardrobe department, described an early encounter with Finney at the Old Vic:

My job was looking after two actors called Patrick Monckton and Michael Keating but sometimes a mate of mine who was looking after Albert Finney would be off and I'd have to stand in for him. Finney had been one of my favourite actors since I'd seen him in *Saturday Night and Sunday Morning*. It didn't matter that he was playing a northerner – I recognised that character, and that was the first time I'd seen the kind of person I could relate to from my own life up there on the big screen in such a convincing way. I used to love watching him in *Hamlet*, giving it the full Shakespearean thing but doing it as a man so I'd go missing during the play to watch him from the seats right at the back … unfortunately I was late getting back once and Albert missed his cue. I went in the bar afterwards knowing I'd fucked up, which I felt really bad about, as I had a lot of time for Albert Finney as a person, never mind how great his acting was. I still wasn't quite ready to face the music, though, so when he came in looking for me I ducked down behind a table. Through the forest of furniture legs I could clearly see Albert's human ones walking across the floor, so I crawled off between the stools in the opposite direction. When I came up for air he was standing right in front of me, like one of the twins in *The Shining*, only with Albert Finney's face. I don't know how he did it. It was like he floated there or something. His first two words were not promising. – they were 'you' and 'cunt' – but when I explained 'I'm so sorry, Albert, I fucked up,

I was watching you from up the back and I just missed the call' it seemed to do the trick. All he said after that was – 'what do you want to drink?'[14]

Perhaps Winstone's story explains why Finney was popular but also why some of the critics disliked his Hamlet. He was simply too virile for those used to the cut-glass delivery of someone like Gielgud. But, as a final comment on Finney's Hamlet, the critics may have sniped, but the box office told a different story. It played to packed houses and some distinguished visitors. Even the Labour Chancellor of the Exchequer at the time, Denis Healey, saw it. 'He and his wife [Edna] enjoyed *Hamlet* very much,' noted Hall in a diary entry.

Maybe Finney was better suited to playing warriors than procrastinators. *Tamburlaine* was another colossal epic, and the first production staged in 'the aircraft carrier', the 1,160-seater Olivier Theatre. A rare performance of Christopher Marlowe's epic play, loosely based on the life of an Asian emperor, it was a four-hour marathon, longer than *Hamlet*. Hall again directed. This time he was more optimistic: 'It's a magnificent part for Finney: tough, vital, funny and with a great tragic dimension at the end. He will be remarkable, I think.'[15]

An entry a few months later confirmed Hall's upbeat mood, 'Albert is in terrific form: one feels all those years of his youth in Manchester studying stand-up comics.'

Denis Quilley and Susan Fleetwood, who had been in *Hamlet*, also co-starred. Unusually, because the completion of the Olivier Theatre had been repeatedly delayed, some of the rehearsals had to take place outside. Hall recalled:

In the hot summer of 1976, in despair as to whether we would ever be able to stage the production, and urgently needing to contact an audience with our work, we performed some scenes outside on the river terraces while the traffic roared by on Waterloo Bridge. The spectators were those who happened to be passing. Many stopped and watched, fascinated by the central figure of Albert Finney in the name part, rakishly wearing a beribboned straw hat against the beating sun … And when Tamburlaine finally inaugurated the Olivier in early October, Albert, surviving severe bronchitis, was magnificent. The drama took the stage and sang. We had successfully launched the second and largest and in my view most exciting of our three theatres.[16]

When the play opened for real, Finney was a sight to behold, with a mane of curly hair, pointed whiskers and a gold-encrusted mini-skirted costume adorned with trinkets and bracelets. At the opening, on 4 October 1976, Finney confronted not just a marathon part, first-night nerves and the dreaded critics but also his lingering illness. Hall wrote:

Albert sounded badly bronchial for the first three-quarters of an hour, but gradually the tubes began to clear and his confidence grew as he realised he would be able to get through. At the end there was the sort of ovation that is usually reserved for opera and ballet, and it was not just for Albert but for the whole company.

This time there were more plaudits than brickbats. Malcolm Macpherson in *Newsweek* said, 'Finney's Tamburlaine was superb, catching all of the character's mad fury and revelling in the colour of the verse to such an extent that he even discovered a hint of humour in the bloodthirsty bully'. John Walker, in the *Herald Tribune*, described Finney's performance as 'very good but not great' – whatever that means.

Tamburlaine was certainly a long test for the human bladder and very hard work for everyone involved.[17] A bonus was that Finney had also found a new girlfriend, Diana Quick, whom he met during rehearsals on the play. Diana, ten years his junior, was still married to actor Kenneth Cranham when she first met Finney. Not only a great beauty but a formidable intellect, she had won a scholarship to Lady Margaret Hall, Oxford, before she had even sat her A levels. She was also the first female president of the Oxford Union Dramatic Society. By 1981 she was starring in Wilkie Collins's *The Woman in White* and, more famously, the television adaptation of *Brideshead Revisited*. Her role as troubled aristocrat Lady Julia Flyte brought her international acclaim and an Emmy.

Diana, serene and sensuous, had an air of maturity about her. She later recalled that Finney once told her, 'You're going to find it very hard to have a career in England. The English don't really like grown-up women. They only like girls.' Finney was usually perceptive about other people, so she worried about her future. Fortunately, however, she has remained in demand.

She and Finney co-starred, albeit fleetingly, in Ridley Scott's first film, *The Duellists*, about an extended feud between two Napoleonic soldiers. Keith Carradine and Harvey Keitel engage in a series of inconclusive, bloody duels. The film was derived from Joseph Conrad's short story *The Duel*, itself based on the true story of a long-standing quarrel between two French officers.

Although the plot seems far-fetched, at least to modern audiences, triggered for no apparent reason other than a ridiculous overreaction to a perceived slight, *The Duellists* is stunning and compelling. It is Keitel's Feraud who keeps the absurd vendetta going. And Keitel acts him well, looking at Carradine's d'Hubert with marvellous scorn as if confronting a bad smell. 'You have the effrontery to invade my space again,' he seems to be saying. The feud may be groundless but that, according to Scott, was the point: 'All the Carradine character needs to say is –

"let's have a drink, shake hands and forget about it". But because of this ridiculous soldier's code they are living under, he can't do it.'

Scott felt he needed a strong player to portray the small but significant role of Fouché, a secret police chief. 'Albert Finney, who's tremendously constructive in the sense that he will help if he thinks a project's worthwhile, did a cameo in exchange for a framed cheque for £25 inscribed "break glass in case of need",' the director recalled.

Finney's Fouché was serpent like, slippery and authoritative. Finney rivets you during his encounter with Carradine. 'I'm something of a virtuoso at survival. You'll be aware of *that*, I think,' says Fouché, a smoky threat rising in his voice. I hate the silly expression 'scene-stealer' but it's apt here. Finney was playing Hamlet at the Lyttelton during his stint on *The Duellists*. Fouché was supposed to be white-haired and beardless but Scott allowed him to keep Hamlet's beard and black hair.

Cristina Raines, who played Adele, remembered Finney's authority in the film: 'God, he just opens his mouth and he just commands the room and he really is a wonderful man'.[18] Many others have commented on Finney's captivating voice, rich, resonant and stentorian, and just perfect for the old actor manager he was to play several years later in *The Dresser*.

Finney went to Cannes in May 1977 to publicise Scott's film, conversing in excellent French as he strolled along the beach. He mentioned his love of rugby, recalling that he had played as a youngster in France. 'I adore the current moment and the infinite possibilities of tomorrow, the secrets of tomorrow … I love that,' he said as the Med brushed his toes. Who wouldn't?

In 1977, the year of *The Duellists*' release, Finney, always testing his artistry, broke new ground. The actual trigger was a play in London that he was involved in producing. Finney recalled:

> I needed a record of organ music for one scene. I rang up Denis King, a friend, who used to be part of the King Brothers, which had been a very important singing group but then broke up. Anyhow, Denis said he would be delighted to make my organ music record. And the man who ran the studio came up to me and said: 'Remember me? Fifteen years ago, I asked you if you wanted to make a record.'

Finney decided to make an album of original material. Within a few weeks they had completed twelve songs, mostly about Finney's childhood and early years in Salford. Many were written during extended rehearsals for *Tamburlaine*. One ditty reflected his feelings about his place of birth:

What have they done to my hometown?
They've pulled the terraced houses down
And put the people in the sky,
In towers twenty storeys high.

Another, 'Those Other Men', reflected Finney's easy come, easy go, play the field attitude to love – with a nod, presumably, to the other men in his girl-friends' lives:

I'd like to thank those other men
They helped to make you what you are
They made you wise in making love
And now your love is shared with me
So how can I regret when I think about those other men?
The gentle warmth of your caress
You didn't learn that yesterday.

Another song, 'Bird of Paradise', could have been an evocation of Finney's exotic Hawaiian holidays, accompanied by the sound of rolling surf and chirping in the trees:

The bird of paradise is very rare
Of a kind beyond compare
You have to handle with great care
The bird of paradise
The way that she moves
To see how gracefully her limbs unfold.

Reactions? Judith Simons said in the *Daily Express*, 'He has a wonderfully poetic, declamatory style … and proves himself a first-class lyricist. His songs should prove a treasure chest for other artists.' Barry Coleman in *The Guardian* merely wrote that Finney 'should have known better'. Lindsay Anderson – surprise, surprise – thought the album was 'dreadful'. My own opinion? I'm sure that the likes of Perry Como or Frank Sinatra would not have lost any sleep.

Some journalists tried to identify the women referenced in the songs. A British hack mentioned Jane Wenham, Samantha Eggar and Anouk Aimée, but, said Finney, the writer had got it all wrong. The list, he said, was too short. (Finney always had a good way of disarming the prying press. In 1982, a journalist interviewing Finney for *Photoplay* magazine told him that she had heard a rumour that he and Diana Quick were about to marry. Finney, laughing, replied, 'Really? I must go home and tell Di. And how many children are we going to have?')

Such was Finney's fame at the time that King's music publisher, David Platz, was able to negotiate a quick deal with Motown. Finney was one of only two white artists ever picked up by the company. Finney and Denis King took off to the US in June 1977 to promote the album which was called, simply, *Albert Finney's Album*. Finney made guest appearances on the Johnny Carson show, with Alan King standing in for Carson.

King tells the story:

Albert was funny and charming as usual and seemed his perfectly relaxed self while being interviewed. Then he was asked to sing and from where I sat at the piano, fingers poised, I could see a strange but familiar light come into his eyes. Not one of total panic exactly but more the look of someone who will be stepping outside his comfort zone. This would not be Albert playing a part or reciting Shakespeare. This would be Albert with no character to hide behind, Albert as Albert, Albert in unfamiliar territory, Albert singing. As an accompanist you learn to recognise this look and you adjust your concentration accordingly; you crank it up to its maximum setting because obviously you want the singer to sound his or her best. Albert walked over from a chair on the dais to the microphone. Behind him, Don Severinson's band struck up, with me conducting from the piano and the number 'What have they done to my hometown?' went as rehearsed. In other words, we got through it. No one screamed for more but it was well received, and Albert seemed much relieved when it was over. Over the next six weeks, across the States, this set the pattern for every time he appeared on TV. He never screwed up but it never got easier for him. And even though we never talked about it I don't think it was really his bag. [19]

Finney echoed his friend's comments:

Singing in front of people was at once frightening and titillating at the same time. When you're acting on stage or acting in a film, you have an automatic out-clause. If the thing goes badly you can always blame it on the director or the writer or whatever. You are part of a group. But when you are up there singing songs you have written yourself, there is no out-clause. It's just you. And, if you're bad, there's no one to blame but yourself. In that way, being a singer is more difficult than being an actor. [20]

Finney, Diana and Denis King had a great time, though, having dinner with Al Pacino in Sardi's. They saw Kris Kristofferson and Rita Coolidge in Phoenix and Diana Ross in New York. Finney also enjoyed a reunion with Liza Minnelli (his co-star in *Charlie Bubbles*) backstage after her try-out musical, *The Act*.

Finney's singing career ended there and then. By 1992, he told Terry Wogan, you could pick up the album as a collectors' item. 'It got to 192 in the Top 200, then sayonara. That was the end of my recording career. The fact that it wasn't a hit doesn't matter. It looks good on my résumé.' Subsequently, Finney denied that he could sing at all, echoing other screen stars like Lee Marvin and Richard Harris who admitted they only sounded good with a professional backing group.

Meanwhile, after that rather strange hiatus, Finney was again ready for an assault on another classic part. Would he fall victim to the jinx of *Macbeth*?

HALL OF DOUBT

I don't give a damn for Peter Hall or his Lear. I want to see the actors' Lear.
Richard Harris, 1988.

John Osborne later referred to Peter Hall, the director of the National, as 'Fu Manchu'. Michael Blakemore called him 'a snob'. For Jonathan Miller he was 'a safari-suited bureaucrat'.

So Hall was never his own worst enemy; others filled that role. Yet Hall could also be hard on himself. His autobiography and diaries, when covering his stewardship of the National in the late seventies, are strewn with rueful admissions of failure. At turns he blames his excessive workload, his subservience to others' demands and his inexperience at handling certain theatrical genres. He also cites his lack of foresight in realising that some productions, although effective in rehearsal rooms, were unsuited to the vast auditoriums of the South Bank.

If there was one word to describe Hall's tenure during this period it was 'beleaguered'. Seldom did a week go by without the press launching new brickbats against the National. Hall's salary, the building's design, the choice of productions, and the rights and wrongs of subsidised theatre – everything was fair game. For some reason, none of his successors attracted this venom.[1] Unfortunately, all these controversies coincided with Finney giving classical acting a last ride out. He has never returned to the National since.

Finney's first work after *Tamburlaine* was with Michael Elliott, the founding artistic director of Manchester's new Royal Exchange Theatre Company, on two plays, Chekhov's *Uncle Vanya* and Coward's *Present Laughter*. Finney won excellent reviews for his Astrov in *Uncle Vanya*, playing opposite Leo McKern (as Vanya) as well as Alfred Burke and Eleanor Bron.

Irving Wardle particularly liked Leo McKern as Vanya. 'In scale, the performance eclipses everything else on stage, but it meets an unyielding match in Albert Finney's granite-hard Astrov, whose dulled responses and wolfish appetites fully confirm his own self-portrait,' he wrote. Hall also visited the production towards the end of its six-week run. He found the version 'definitive' and added, 'Albert's Astrov was a country doctor wading through shit and mud to save the peasants from cholera'.

Finney's second play with Elliott, *Present Laughter*, co-starring Diana Quick, seemed so *not* Finney that it ran the risk of provoking unintentional laughter. Think of Coward, and one pictures a leading man with cut-glass, strangulated Oxford English delivery, a suave, debonair air, tall and slim with impeccably coiffured hair and cigarette holder. Finney, with his hefty build and bulldog appearance, did not particularly fit this kind of light comedy. And even less was he Garry Essendine, the preening, self-conscious comedy actor of *Present Laughter*. (George C. Scott also played the lead in a Broadway production of *Present Laughter*, perhaps a similar case of unusual casting.) You could see the role being played by Nigel Patrick, certainly O'Toole, with his slightly passé air of rakish sophistication, or Simon Callow – the star of a more recent revival. Finney seemed all wrong for it, yet somehow he succeeded.

Finney's conviction finally swayed Irving Wardle:

In the role of the champ, however, we find the irredeemably post-war figure of Albert Finney, the least likely sucker for a silk dressing gown or target for request that he should abate his 'devastating charm' ... What counts, however, is just how far he does go. As on past occasions with this actor, any opening incredulity is finally swept aside by the sheer energy and stamina with which he fights for his view of the character.

Finney made an unexpectedly early return to the National to replace the recently deceased Pitt Wilkinson in *The Passion* at the Cottesloe.[2] He took the relatively minor roles of Annas and the blind man. Mark McManus, later to find fame as Taggart, was Jesus and Brian Glover, the actor usually described as a 'gritty northerner', most famous for his role as the bullying sports master in *Kes*, played Cayphas. One scene called for Glover to consume a flagon of wine to the accompaniment of a drum roll. Grape juice, rather than wine, was the usual liquid for the occasion. But one time, Finney, ever the prankster, decided to substitute the juice with some fine red wine. Doubtless, Finney expected that Glover would detect the ruse and sip the contents more slowly than usual. Not at all – Glover downed the whole flagon in one go, then scurried off to the dressing room during a break in his performance where he threw up before returning to the stage.

Finney's parts in *The Passion* were unusual territory for an international star. Someone in his position might have been tempted to snooze in the wings and whistle through it; but not Finney. His blind man was as finely etched as any of his leading roles at the National. Jack Shepherd caught a pivotal moment in the production:

> Finney played it like the blind people he had seen on the streets of Salford, upright but leaning away, with a worn, pressed suit, and a gabardine raincoat that his mother had folded over his arm before sending him out. To stand behind him and read on the faces of the spectators the moment at which his sight returned was as powerful a theatrical experience as I have known.[3]

While in *The Passion*, Finney was simultaneously learning lines for *The Country Wife*, Hall's version of William Wycherley's Restoration comedy in which a rake feigns impotence to have clandestine affairs with married women.

'The general impression is of waiting for a dance that never begins,' said Wardle of *The Country Wife*. 'There are a good many nice individual details; as where Albert Finney's Horner drops his hat to a strategic position to allow the suspicious Lady Fidget to approve his manhood.' He thought that Ben Kingsley, pre-*Gandhi*, had emerged best, hailing his 'brilliantly inventive and entirely traditional portrait of a Restoration fop'. But he went on to judge that 'good or bad, the separate details never coalesce into any rhythmic patterns.'

Hall himself noted in his diaries that *The Country Wife* was 'full of stridency and nothingness'. And he blamed himself for the poor reception:

> I tried to rehearse *The Country Wife* during the height of the financial crisis. To make matters worse this was my first [and only] attempt at Restoration comedy, so I was dealing with an unfamiliar world. Although there were pleasures along the way – among them a cast including Albert Finney, Susan Littler[4] and Richard Johnson – the production was a failure. The energy I draw from rehearsals and then reapply to administration just wasn't there.

Better was Hall's production of *The Cherry Orchard* at the Olivier in early 1978 which some thought featured Finney's finest work at the National. Michael Billington noted:

> The quality I most remember was that instead of playing Lopakhin in the obvious way, which is a kind of country peasant who has become part of the middle classes, the motivating factor here was that he was obviously in love with Ranyevskaya [Dorothy Tutin].

Ralph Richardson was also singled out for his 'spellbinding performance'. Nevertheless, Hall was once again dissatisfied:

> It had a dazzling cast, Albert Finney, Dorothy Tutin, Robert Stephens, Susan Fleetwood, Ben Kingsley and – crowning it – Ralph Richardson as Firs. Rehearsals were exhilarating ... But once we moved from the rehearsal room into the great space of the Olivier, the play simply vanished. All the interplay between the actors seemed to disappear. The Olivier is a theatre for dialectical discussion and big epic statements. Irony, ambiguity, delicacy and the eloquence of the unsaid are very difficult to convey in it.

Dorothy Tutin's daughter, Amanda Waring, remembers Ralph Richardson arriving at the theatre on a motorbike and that he and Finney taught her mother to ride one too.

All these plays were a preparation for Finney's assault on *Macbeth*. (So superstitious are some actors about this play that, for example, Peter O'Toole would not even refer to it by name, calling it 'Harry Lauder', when he played the part in 1980.) And from the beginning it seemed that the Hall/Finney version was troubled.

Hall always maintained that he had never wanted to stage it. A diary entry from 15 February 1978 tells the story:

> Dinner with Albert. He just wouldn't give up on *Macbeth*, which I desperately don't want to direct. 'Why worry,' he says, 'it's only a play? Let's continue our adventures. We have a fine company, a fine theatre, you know *Macbeth*, I know it, why be so intense about it?' Difficult to argue with, especially when we need it to add weight to the repertoire. And he did a lot to put my confidence back ... The real reason for doing *Macbeth* is, I'm afraid, this: Albert has stuck by me through thick and thin. If he wants me to direct the play, I must stick by him.

Rehearsals saw gradually deteriorating confidence. Hall began to realise that, for whatever reason, the production lacked that certain something. 'Final run-through of *Macbeth* this morning,' Hall wrote on 22 May 1978. 'Albert is sporadically superb, Dorothy very deep and complex, but I don't know what the production's like. Rather ordinary, I think. It's not wrong-headed; it just perhaps doesn't have a head at all.' Hall wrote that Finney's performance was variable, at times 'dry and uninventive' and with a 'staccato delivery'. Tutin, according to Hall, was 'too breathy and fading'.

Nicky Henson, as Malcolm, said he and the rest of the cast knew the critics would be gunning for them. Nevertheless, he found it 'rather extraordinary' when Hall, on the day *Macbeth* opened for press previews, told the company to expect bad notices. (Crying foul before battle commenced?) Finney responded by trying to drum up morale – literally – by taking to the glass roof and banging a drum. According to Henson, 'it gave us a lift and we then all hung out the windows, cheering away'.

Remember Peter Bowles's recollection of the 18-year-old Finney's approach to *Macbeth*? 'I'd learn the fucking lines and walk on.' That implies tremendous bravado if nothing else. Yet, ironically, Hall admitted the final result was dull. 'John Bury [set designer] and I tried to set an example by doing it economically. We ended up doing it boringly. The notices for me and for Albert were terrible.'

Dorothy Tutin's daughter, actress Amanda Waring, remembers her mother's dissatisfaction:

> She wasn't fabulously happy. She loved working with Albert and with Peter Hall but she felt let down by the stark production. The Olivier is a ginormous auditorium, allowing for little feedback with the audience. And there's no comedy in *Macbeth*, so little sense of how the audience feels. She didn't particularly like performing at the Olivier – the Lyttelton and the Cottesloe are a bit more intimate – and she would take the work home.[5]

She also remembers that Finney would sometimes 'corpse' on stage, play a few practical jokes, which sometimes unnerved the cast. Perhaps Finney did it on purpose, to lighten up the atmosphere, because reviews were critical.

Ned Chaillet, in *The Times*, led the assault, comparing it unfavourably to Trevor Nunn's 'superb' production starring Ian McKellen which had just ended at the Young Vic:

> The bare stage is used only to make the text pedantically plain, not to illuminate its drama. The moments in Mr Finney's performance which are memorable are all near the end, when his face becomes a mass of nervous twitches, revealing the despair that the witches' prophecies have brought.

Geoffrey Wheatcroft, in *The Spectator*, compared Finney's Macbeth to Alan Howard's Coriolanus: 'The National's Macbeth is another man who can convey great physical excitement, but Albert Finney lacks Howard's resources as a classical actor and as a verse-speaker'.

Finney's Macbeth might not have attracted great notices, yet once again, Finney had dared to tackle a colossal role. It's as well here to take a step back and acknowledge his sheer guts: Tamburlaine, Hamlet and now Macbeth. All three were gargantuan classical parts demanding not only talent and self-discipline but also the toughest mettle.

Occasionally even Finney's resilience had crumbled. Hall records visiting Finney during the interval of *Hamlet*, after the play had transferred to the Lyttelton, in which Finney was clearly struggling:

> He sat there covered in sweat, crying his eyes out. He cried and cried and cried. I asked him if he would like me to go. No, he said, he felt tonight he'd unblocked something in himself. I agreed. What we'd had before was energy, ferocity, and agility. What we had tonight was a man exposing his own heart in return for the audience's gift of those few hours of their lives.

Although Finney would face subsequent jibes that he was avoiding classical theatre, in the late seventies the whisperings were just the opposite. Some people said that he had rejected a glittering Hollywood career to do theatre. His friend Tom Bell, speaking in 1978 about Finney's long stint at the National, said, 'I wouldn't want to work there. Albie climbs mountains there. I'd rather think in terms of films.'[6]

'Climbing mountains', Everest even, was a good analogy for Finney's repeated efforts. *Hamlet* and *Macbeth* were seen as the ultimate tests for an actor. Consider the 1980 Old Vic production of *Macbeth* starring Peter O'Toole. Audiences were rolling in the aisles as critics took shots at O'Toole's poor timing and lisping delivery. 'A cross between Bette Davis and Vincent Price,' said one. The following day it seemed that World War Three had erupted. As O'Toole told Russell Harty, 'the house was besieged by the press'. Harty said, 'You mean the box office was besieged?' O'Toole: 'No *my house* was besieged.'

Ironically, the terrible notice boosted ticket sales for O'Toole's *Macbeth*. O'Toole's continuing in the run was saluted as a feat of heroism, given the bile thrown at him. And although Finney's *Macbeth* was not nearly so skewered (compared to O'Toole's at any rate), to perform it when his *Hamlet* had not attracted universal adulation also took courage.

Peter Hall, in his diaries, noted the intensity required for performing *Hamlet*, *Macbeth* and *Lear*: 'Each of the tragedies is a microcosm of a man's life, full of effort and then exhaustion. So is the actor's performance. It is a metaphor as potent for the life of the individual as the metaphor of the Globe Theatre is for the world itself.'

Finney deserved praise for tackling the roles and they were a rebuff to those who (subsequently) said he had somehow shirked the classics. But people have short memories. After *Macbeth*, there was the possibility of another National

Theatre production, of *Galileo*, to be directed by Lindsay Anderson. But Anderson declined. In a letter, he outlined his reasons for turning down *Galileo* and then added a damning judgement on Finney's period at the National. (Anderson's repeated criticisms of Finney are usually a lone voice in the wilderness. And, ironically, Finney would also come to echo Anderson's dislike of the National Theatre building itself):

> I nearly accepted, but at the last moment my heart failed me. I dislike that building, and the people in it, so much. And when I read the play again, it seemed to me forced and schematic. And not particularly relevant to our time and our problems. Was I wrong? Also they wanted me to work with the National Theatre 'Company', which meant Peter Hall's choice, not mine. And they seemed to me an unexciting bunch, including Albert Finney, who has been acting badly ever since he started at the National, I'm sorry to say. His Hamlet was very disappointing. Of course, he should not be playing Hamlet but Claudius – and I didn't see his *Tamburlaine*. Then *The Cherry Orchard*, which was really a lamentable production altogether by Peter Hall, and most recently a disappointing *Macbeth*. It is sad when you think that he was undoubtedly the most promising talent of his generation.[7]

Finney had one final commitment to the National. He played John Bean in *Has Washington Legs?*, Charles Wood's comedy about filmmaking, written to mark America's bicentennial celebrations. 'Finney dons a cloak and prowls incognito over the set, thus precipitating a deliciously funny parody of the tent scene from *Henry V*,' said Wardle.

On 23 November 1978, Finney was granted a decree nisi from Anouk Aimée on the basis that they had lived apart for two years. It was the end of his marriage and also the end of his stint at the National. Finney had finally tired of what he viewed as Hall's 'academic' view. He felt that Hall's insistence on getting the text right smothered the spirit.

Hall had once said, in 1977, that he wished 'dealings with all actors were as pleasant as they are with Albert', but, a year later, the relationship seemed fractured. Hall's diary entry, dated 17 July 1978, records that their mutual agent, Laurence Evans, told Hall that Finney was now 'disgruntled' at the National and felt that he had been 'overworked, abused and mishandled'. Hall felt it was just sour grapes on Finney's part after the poor reception to *Macbeth*. 'I'm afraid I let Laurie have it,' recorded Hall. 'I told him how little I had wanted to do *Macbeth*, and how dishonourable I felt the accusations were. These things nearly always happen when a production doesn't succeed.'

Later, Finney declared he was never a fan of the National's stages, in particular
the Olivier Theatre:

If you stand on the stage of a 'proper' theatre, there is a circuit of energy flowing out to the audience and back to the performer again. Here the circuit
wasn't completed. The energy going out of me didn't come back. Instead of
being recharged, like a dynamo, I felt like a battery running down.[8]

(But Finney was never as rude as Jonathan Miller, who likened the building
to the Brent Cross Shopping Centre, or John Osborne, who called it 'Colditz
on Thames'.)

Hall, as we have seen, was not without his critics. Some actors I have interviewed, such as Bernard Hepton, have simply said they disliked his approach.
Hall's insistence on adherence to the text, while endearing him to playwrights,
could irritate actors. Richard Harris, speaking to Michael Parkinson in 1988,
said, 'I don't give a damn for Peter Hall or his Lear. I want to see the actors' Lear.
I want to see O'Toole's Lear.'[9] (In the same interview, Harris said that he had
never seen himself in the same league as 'the greats – Peter or Albert'.)

Simon Callow described Hall's approach more diplomatically:

Hall's theatre is always about preconceived ideas rather than creative intuition,
and it is always dependent on a unanimity of approach from both performers
and the creative team. Hall, like every subsequent director of the National
Theatre, has a degree in English from Cambridge University, and the values
of textual rigour and moral judgement famously inculcated by F.R. Leavis
were at the centre of his work.[10]

Finney, after 1978, never acted in Shakespeare. Neither did he work with Hall
again. To movie audiences, Finney had disappeared altogether. Yet he believed
this 'block' of theatrical work required a long commitment:

Just because I wasn't making movies, people thought I'd retired. I think it's
important to stay with the theatre for some time when you're doing the classics, because they require a particular breathing technique for control. In order
to go as far as you'd like to go, it requires getting on the boards and doing
it for a while. It's the same with cinema. You have to do a few movies to be
comfortable in front of the camera.

There had been movie offers along the way. Finney had even started filming one
of them in August 1975 – a French drama called *The Story of Marie and Julien*,

directed by Jacques Rivette and co-starring Leslie Caron. But the director had suffered a nervous breakdown only a few days into shooting and the project was abandoned." Then Finney had been considered for the W.C. Fields biopic, *W.C. Fields and Me.* The part went to Rod Steiger. Probably Steiger, with his off-screen eccentricity, was better suited to portray such a misanthrope.

Finney was also set to play General Zod, the villain in *Superman.* Finney's only caveat was that a stage commitment meant he had to be released from filming no later than 5 p.m. No deal – Terence Stamp played Zod instead. Producers tried to get Finney to re-team with Audrey Hepburn, playing Robin in *Robin and Marian*, but negotiations broke down.

Finney wanted to get back to making films. He ended up making three misfires in a row. But before that he got 'lost' up the Amazon.

14

LOSING HIS HEAD

If you're not in the movies people think you've either died or are in a sanatorium.

Albert Finney.

After such a long stint at the National, Finney decided it was time for another extended period away. He and Diana travelled to South America in early 1979, conveniently missing London's Winter of Discontent and one of the coldest on record.

The Times, on 10 April, reported that Finney and Diana were now five days overdue from a Latin American trip that was to include a boat journey up the Amazon and a visit to the Galapagos Islands. Friends waiting for them in Los Angeles were now 'seriously alarmed', according to Michael Medwin. He added that the couple had no planned itinerary, making it difficult to know where to start looking for them.

Medwin said he had left Finney and Quick in Rio de Janeiro on 26 March. He had then flown to Los Angeles to set up some business meetings. Finney had been scheduled to arrive on 4 April. Medwin had been unable to trace anyone who had spoken to the couple on the islands. He even wondered if they had got there at all. (Ah, the days when people could go completely incommunicado!) 'This is uncharacteristic of Albert,' said Medwin. 'We were to have had talks with 20th Century Fox and when it comes to business Albert is always on time.' Medwin then said he had phoned the Foreign Office in London to make enquiries.

Yet the drama was short-lived. On 11 April 1979, *The Times* reported that Finney and Diana had arrived in Quito. The couple had visited the Galapagos Islands and were expected to leave for LA soon. Finney later claimed that he had sent a cable to postpone the meeting with 20th Century Fox but it had never arrived. They were having breakfast in bed in a five-star hotel in Quito

when Diana saw her boyfriend's picture on the front cover of a local newspaper. 'Something awful has happened to you,' said Diana to Finney in between
mouthfuls of croissant. But it hadn't; they had not, after all, been eaten alive by
marauding Amazonian cannibals.

Perhaps the trip stirred some unconventional ideas in Finney (man versus
nature?), because when he returned to acting after a ten-month hiatus it was
in the most unlikely project imaginable. Sporting unkempt shaggy locks and,
ironically, a vaguely lupine look, Finney played an over-the-hill unshaven cop,
Dewey Wilson, in Michael Wadleigh's *Wolfen*, based on the Whitley Strieber
novel. It's no classic but it's the best of the three misfires Finney made in the
1979–80 period – gory, macabre and totally risible, but a guilty pleasure for those
who enjoy seeing decapitations.

It's also a grim portrait of a bombed-out, run-down South Bronx circa late
seventies. New York has never looked so unappealing. *Wolfen's* premise was that
the destruction of the area had raised the ghosts of Native American wolf spirits.
Finney explained his attraction to the story, and he made clear that Wadleigh's
inexperience did not faze him:

> If somebody wants me to do a project, I don't think there's any point in
> having a long meeting with the director, even if he's one of my heroes. I'd
> rather read the script, and if there's something in it that intrigues me, that's
> the time to meet the director. Everybody can talk a great script. But it has to
> be on the page.
>
> *Wolfen* hinted that there are more things in heaven and earth than we
> understand in our philosophy. Certain animals have a fascination for us. Wolves
> are very powerful in European mythology. And there's all this research being
> done now with sea mammals. What drew me to *Wolfen* was the sense of
> mystery surrounding those creatures. If I respond to the script, and if I then
> talk to the director and feel sympathy with him, I don't worry about his track
> record or lack of track record. I've done other films with first-time directors
> if I trusted them.[1]

Finney insisted on calling *Wolfen* 'a surrealist thriller' until the studio objected.
They didn't think such a description had much box office appeal. 'Nevertheless,
that's what I felt it was,' said Finney. 'I certainly hoped it would be scary, but
I also hoped there would be something rather haunting about it.'

Gregory Hines made an impressive film debut as Dewey's mischievous medical examiner friend, Whittington. Hines, who died prematurely in 2003, and
memorably tap-danced at a tribute to his cancer-stricken idol Sammy Davis
Junior in 1989, apparently spent some time drinking with Finney off-duty.

And, just occasionally, it shows. Not that Finney ever looks as hungover as Richard Burton in *Villain* or *The Klansman*, but he is surprisingly piggy-eyed and unkempt. Luckily, the dishevelled look suited Dewey.

Playing a militant Native American activist was Edward James Olmos, a conscientious social activist off-screen who took a shovel to the streets in the wake of the 1992 LA riots. God knows what he made of the South Bronx; the area was at its worst in 1979. It looks like a demolition site – so much so that some German filmmakers even used it for a film about the bombing of Dresden. David Gonzalez in the *New York Times* remembers:

> Community School 61 was about the only occupied building on Charlotte Street when I arrived in September 1979 to teach photography. It was an old-style red-brick schoolhouse, unlike the Brutalist concrete learning factories that had become popular that decade.
>
> The classroom overlooked a heart-breaking panorama of rubble, on streets that had incongruous names like Suburban or Home. One week, a Hollywood film crew descended on a nearby block and built a wood-frame church. Just as quickly, they torched it, so it could serve as a suitably charred ruin for their movie, *Wolfen* ... If wolves had actually roamed this area centuries before, one could see why they were upset with how things had turned out.

Wolfen begins with a chauffeur-driven, cocaine-snorting couple of socialites (former Miss World Anne Marie Pohtamo plays the 'rich bitch') getting slain in Battery Park. And in a particularly grisly fashion, one might add.

'How would you like to see your own body and know you're dead?' asks Whittington. 'The brain can live without oxygen for a minute.' Well, you know what's coming after that ... Those of nervous disposition better turn off. It gets even more bloodcurdling when Dewey, casually munching cookies, visits a blood-strewn morgue. Whittington makes a startling discovery – there's not a trace of metal anywhere in the victims.

The death of Dewey's NYPD superior, Warren (Dick O'Neill), is a veritable party piece. His severed head rolls around the street and appears to speak, to voice horror at the sight of his own headless body (Whittington warned you!). Whittington, on the other hand, likes to think he is prepared. 'If violence comes, I'm ready,' he says, demonstrating his karate skills. (Hines later said it was the first time he had ever undertaken any kind of showbusiness work that didn't involve dancing. He would have needed deft footwork to get away from these monsters.)

It's all rather difficult to take seriously. How Finney or any of the other actors can keep a straight face in the midst of all this carnage is a mystery. Wadleigh,

whose chief claim to fame before this was as a documentary maker of the
Woodstock 1969 music festival, directs as if determined to maximise the gore.

The studio wanted Dustin Hoffman to play Dewey. And, Hoffman, a native
New Yorker, would have been more authentic casting if nothing else. Perhaps
Finney was better able to portray a bruised, boozy burnt-out cop. Yet it's still a
strange choice.

Wadleigh lured Finney into some brave feats; walking atop Manhattan Bridge
afforded spectacular views. And there's a creepy lunar transformation by Olmos
as he dances across the sand. But rewards are few, although fans of the genre still
like it. By the ludicrous climax, whereby some understanding appears to have
been reached between humans and wolves, the movie's message, presumably that
capitalist development is interfering with things best left untouched, has been
lost in blood and gore. Finney's cop is believable enough, even if his accent does
occasionally stray. Perhaps the best thing about *Wolfen* was the camera angles,
courtesy of a handheld Steadicam so that the humans were seen through the
wolves' point of view.

Hines found Finney a great teacher, not complex motivational psycho-babble,
but simple 'think it through and it will show' mechanisms:

> I knew the director, Michael Wadleigh, from when we were hippies together.
> Once I got the part, I was with Albert Finney, and I was hooked. Just a small
> conversation with Albert Finney is like Acting 101. I remember one time
> when we were supposed to come through this doorway, walk through the
> morgue, and have some dialogue. I was back there trying to figure out how
> to do this thing.
>
> Wadleigh wasn't the type of director who'd really talk to you, unlike Francis
> [Coppola], director of *The Cotton Club*. If you even look like you don't know
> what you're doing, Francis will say, 'Wait! What do you need?' Or he'll just
> start talking to you about the way you should be feeling. Anyway, Albert was
> sitting down, waiting for our cue, and he said to me, 'If I were you, when I go
> through that door, I'd feel anxious because I'm late. I have someplace else to
> go, yet I'm intrigued by the possibility that this will be an interesting case.' It
> was like a light bulb going off in my head. Then I knew exactly what to do.[2]

Joy Gould Boyam, in *The Wall Street Journal*, summed up the overall mood:

> As terrifying a movie as you're likely to see. But you're also unlikely to see a
> movie that is quite this gory (lots of dismembered body parts lying around
> and scenes in a morgue) or quite so pretentious, thematically muddled, and
> just plain mad.

Loophole should have been better – given its illustrious cast – but wasn't. A one-dimensional heist caper, filmed over nine weeks in London in 1980 by first-time director John Quested, it featured a criminal godfather (Finney) who recruits an architect (Martin Sheen) to carry out a bank robbery. The movie barely comes alive despite a fine cast that included Susannah York (a last-minute replacement for Julie Christie), Martin Sheen, Colin Blakely (in his fourth movie with Finney and, needless to say, his name is misspelled as 'Blakeley' in the Brent Walker trailer), Jonathan Pryce and Robert Morley. The film was solid, professionally made but rather forgettable, thoroughly eclipsed by *The Long Good Friday* with rising star Bob Hoskins.

For Finney, the most enjoyable part of *Loophole* was his friendship with Martin Sheen. The American actor remembered, while working as a cinema usher in New York, seating Finney during a break in *Luther* when Finney decided to catch a movie. Finney and Sheen were both interviewed by American television on the set of *Loophole* and joshed each other throughout, staging mock rivalry. During Sheen's interview, Finney bellowed, in his best Shakespearean manner, 'Must I wait until the last syllable of recorded time?'

Sheen shot back, 'I'm going to tell them about my film successes.'

'Oh,' said Finney, 'We'll not be waiting long then.'

Sheen had nearly died during the shooting of the picture *Apocalypse Now*, made the previous year, but that did not stop him drinking copious amounts alongside Finney. Sheen's staple was Guinness, whereas Finney's favourite tipple was always wine.

Director John Quested, who had initially wanted Michael Caine to play the part of Daniels – somehow he had the idea that the central character should resemble Great Train Robber Bruce Reynolds – praised Finney's approach:

> He's always prepared to take that extra risk as an actor, not necessarily keeping to the trunk of the tree but sometimes bouncing on the branches instead. You have to know what you're doing with him. But he's always very professional, loyal and kind to other actors. Albert came up to me during filming and said, 'you're very lucky to get Martin Sheen'. He didn't seem to realise that Martin was in it only because of him [Finney]. Finney contributed in every way he could. He even used his own car in the film. He was always so helpful during filming and is that rare case of a famous actor who's well-adjusted and with a great sense of humour. He could have pursued more classical roles later in his career. But it's up to him. He made his choices. I wanted to work with him again but it was always a case of finding a part that interested him.[3]

Quested said that once you got a star like Finney then others always wanted to jump aboard, great names like Robert Morley, Jonathan Pryce and Blakely. Quested added, echoing the views of many people I interviewed, that it would be hard to assemble such a cast of old 'reliables' these days: 'I'm not sure those kind of people exist anymore. Where are they?'

Unlike *The Long Good Friday*, which was more about professional gangsters, Quested said he 'wanted to create a story about what it takes to corrupt somebody, how much has to happen before someone is tempted off the track'. He remembers, as an aside, that Finney corrupted Sheen into betting on the horses. But the film did not stretch Finney much and is now rather obscure. (Although Quested, interviewed in 2016, wondered, as others did, if London's Hatton Garden jewel thieves had seen it!)

Vincent Canby in the *New York Times* described *Loophole* as 'a film of such ineptitude that you are allowed to suspect there's a far more interesting (and possibly more cautionary) story behind the screen than anything that's on it.' Turning the knife, he added, 'Jonathan Hales's screenplay, an anthology of irrelevant detail, appears to have been directed by John Quested by long-distance telephone and then edited by a committee of financial receivers. The actors look bewildered.'

Looker, which Finney made late in 1980, completed a mediocre movie medley that augured little for his return to film. Finney played, rather lackadaisically, a plastic surgeon uncovering a dastardly plot involving supermodels. Director Michael Crichton had made the engrossing *Westworld*, which raised some interesting questions about holidays of the future and the 'independence' of robots. From Finney's public comments at the time it's possible that he just accepted the film because he wanted to experiment with different genres. 'Instead of playing a slouch, boozy, burnt-out cop, as I was in *Wolfen*, I'm playing a very chic and successful California plastic surgeon, almost a Cary Grant role. So that was a nice contrast,' he said in 1981.

Looker might have had something to say about the craze of plastic surgery which was to overtake Hollywood a little later. It might have accurately foreseen the future, yet that didn't make it entertaining. Critics ridiculed it and it failed at the box office. Vincent Canby wrote:

> The plot is pretty silly but Mr Crichton's handling of it is even sillier. Mr Crichton has fun sending up television commercials in one extended sequence, but his direction of the rest of the film is so sloppy one suspects that if he himself were a plastic surgeon, two ears might wind up on one side of the same head.

Coincidentally, the period around 1980 was also a dreadful time for many of Finney's talented contemporaries. O'Toole had bombed in *Macbeth*; Harris was making instantly forgettable movies like *Highpoint* (better titled *Lowpoint*) and *Your Ticket is no Longer Valid* (all too true!); Burton had made the lamentable *Circle of Two* and *Tristan and Isolde*. As for Finney, he had not made a truly good film since *Murder on the Orient Express*, seven years earlier.

At the box office it was all Caine and Connery. By 1981, Finney was no longer famous enough to 'open' a film and his name was increasingly mentioned only in cinema retrospectives, restaurant and racetrack sightings and at glamorous events with Diana Quick. Not that this really bothered Finney. In many ways it suited his personality *not* to be recognised. 'Nobody knows who I am because I'm not in that many films and I look different in almost every role. Even people who saw me in *Tom Jones* are convinced I haven't made a picture in the last twenty years,' he once said.

But a meaty screen role was long overdue. And who better than the director of *Midnight Express*, one of the most harrowing movies of the late seventies, to provide Finney's return to form on film?

15

BACK IN THE GYM

I used to wake up in the middle of the night, weeping at the impossibility of relationships.

Albert Finney.

'What the HELL do you want from me?' screamed Finney. And, for once, it was not in character, in this case as the violent, self-pitying writer George Dunlap. Finney was shouting at his director, Alan Parker, in the middle of San Francisco. It was several weeks into the filming of *Shoot the Moon* and Finney was not a happy man.

Shoot the Moon typified the family histrionics genre that was trendy in the early eighties. Throw in the essential ingredients to cause mayhem – usually the three D's of death, divorce or disease – and audiences left cinemas feeling that their own problems weren't so bad. Movies such as *Kramer Versus Kramer*, *Ordinary People* and *Terms of Endearment* were also great actors' vehicles from which stars could, hopefully, emerge Oscar-laden.

Parker had approached 'the usual suspects', Al Pacino and Jack Nicholson, to portray George Dunlap, a celebrated writer, four-time father and philanderer. (The backdrop of success is essential for this kind of film. Viewers must home in on the trauma. The usual problems afflicting couples, especially mundane money concerns, must be extraneous.)

After Pacino and Nicholson declined, Parker searched out Finney:

Albert had been a hero of mine and to most of my generation of filmmakers, but when we started to get the chance to make films, he wasn't there and it was very frustrating. You'd see him having lunch, telling wonderful stories, but offer him anything, and he'd always say 'no'. I originally thought he was plain lazy, but then he did things like *Hamlet* and *Tamburlaine* on stage, so it wasn't that. Suddenly it all changed and I got lucky. I knew he'd done that weird thing *Wolfen* but I probably thought that was just him being bloody-minded, choosing some weird subject, considering that he turned down anything that was good in previous years.[1]

Parker sent him William Goldman's script. At first Finney declined, but some gentle coaxing persuaded him. It was the right decision. *Shoot the Moon*, a gruelling actor's piece about a marital break-up, was just what Finney needed after three turkeys. He joined the set in San Raphael, north of San Francisco, in January 1981, straight after *Looker* wrapped.

The 'trouble' for Finney, if one can call a heavy part 'trouble', is that he had to summon deeper emotions than he had done recently on film. Yes, Finney would bare his soul in *The Dresser*, but that was for a totally different character. George Dunlap was a modern protagonist, recognisable to many middle-aged, unhappily married men. George, however, is not only a cheating husband. He's also a child-beater and a bit of a nutcase. For Finney, an actor who shunned introspection, the film proved tortuous but ultimately rewarding.

Parker and Finney disagreed from the outset, not over interpretation but voice. At the first reading Finney mustered his best American accent, one that had served him well in *Looker* and *Wolfen*. Parker objected and urged him to play the part as a Brit. After all, many successful British writers would be married to American women in California.

Maybe Parker had made a bad start. Finney, a gifted mimic and observer, can take a funny walk, a posture, an accent or a squint and incorporate them into the part, then he draws upon his superb actor's toolkit to bring the character to life. Perhaps also Finney felt more comfortable becoming someone else, especially for such a flawed, hostile character as George. But Parker said that he 'was never fond of Finney's American accent – you never know whether he's taking the piss or not'.

The opening scene called for Finney to walk to his study and cry. Parker congratulated him and Finney brushed it off, 'That's acting. If you don't feel it, fake it. That's what I do for a living.' Parker bristled; he contrasted this with Diane Keaton who lived the character – no faking.

The early scenes are relentlessly downbeat, accompanied by a melancholy piano beat. Finney and Keaton, playing George and Faith, travel to San Francisco to collect an award. George looks anguished and momentarily speechless. Ironically, by then she knows he's cheating on her with a younger woman, Sandy, played by Karen Allen.

Explosions come next morning. Finney breaks a plate in the kitchen and Keaton responds by serially smashing more. With less skilled actors it could have seemed staged; to their credit it seems truthful. But Finney was getting testy about what he saw as Parker's effusive praise of Keaton. So much so that he cornered Parker in between plate-smashing. 'You always say, "great Diane, very good Albert".' To which Parker would reply. 'Well, Albert, she always *is* great.'

Parker was becoming concerned by the disparity in their performances:

You watch someone walking and you want them to run. You know they can run but won't. There's something holding them back. They're not trying too hard, as if it's rather vulgar. To Albert, I never seemed happy, and he'd become irritated by that and would ask me why – and maybe I couldn't probably articulate it. ... He'd never been acted off the screen before in his life and now this was actually happening. Yet I was also beginning to think that if he could get away with walking through a scene, he would. That's nothing to do with laziness; it's to do with the fact that he had to rekindle the passion he once had for the job. For the moment, after walking through his last couple of films, he seemed to have lost it. For too long he'd been enjoying lunch more than acting. I knew that in order to push him where he knew he had to go, and for the sake of the film too, I had to risk my friendship and confront him head on.

The screaming between Parker and Finney occurred outside San Francisco's Fairmont Hotel. Although an early scene in the film, it was shot six weeks into shooting. Parker can't remember the exact trigger, but it appears that he told him off in front of extras and the crew while a rain machine spewed water in the background. Parker recalled:

Suddenly there we were, both of us, face to face, standing under the rain machine getting drenched. Here were the same lungs that had stood on stage declaiming Hamlet and Luther yelling at me in the middle of San Francisco. It was not an experience I would recommend, after all that, and more than a bit dampened, I said to him. 'It's good you're letting me know what you feel.' He said: 'What is it? What is it?' So I told him it's just that I know you can be great. That's all I want.

Finney described the incident differently. He remembered a night scene where he and Keaton, as George and Faith, leave their car to attend an awards dinner. After the shot, they retired to Finney's camper where he offered Keaton a glass of wine. She said no, but Finney poured himself one. According to Finney, Parker suddenly entered, saying the scene had to be redone because the camera-man suspected a technical problem. Finney recalls:

Parker came up to me and got very angry because I'd been having a glass of wine – remember, I had thought the shot was done – saying I was treating everyone with disrespect. And I was terribly pissed off, because this was nonsense. I got angry at Parker, but then I got angry with myself afterward for being angry at him. It was an irrelevant incident. I don't get angry that often.

Finney was unusually contemplative for the rest of the shooting:

> Trying to do the real thing, in this case intensely harrowing marital scenes, for make-believe purposes can really put you through the mangles. I didn't feel like going home at night and having a giggle after screaming at Diane Keaton, an intelligent and particularly 'live' actress, all day. So many of the scenes in the film were so realistic they were uncomfortable. We've all had relationships somehow of this sort at some time in our lives. I must say I've never lived through a marriage quite like the intensity of that one and the experience taught me that so often things become vicious and break up because you are simply unable to articulate. It's the kind of role where you have to dig into yourself and present yourself on the screen and that's always tough. Particularly in scenes where we were fighting or arguing, it's not pleasant to be reminded of times when my own behaviour has been monstrous.[2]

George becomes more unhinged. He turns violent when he tries to deliver a typewriter to his oldest daughter (Diane Lane) and she doesn't want to see him. George breaks into the house, surrounded by Faith and four screaming girls (a nice authentic touch rather than the usual boy/girl split) and threatens her. (She should have heeded a police officer's advice to put bolts on the doors.) It's a nasty scene.

Suddenly, he explodes. David Denby, writing in *New York Magazine* in 1982, captured the full force of the assault:

> The scene is terrifying. Albert Finney's full, bullying strength, which up to now has looked useless, even ridiculous, breaks forth with horrible fury. The children are frightened and ashamed for their father and finally George is ashamed too. And yet, although he has disgraced himself, perhaps unforgivably, he is never more their father than at this moment. In the ghastly silence as he walks out of the house, a little voice pipes up, 'Daddy, do you want a Band-Aid for your hand?' This extraordinary scene, almost Sophoclean in its combined power, complexity and piteousness shows up a similar bit of hanger whomping in *Mommie Dearest* for the flamboyantly absurd atrocity that it is.

George gets worse. Even at the deathbed of Faith's father, supposedly a friend of George, anger simmers. 'Fight it!' he screams at his father-in-law as the old man struggles for breath. Predictably, the next scene is a funeral.

Goldman's screenplay doesn't really probe the reason for George's rage. Many years later, Finney told Melvyn Bragg that he believed the character of George had 'resorted to a violent act because he couldn't cope with the fact that he'd fallen for someone else; he just didn't have the wherewithal to cope with it'.

Finney became depressed during the fourteen-week shoot:

> I used to wake up in the middle of the night weeping at the impossibility of relationships – that forever isn't going to happen. You get into your own memory vault, the emotional memory of it, and drawers used to fly open and infuse your body with the blues.

An accident outside filming only made matters worse. Diana visited Finney during shooting, between completing *Brideshead* and its transmission. In San Francisco, with Finney, she was leaving a Ry Cooder gig when she fell on her chin and fractured her jaw in two places. She lost sixteen teeth, her voice box was badly damaged, and she needed a year's recuperation to rebuild her voice from scratch. 'For a while I thought I wouldn't be able to earn my living as an actor,' she said.

Meanwhile, the movie became more melodramatic. A restaurant scene where Finney and Keaton have a chance meeting after their break-up seems overblown. They scream at each other and George even thumps a fellow diner while a pianist struggles to keep tune in the background.

Parker gave a contemporary interview in which he conceded that this was his most personal film:

> I'm constantly walking the tightrope, as everyone does, of trying to stay married. In that respect it's the first film I've made that's close to my heart. Although it was Goldman's screenplay he said he 'put in as much of myself as it is possible to do'. Bo and I sat there in a hotel room and we became amateur shrinks for one another. I believe the film's strength is that it does hit certain truths about our relationships, all our relationships.

Dave Smith, interviewing the director in 1982 for *Photoplay* magazine, suggested the film was perhaps too violent. Parker seemed unsure:

> I think where we have shown violence it is a cinematic extension of a lot of the rage and anger that we have within us. I certainly have it in me and it's

anger that we don't often admit or often express. For the film that safety valve was overridden and suddenly emotions do explode. I stand by my decision to do it that way but I know many people do feel it to be a little too much.

Parker, perhaps keen not to fall out with Finney, later praised his performance:

His was the more demanding role, and I think it was more taxing for Albert than many of the films he'd been making. It's not simply acting out a charade. You draw on your own pain, and very often, for extremely emotional scenes, you ask of yourself things you don't really want to open up. Albert taught me how much an actor gives of himself. As a director you have to be as sensitive as possible to an actor's feelings. I could shout 'cut' and start chatting to the cameraman or something. But Albert would sometimes have to go away and sit down for half an hour or so after a particularly emotional scene.[3]

Finney thought Keaton was great:

Shoot the Moon was very exciting because of Diane. She's very spontaneous as an actress and that's a quality you tend to lose or at least restrain when you're trained in the theatre as I am. I try to reproduce a performance once I've got it. Whereas I noticed she'd try something new in every take if it occurred to her. She was terrific to work with. It was real proper tennis. One has to respond to that, not the way you did it in the last take. You have to be relaxed about it.

Karen Allen, a great Finney fan, said she 'adored' him: 'He was a pleasure to work with and we remained friends for some years after. He was one of the best storytellers ever. He had such a spirit of fun and mischievousness.'

Overall, *Shoot the Moon* doesn't quite convince. Parker offers many picturesque shots of northern California and an anguished Finney hunched over his typewriter as the surf rolls in, or sitting on his boat under a starry sky. Yet there isn't enough insight into George's character. Feminist groups were appalled at the violence George meted out to Faith and, in particular, the veiled suggestion at the end that she might take him back.

The final scene saw more mayhem. George mows down a new tennis court that Keaton and her new lover (Peter Weller) have built. According to Finney, 'we made three endings for the film but none of us could actually articulate about how we felt so Alan went round canvassing the unit to see which one they felt suited best.' As it turned out, the film stopped before any of the endings began. Perhaps the film's abiding message is 'pity the children caught in the carnage'.

For Finney it was a step back on to the pedestal of great movie acting, although the film was far from universally acclaimed. 'A halfway decent actors' piece which doesn't really justify its time or leave affectionate memories behind. In essence it adds nothing except noise to what was being done in this field forty years ago,' said Leslie Halliwell.

After the anguish of *Shoot the Moon*, Finney wanted some light relief. Like Arthur Seaton in *Saturday Night and Sunday Morning*, he believed that life and art should be enjoyed. Recalling failed relationships had unsettled him. In that respect, the actor's life suited him, 'For a very brief span you get obsessed by something. Then it's over and you move on to something else.'

So it was that Finney went from gut-wrenching adult drama to dancing with little Aileen Quinn in *Annie*.

For Finney the joy of *Annie* was getting to know John Huston, one of his favourite directors. He claimed that he'd seen more films by Huston than anyone else. It was the beginning of a firm friendship between the 45-year-old and the 75-year-old, the latter a bizarre choice to direct this slice of American slushy mushy apple pie. But Finney was also an unlikely Daddy Warbucks, the bullet-headed, bald, billionaire sugar daddy who becomes surrogate father to orphan Annie during the Depression.

Finney went straight into *Annie* on the back of *Shoot the Moon*. He told interviewers he needed to get back into making movies:

> I think I probably did this run of films because I know how much it helps if you do a bit, however easy you are in front of the camera. Stage and film work use a totally different set of muscles. And acting anyway is like being a fighter – once you're back in the ring, you're also back in the gym.

Columbia Pictures gambled £30 million in the hope that *Annie* would lure families to cinemas. It all started in 1924 when a cartoonist offered the *New York Daily News* a strip called 'Little Orphan Otto', featuring a boy with frizzy hair. 'Looks like a pansy to me,' said the publisher. 'Put a skirt on him and call it Little Orphan Annie.' So it was that little 1-year-old Annie and her dog Sandy were born, all alone in the world until taken in by Warbucks.

In 1977, a musical adaptation opened on Broadway, winning twenty-two major awards, including seven Tonys by the time the film started to roll on 29 April 1981. Producer Ray Stark offered his view of the story, '*Annie* is basically a love story between a little girl with nothing but the courage to dream and an adult with everything except someone to share it with.'

The quest for Annie took two years. Casting directors scrutinised more than 20,000 photographs, interviewed 8,000 children and auditioned another 550 on videotape. Eventually the search was whittled down to several girls, among them 9-year-old Aileen Quinn, already a familiar face on commercials. English choreographer Arlene Phillips, famed for her creation of Hot Gossip, was responsible for the song and dance numbers.

At Columbia's Burbank Studios a million dollar tenement was constructed, based around the orphanage. It was a four-storey street, designed to allow filming from any angle; it took five months to build. The other major location was the cavernous home of Warbucks. Nothing short of a mansion would do and the ideal place was found in New Jersey. It was the former home of the president of F. W. Woolworth, built on the site where Woodrow Wilson's summer White House had once stood.

Finney had sung before, notable for his Motown contract as well as in *Scrooge*, but he also had to dance for *Annie*:

I was very self-conscious when I started the dancing rehearsals. My partner was, much of the time, Ann Reinking, who is a terrific dancer and I kept thinking I'd break her legs while trying to get the tango right. The whole thing was new stuff to me. I had to shave my head twice a day because by lunchtime there'd be a five o'clock shadow. My bonce, being all virgin soil, burnt terribly and I had to wear a beret. Anyway I felt quite rude and naked sitting there bald. I tried wearing a wig on set but nobody knew who I was and when I went off-set bald everybody thought I was into martial arts. I also found myself assuming a sitting position rather like Yul [Brynner] like a king on a throne. People would come up to me and murmur to me how good I'd been on stage the night before in, I presume, *The King and I*.[4]

Finney was clearly nervous about the dance routines. Elaine Kaufman, owner of one of the city's most famous – and star frequented – restaurants, Elaine's, remembers a frantic call from Finney on the eve of an important number:

He says, 'Elaine, darling, you've got to help me. I've got this big number before the cameras tomorrow – I'm Daddy Warbucks singing and moving all over the place but I'm not ready.'
'So, what can I do?'
'Singing's not my strong suit and I need to rehearse.'
'Where?'
'Here. With you and all your waiters.'
'Albert, this is a restaurant. We don't rehearse.'
'If you don't do this for me, you're all poofters.'

Elaine recalls, 'So he takes the recorder from his pocket, turns on the music for "I Don't Need Anything But You" and he rehearses, me as Little Orphan Annie, would you believe? Got all my waiters to dance up and down around the tables with him.'[5]

Finney certainly gave it his all. Aileen Quinn, who stayed friendly with Finney, recalled:

> One of my favourite memories of him is [Finney] learning to really sing for the first time. He did that beautiful version of 'Maybe'… As he was taking singing lessons on the set, I can remember him with a cigar out of his mouth and going 'la la la la la la la,' pause, 'la la la la la la'.

This, plus Finney's habit of putting bottle caps under his loafers to practise his tap routine, thoroughly charmed Quinn. 'He was, like, in it to win it … so adorable.' Quinn also revealed how when she was sleepy between takes, Finney would tickle her knees to keep her awake when they were sitting in the back of the Duesenberg.

Was *Annie* worth it all? It would be nice to say it was, but the film bombed big time, failing to break a bad run from Huston. 'Misguided opening-out of a charming stage musical based on the comic strip which is basically a reversal of *Oliver Twist*. Some of the best moments have been discarded, the dancing is ponderous, the acting distinctly uneasy, and the choice of director stupefying. None of it works at all,' said Leslie Halliwell.

Finney's one-pitch, bellowing performance is a little indelicate. He simply didn't convey tenderness well at this point in his career. With time, and when his features cracked, he could convey vulnerability beautifully. In *Annie*, however, he is simply too explosive. When Warbucks screams, 'I love money, I love power, I love capitalism!' it's difficult to believe he'll ever change. Only towards the end, when he is separated from Annie, does he invest a little softness into the part which, as has been observed, seems like an all-out impersonation of Huston.

Finney, as always, was a hit with his co-stars. Carol Burnett remarked of him, 'He's charming. He makes you think you're the only girl around. But I certainly never took him seriously. And I don't think he expects you to take him seriously.' And, perhaps most importantly, Finney and Huston got on marvellously. Both shared a passion for fine wine, consuming bottles of Dom Pérignon and Mouton Rothschild 1959 at a restaurant called Fromagerie to which they were constant visitors.

Finney's other great activity during *Annie* was attending the races. Not that he ever gambled huge amounts. 'The most I ever bet is $2,000, but generally, considerably less,' said Finney. 'And I don't believe in simply betting. One prefers a knowledgeable gamble.'

As always, Finney enjoyed talking to everyone, cherishing even short exchanges. One particular encounter showed that Finney was not just making small talk but had his wits about him. Executive chef Jack Stierer takes up the story:

As a Captain in the Continental Room at the world-class Rancho La Costa resort in Carlsbad, California I certainly had my chance to serve a number of celebrated personalities – from golf and tennis superstars to Hollywood household names to movers of industry. But one such experience I always remember as being unique: the day I served Albert Finney both lunch and dinner at two different venues some 20 miles apart.

La Costa was a union house, and when the racetrack in Del Mar (also union) opened for the seven-week summer season, many of us signed on and moonlit there during the day. In other words, in addition to evenings in the Continental Room, our standing gig, and exhausting work, we reported to the race track six mornings a week at 9 a.m. and waited on the Turf Club tables until the last race at 4 p.m. This was a breakneck schedule, but we were young and willing to blast through the seven weeks for the perks, the tips and the prestige.

Plenty of celebrities took tables at the Turf Club. I can remember brushing shoulders with Desi Arnez, Dustin Hoffman, Kim Novak and more. But I was especially thrilled when Albert Finney sat in my station one day. He was on a break from the filming of *Annie* and all but unrecognisable with his shaved head for the role of Daddy Warbucks.

After lunch was served and the first few races run, the pace of service became relaxed and I was needed only for the occasional drink order during the late afternoon. At one point Mr Finney approached me, off to the side rail in my starched white Eton jacket, and we started to chat ... about the horses, the area, his current film project. Quite a conversation ensued until finally he returned to his box, and I to my other diners' needs.

Once the last race was in and our checks closed out, off we dashed. Twenty miles up the coast from Del Mar to Carlsbad and a quick change and we were in our places for the evening dinner service at La Costa. Imagine my surprise, then, on seeing Albert Finney's name down for a party of six in my station!

Well, he and his group were seated and I proceeded to confer with him on the wine selection. He was looking at me quizzically, but out of context, and, now in a black tuxedo, he didn't seem to know me from earlier in the day. I returned with the wine, and poured for the table, and only then, returning the bottle, did he take another, closer look at me and say, 'I say, didn't you serve me lunch today?'[6]

Finney went on a three-city 3,700-mile promotion tour for the film when it came out in 1982. For Finney, a man who likes to do the work and then disappear, the tour was laborious. But he went through it like a pro despite his disdain for publicity. On one occasion, however, attending yet another premiere in Dallas, he grew restless: 'I will go to the theatre and I will leave before the film starts. What I want to do is have a good dinner, and what I do not want to do is sit through that movie yet again!'

The publicity people later caught Finney, as good as his word, tucking into a hefty dinner of scallops, calf's liver and wine. Finney now had the beginnings of a double chin and an expanding waistline but the passing years didn't worry him:

> I don't yearn for how I used to look. I don't think I'm particularly handsome. I think maybe I'm attractive. I remember with *Tom Jones* being very concerned to tell people that I was not just another pretty face, and that's why I took all those character roles. Why I played Luther on Broadway, for instance. All those character roles were perhaps an overreaction to being treated like some kind of sex symbol.

On the publicity tour Finney was seen cheerfully blowing smoke up the nostrils of anti-smoking fanatic Herbert A. Allen Jr, the investment banker who was also chairman of the board of Columbia Pictures. 'The habit of a filthy animal,' snaps Allen, fanning away smoke.

'I smoke because Picasso smoked. And because Hitler didn't,' replied Finney, but it was all in jest.

A magazine profile noted that Finney was 'pliable and amiable up to a point but that point is ringed by electric wire'. As ever, Finney stressed his determination to go his own way:

> One of the terrible things about the sense of permanence is that you're not open to possibilities. I find possibilities very pleasurable and sensual and exciting. … What I do is resist seeming to be one thing. I may be deluding myself, but there is a sense of the rogue and vagabond, the strolling player, seeing what comes up – where do I want to go next, how do I feel. It actually means I don't have to fit within society, into a particular mold. I like the sense that one might still be surprised by life.

And Finney was about to surprise audiences with a magnificently observed portrayal of stage crucifixion that, by rights, should have won him an Oscar.

STOP THAT TRAIN!

Once he's assumed the disguise, he's a different man.
                    Tom Courtenay (as Norman) on Finney (as Sir).

We don't like to think of actors' deaths, but when a great star finally takes to the celestial stage, news bulletins tend to run a valedictory clip showing the performer at the peak of his or her powers. For me, Finney's finest moment on-screen comes when he issues a thunderous, even volcanic, command that halts a departing train in *The Dresser*.

Acting students would do well to study this thumbnail illumination of character. Courtenay – breathless, prissy, effeminate, begging and pleading – is pushed aside like a poodle yapping at someone's heels as he reasons with the driver. Then we catch sight of Finney as Sir, surrounded by his luggage-laden players, striding briskly and proudly, stick and chin thrust forward, clearing a path. When Sir raises his stick and brings the wheels of the train screeching to a halt with a stentorian roar 'Stop that train!' – Finney is fleetingly showing what this great actor was before old age debilitated him.

It was just as well that Finney was still living in London, not Hollywood, because *The Dresser* might not have come his way. By 1982 he was sharing a mews house with Diana in Chelsea. Diana had knocked down some walls while Finney had been away and redecorated the house, painting the living room apricot. Visitors noted few theatrical mementoes. Instead, photographs from their trip to Macchu Piccu in 1979 lined the mantelpieces.

Finney liked to live well but, unlike other stars, had resisted moving to America. He felt that London offered him the ideal balance between theatre and film:

It's much easier in England than America. London is the centre for theatre, film, television and radio. In America, the theatre and the movie industry have two different centres. An actor has to make a decision where to live. If he wants principally to be a stage actor, he stays in New York. But then if he wants to try movies, he has to move his family 3,000 miles. We don't have that problem in England.

His other reason for staying in the UK was that he felt that, in America, a commercially successful film brought untold pressures on its leading actor:

In America, there's pressure to stay on the treadmill and follow up a movie with a more successful movie. That's impossible of course. Nobody's career has ever continued to go upward and onward without a few backward steps. The graph of any life fluctuates. All graphs go up and down. Look at the great acting careers in England – Olivier and Gielgud and Richardson. They're working actors. They don't worry that they shouldn't do theatre or television because they're movie stars. Picasso didn't paint a masterpiece every time he stepped up to the easel; sometimes he just did little sketches, but he kept working. That's how Richardson, Olivier and Gielgud feel. If they're not doing a movie or play they'll do a television play or radio play, just to practise their craft. It's tougher to do that in America.[1]

Finney remained determined to control his own destiny. By now he had had the same agent since the sixties, but he saw his agent's role as strictly to negotiate a deal, not recommend a script:

He's a friend as well as an agent. But I don't look to him for advice in creative matters. I'm not saying he's not allowed to speak. But his function is to take care of business. My function is to decide which way I'm going and choose the script I want to do. I've never been 'handled' in that way. I've been making my own decisions for twenty-five years.

And living the way he wanted.

Food and drink were always important to Finney. In 1981, *Rolling Stone* magazine was invited into Finney's home:

Sunday dinner at Albert's place was an elaborate affair. Now setting the white marble-topped dining table, meticulous as ever, a pride of careful movements, wiping a wine-glass that looks fragile beside his imposing frame – economical gestures from an unextravagant man, Diana emerges from the kitchen. Albert arranges the last plate and snubs out a Marlboro. A switch from Bloody Marys to wine. It is dinner at the Finney household.[2]

It all seemed rather pleasant. *Rolling Stone* continued:

> Four people consume an elegant fruit course, roast beef with Yorkshire
> pudding, greens, vegetable purée and bottles of Orvieto, Bordeaux and cham-
> pagne. Caramelised pears appear and disappear. Then, biting off the end of a
> fine Havana cigar, Albert excuses himself and descends to the basement, where
> he sprawls out upon a black leather couch to digest his meal before the TV,
> which was replaying the big football match at Wembley between Liverpool
> and Tottenham.

Finney had always been interested in sport, especially his beloved Manchester
United. He was a regular visitor to Epsom to inspect his horses, driving himself in a blue-grey Mercedes sports car. Finney also enjoyed watching cricket,
especially with his close friend, Julian Holloway. Golf was another favourite. In
1983, he partnered Lee Trevino on International Pro-Celebrity Golf. Peter Allis
recalled that Finney 'was not a great golfer but that he loved the game', noting
also his great sense of fun.[3]

Ken Bowden, one of the programme's behind-the-scenes organisers, recalled
Finney's friendliness and lack of vanity:

> At the time of his appearance for us, Albert Finney was one of the world's best,
> busiest and most highly acclaimed actors, but there was no misunderstanding the
> singularity of his personality as a famous person. He was, in a nutshell, at all times
> the least 'starlike' star any of us involved in the shows had ever encountered.
>
> Most striking to me was Finney's clearly genuine lack of even an iota of the
> self-absorption – the 'me, me, me' syndrome – so innate to the bearing and
> behaviour of the majority of super-successful and/or 'celebrated' people. Out
> of genuine interest I recall asking him more than once about some element of
> his work, but the response was always a dismissive wave of the hand and a turn
> to either a non-personal subject that had engaged his interest, or an inquiry
> or a comment related to his questioner's life or thoughts.
>
> Those of us who came to know him that week found this depth of interest
> in whomever he happened to encounter, regardless of what some might call
> 'station' in life, especially fascinating. Invariably, one completed a conversa-
> tion with Albert Finney with an overpowering sense that the lives, styles, and
> perspectives of whomever he happened to meet were vastly more interesting
> to him than his own. Which, of course, I quickly realised, must surely have
> been a major contributor to his stunning range of thespian 'personalities'.
> Whatever the fount of that characteristic, however, it surely made the man a
> joy to be around.[4]

Cynics may say that Finney was taking an interest in others to help his characterisations. (Just as, for example, Woody Allen seldom says anything funny
but waits for someone else to make an amusing comment. Then he takes out a
notebook and jots it down.)[5] Yet Finney tended to play characters in extreme
situations – alcoholics, burnt-out classical actors, gangsters and real-life figures –
for whom his encounters with 'ordinary people' would offer him little material.
More likely, Finney has the healthy ego of a confident performer. But he realises
that celebrity is not to be taken too seriously.

Rolling Stone also noted Finney's reluctance to talk about himself – or a
similar lack of introspection. He always had plenty to say but it was seldom
personal. And here lies a certain contradiction. Finney is in many respects very
'un-actory' – were there such a word. He does not spend much time talking
about the craft of acting and his profession is not – pardon the awful phrase –
an all-consuming passion. He takes his work seriously but will not be found
discussing his approach to a certain part. He just lives it. Away from the stage or
camera, he doesn't discuss acting much, yet his conversation brims with theatrical anecdotes, stories not about himself but about the glory days of Olivier,
Richardson, Wolfit or Lawson. It's a way of engaging his audience without
having to be too personal. As he says:

> I've always found it very, very hard to get up in front of people and talk as me.
> Cause what am I supposed to be? What do I represent when I get up as me?
> In this part of the 20th century, we're all supposed to be clear about what we
> are, the manifestations of me, the finding of me. But I think there are probably
> many me's. And what I'm probably about is acknowledging that … There's
> no deceit intended.

Rolling Stone noted Finney's perpetual friendliness and charm. The magazine noted that he pretended to recognise a waitress at Fortnum & Mason in
London's Piccadilly, where he was having afternoon tea, who claimed to have
served him before. Later, he admitted that he couldn't quite remember the lady
in question. But it didn't matter, everyone received his winning smile.

Pat Pearce, cleaner at the Bristol Hippodrome, billed by the *Daily Mail* as 'Mrs
Mop to the Stars', recalled Finney's friendliness. 'My all-time favourite [star] was
Albert Finney. He was so sincere. After we'd been photographed I thanked him
for posing with me, and he said, "You must not thank me, it is for me to thank
you." I thought that was so lovely.'[6]

Finney might not have talked about himself, at least not in any great depth.
The trouble was that, rather like Richard Burton, he was such a forceful personality that he tended to dominate any room he entered. So filmmakers naturally

thought of him when it came to casting larger-than-life characters. Fortunately, Finney could be generous (considering actors usually dream of nabbing a showy part for themselves) when he thought a script better suited to someone else. Author Robert Sellers tells how the part of Alan Swann, the Errol Flynn–like character in *My Favourite Year*, was offered to Finney:

> Mel Brooks's co-producer on the film, Michael Gruskoff, first sent the script to Finney. He got an unusual reply back. Albert read it and said 'you've got the wrong guy, Michael. Peter would be better for this part than me.' Finney even made sure that a copy of the script made its way to O'Toole.[7]

Richard Benjamin, the film's director, remembered going to California, where Finney was still involved in *Shoot the Moon*, to persuade him to do it. They spent a day on a houseboat. Finney, he said, was 'charming' and 'delightful' but Benjamin said it was clear instantly that Finney didn't want to do it.

Finney was wise to decline the role of Swann. In the end he accepted a much better part, one that all actors dream of. The background to *The Dresser* was inauspicious. Playwright Harwood recounts its inception:

> I wrote *The Dresser* as a play of course, and the day I was to deliver it to my agent I went to the Garrick Club, of which I'm a member.
>
> And as I was going in, John Gielgud was coming out, and he said, 'Oh, what have you been up to?'
>
> I said, 'Well John, I've just written a new play about an English actor manager, and his dresser.'
>
> And Gielgud said, 'Aah, backstage plays never do well.'
>
> I went into lunch absolutely crushed. So when I delivered it to my agent, Judy Daish, I said, 'This won't do anything, John Gielgud says backstage plays never do.'
>
> She read it and said, 'I don't know.'
>
> I said, 'Judy, John Gielgud knows more than you.'
>
> It was done in Manchester and I think from the first night to now as we sit here I don't think a night has passed when it hasn't been performed somewhere in the world. Which is lovely.[8]

The Dresser was a stage hit in London and New York. Tom Courtenay played Norman, the fussy, prim, whisky-soaked gay dresser who tries to prevent an old actor having a breakdown. Norman somehow manages to get Sir, played by Freddie Jones and Paul Rogers on stage, through a final production of *King Lear*. Or is it Norman who's really collapsing?

Peter Yates was persuaded to direct a film version for profit 'points' rather
than an up-front fee. He was also determined that Courtenay, who had played
Norman 500 times on stage, would get the part on film. Yates said:

I'd been looking to do a story about the theatre for some time but all the
ones I found only treated the subject of the theatre in a very peripheral way.
When I saw *The Dresser* I immediately thought it would make a wonderful
film because of it being so strongly rooted in the traditions of the theatre.[9]

Finney and Courtenay, who proved a magical teaming, were also persuaded
to take points. Curiously, although they had 'emerged', as the saying goes in
theatrical circles, at around the same time (the early sixties) not only had they
never worked together but Finney's recollection is that they had not met. By
1983, Courtenay had triumphed in *Billy Liar*, *The Loneliness of the Long Distance
Runner* and *One Day in the Life of Ivan Denisovich*. Yet their careers had taken
them on separate paths.

Courtenay and Finney quickly became buddies. In a contemporary interview
Finney named three close showbiz friends: Michael Medwin, Julian Holloway
and Tom Courtenay. It's now difficult to think of any other actors who could
have breathed such life into these two egomaniacs. Although Anthony Hopkins
and Ian McKellen gave sensitive performances in a recent television adaptation,
actors tend to be more interesting when playing old than being old.[10]

Courtenay was touched by Finney's lack of grandeur:

Albert is not impressed with being a star, probably because he is still so involved
with the theatre. It would have been easy for him to pull rank on me during
the filming and demand a limousine and all the rest. But he has no pretensions.
He rode home with me each night, discussing how to improve our scenes.[11]

Finney was Sir, an actor manager well past his prime, clearly modelled on
Donald Wolfit for whom Harwood had once been a dresser. The play, set in the
Second World War, depicts Sir's disintegration during a German bombardment,
an attack which he seems to take personally as if Hitler were trying to disrupt
his performances. Other roles in the company were taken by Edward Fox and
Michael Gough. Zena Walker played his long-suffering wife.

Finney, 47 when the cameras rolled, was made up to look much older with
a lined face and wisps of hair covering a largely bald pate. Even Finney's deep
oak-like voice, deliciously rich and fruity, suggested an older man, perhaps
helped by decades of Marlboros and fine wine. Yet Finney decided not to make
Sir too decrepit. He told Michael Billington that he wanted to suggest that his

character still had 'flashes of greatness'. To that end Harwood, rather ingeniously, inserted the key scene where Sir and his troupe are late and he stops the train. Finney – we will recall – was said to have based the scene on his old RADA teacher Ernest Milton whom he remembered trying to halt a departing tram.

Finney's Sir was an amalgam of various theatrical greats who spoke with extended vowels and the deliberate, delicate declaiming of the period. Not just Wolfit but also Wilfred Lawson and Ralph Richardson spring to mind. If the delivery sounds rather like a more thunderous version of Brian Sewell, with its peculiar emphases and intonations, then this was intentional.

In some of his performances we don't lose sight of Finney the actor. By this I mean that he is merely called upon to play 'a personality' as leading men are required to do. *Tom Jones* was the prime example. Here, however, Finney totally transforms into Sir. As he sits in front of bombed-out buildings and consoles displaced families with free tickets to the theatre – 'I trust you will find comfort there' – Finney looks as shell-shocked as the people he seeks to reassure. Even the phrase 'I may do something vio … lent' is delivered as if he's in a daze, gripped by a mental disorder so great that even commonplace words sounds stilted.

Finney's portrayal is a brilliant depiction of deteriorating powers and broken nerves. At times Sir looks quite ready for the asylum. 'My name is on the door,' he says in a peculiarly melancholy way as he enters his dressing room. When he sees his reflection and etches lines on his face to play Lear, he seems transfixed. 'There was a time when I painted in all the lines. Now I merely deepen what is already there.' And when Sir tells Norman, 'you're put through it night after night', it's not with the exhaustion of the factory worker but rather someone terrified of public exposure.

Finney conveys Sir's growing stage fright and the sense of imminent collapse, the horror in his eyes as Norman tries to get him onstage. Harwood's script is also funny in places – Sir blacking up for Othello, rather than preparing for Lear, and taking curtain calls with exaggerated false modesty. It's a withering portrait not only of decay but of self-importance, of the kind that is impervious to reason. It's Finney's greatest performance on film.[12] It's difficult to think of any other international star with the presence, command and majesty to pull it off. Possibly O'Toole, but he might have made it too broad.

Courtenay's performance is mostly brilliant too, the ideal complement to Finney's Sir. Yet his fluttering prissiness is occasionally an overplayed hand, especially on film where the camera detects excess. In the final scene, when Sir has died and Norman is left bewailing not only his death but his exclusion from his master's autobiography, his reaction is over theatrical. Ironically, Courtenay once commented in a recent interview that he thought there was a scene where, if Finney had played Sir on stage, he might have done it differently. One can return the compliment.

The bickering and backstabbing depicted in the movie were not part of the actual filmmaking; everyone got on superbly. Eileen Atkins, cast as Madge, recalled:

> Here we were, a lot of theatre actors who suddenly struck it lucky and were in a film ... they [Finney and Courtenay] have a wonderful sparring relationship in the story, gently sending each other up. They're both lovely people. I know Albert – who introduced me to vodka – a bit better than Tom, whom I didn't know before we started. He looks so serious. I thought he wouldn't stand a chance against Albert because he seemed so bland.[13]

The Dresser undeniably had two great performances, yet two triumphs in the same film can cancel each other out come award time. Finney and Courtenay were both nominated for the best actor Oscar but Robert Duvall won for *Tender Mercies*.

Critics rightly hailed the film and the performances but most, again rightly, gave Finney the edge. Richard Schickel, in *Time*, called Finney 'a revelation'. David Robinson in *The Times* agreed:

> The marvel of the film is Albert Finney's performance. It is the kind of fruity role that might tempt an actor to get by with the easy superficial effect but Finney intimates unfathomable depths. This old man really appears to have a past, a soul, secrets. By turns his mind and intellect surface into the light, wily and autocratic, and then recede again beyond pursuit – and all the coming and goings are visible in his eyes. The gestures are large and theatrical but the nuances infinite.

Roger Ebert wrote, 'Sir is played by Albert Finney who manages to look far older than his 47 years and yet to create a physical bravura that's ideal for the role.' Ebert went on to call it 'the best sort of drama, fascinating us on the surface with colour and humour and esoteric detail, and then revealing the truth underneath.' Ebert nailed it, and *The Dresser* is my favourite Finney film, not least because it shows his Lear that never was.

Yates summed up Finney's appeal:

> Finney maintains his sharpness and enthusiasm by taking on challenging roles and treating his job as a craft. The Dresser required him to put forth great effort to meet the challenge. I see so many actors become bored and finally

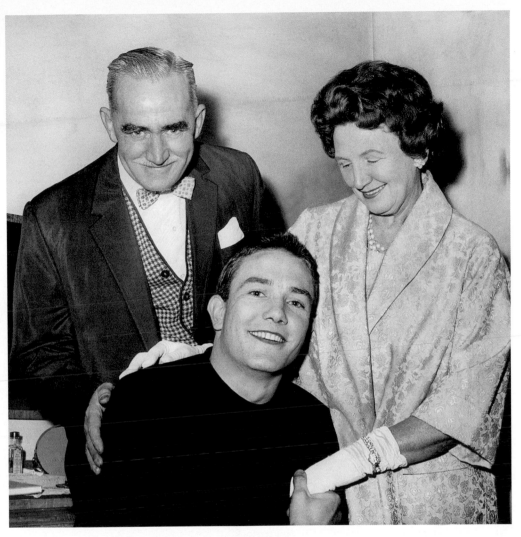

Albert with his father, Albert Senior, and mother, Alice, in 1960. Unlike so many great artists, Finney had a happy childhood and a close-knit family. (Talbot/ANL/REX/Shutterstock)

Albert and Audrey Hepburn share an intimate moment in *Two for the Road*. 'She was rather like a blooming flower and then when her husband arrived, the flower closed up and shrivelled,' he recalled. (Everett/REX/Shutterstock)

Finney was a last-minute replacement for Trey Wilson in the Prohibition-era drama *Miller's Crossing*. But he quickly made the part of quick-witted gangster, Leo, his own. Here with Gabriel Byrne, 1990. (Everett/REX/Shutterstock)

'Albie climbs mountains at the National,' said Tom Bell. But the critics knifed Finney and he never returned to Shakespeare. Pictured here with co-star Dorothy Tutin in *Macbeth* at the Olivier Theatre, 1978. (Reg Wilson/REX/Shutterstock)

An Olivier award-winning performance as Harold in *Orphans*. Here, giving a little tweak of 'encouragement' to Kevin Anderson as Phillip in the original Hampstead Theatre production in 1986. (Alastair Muir/REX/Shutterstock)

In 1996 Finney appeared with frequent co-star Tom Courtenay in *Art*, Yasmina Reza's acerbic study of strained friendship. This was Finney's final stage appearance. (Alastair Muir/REX/Shutterstock)

Pipped to the post again? Finney should have (finally) won an Oscar as best supporting actor for his portrayal of a careworn lawyer in *Erin Brockovich*. Pictured here with co-star Julia Roberts. (Everett/REX/Shutterstock)

Finney inherited what would have been Oliver Reed's role in the television series *My Uncle Silas* and captured the charm of H.E. Bates's old country rascal. Pictured here with the late Lynda Bellingham. (ITV/REX/Shutterstock)

With third wife Pene at a London ceremony marking his BAFTA fellowship in February 2001. (Richard Young/REX/Shutterstock)

As slaver turned ascetic abolitionist John Newton in Michael Apted's *Amazing Grace*, Finney showed he could still rivet audiences with his intensity, 2007. (Goldwyn/Everett/REX/Shutterstock)

angry at themselves, because they do things for money that they don't care about. Albert won't do that.[14]

Orson Welles let it be known that he had been hoping to film *The Dresser*.[15] He thought that Michael Caine would have been good as Norman. He also said that Ralph Richardson would have made an excellent Sir. But it was Richardson's bad luck, or Finney's good luck, that Richardson was 80 by the time *The Dresser* started filming, and, sadly, Sir Ralph died shortly afterwards.

The Dresser also marked the beginning of the end of Finney's relationship with Diana Quick. Finney always liked to flirt. Petronella Wyatt, in an interview with the *Daily Mail* in 2013, recalled an encounter with Finney in about 1983:

He was a keen racegoer and at the time we met, my father [Woodrow Wyatt] was chairman of the Tote. Finney often lunched in our private room at various race courses. I was 15, but looked older, when he turned to me over the Chablis and began to pay me extravagant compliments.

'You look like the young Liza Minnelli. She was a very sexy woman,' he told me on one occasion, then, possibly inadvertently, placed his hand on my thigh.

'May I take you out during your school half-term?' he asked.

'Yes, please,' I gushed.

My fury knew no bounds when I told my mother about the invitation and she forbade any such meeting on the grounds that Finney had a regular girlfriend, the actress Diana Quick.[16]

But by 1983 Diana was no longer with Finney (and it's possible that Petronella Wyatt's account came after their break-up). Finney's new girlfriend was Cathryn Harrison, the granddaughter of Rex Harrison, who played stage assistant Irene in the film. Quick's next long-time partner was Bill Nighy, who hit the big time with his portrayal of a fading rock star in *Love Actually*.

Finney should have been on a roll after *The Dresser*. It was strange then that he agreed to play Pope John Paul. The lacklustre script can't have been the deal clincher – standing up to Communism, keeping spiritual values when religion is effectively banned, and rising to become the first Polish Pope should have made a compelling story. Yet there was little to hold the attention in Herbert Wise's plodding and murky-looking biopic which occupied Finney during the spring of 1983. The film has little dramatic cohesion, instead a surfeit of close-ups of sombre-looking characters and earnest deliberations.

Pope John Paul was filmed in Graz, Austria. Michael Crompton played the young Karol Wojtyla. He remembered Finney's advice at the first read-through in London: 'Albert had agreed to read with all of us. I was incredibly nervous, but

Albert told me to "relax and just speak it, the camera will do the rest." Anyway I got the part, probably because I looked more like Albert than the others.'

Crompton recalled Finney quickly learning the name of every crew member and treating new cast members to dinner. Towards the end of the meal Finney would suddenly disappear, only to return with the news that the restaurant owner had decided to cover the cost because he liked his guests so much. This was just an Albertian ruse. Finney, alias the Pope, was being his usual generous self.

Finney captured the cadences of speech, presence and wisdom of the Pope,[17] and he's well supported by a team of old pros – Malcolm Tierney, Nigel Hawthorne and Alfred Burke. Yet somehow it all comes across as laborious. It also strains credibility to see Finney playing the Pope from such a young age. Even moments when the Pope and his supporters stand up to the authorities lack punch. 'How can I talk to someone who doesn't recognise we [the Church] exist?' Finney asks a minister in the Polish government when they try to resolve a dispute over a holy site. More baleful stares.

Finney was always more Churchillian than papal, a sensualist not an ascetic. Thankfully, Finney's next film, which would reunite him with John Huston, was to prove far more ambitious and test him to the limit. Lee Marvin, who won an Oscar for his portrayal of the drunken gunslinger in *Cat Ballou*, used to joke that he'd had a lifetime of experience. Could Finney, the consummate connoisseur of fine wines, fall to the challenge of playing a shambolic drunk? It was time for his second act with Huston.

SOUSED IN MEXICO

I kinda loved John. He was like a second father to me in many ways, which I know may sound odd considering I was 45 when I first worked with him, but when you had to say goodbye there was always this feeling of loss, that terrible sadness that you'd be deprived of his company.

Albert Finney.

I once entered the home of author Malcolm Lowry[1] in the idyllic-looking town of Ripe, East Sussex, where he was living at the time of his death in 1957. Lowry, destroyed by drink and depression, had retreated there on doctor's orders. The cottage, with its low ceilings and exquisite vantage point, took the word 'quaint' to the extreme, but when you entered the master bedroom, you had a tangible sensation of its tormented resident.

Lowry's great novel *Under the Volcano* had fascinated, and frustrated, film-makers for years. It has been acclaimed so often as a masterpiece that it may deter people from reading it. (And much of the praise probably comes from people who think Lowry was the famous painter!)[2] Many believed that this story of self-destruction, essentially a portrayal of ever advancing drunkenness, defied filming.

Lowry inhabited his own drink-sodden hell. A chronic, incurable dipso-maniac, he suffered from what he claimed was a kind of 'free-floating anxiety neurosis' which he variously blamed on sadistic nannies, locker room ridicule at school and an authoritarian upbringing. He was a man who wrote about what he knew, so it's no surprise that alcoholism should be *Volcano*'s theme.

Screenwriter Guy Gallo, who died aged only 59 in 2015, had written a screenplay of *Volcano* while he was at Harvard. Fascinated by the novel, Gallo had managed to pare it down, shunning the extravagant stream of conscious-ness narrative. His script featured a drunken consul, now resigned, living in Mexico in 1938, his wife Yvonne, and his half-brother Hugh, with whom she has dallied. Gallo wrote the initial screenplay in a matter of days, although there were many revisions.

The consul was a haunted, self-destructive figure, so it would have seemed ideal for another Burton/Huston collaboration, similar to *The Night of the Iguana*.[3] After all, Burton's own poisonous relationship with the bottle had filled thousands of magazine articles and about ten posthumous biographies. Yet Burton was in poor health. He had collapsed during the run of *Camelot* back in 1980.

Burton was also committed to a run of *Private Lives* with Elizabeth Taylor on Broadway. The crowds flocked to see Liz and Dick 'selling themselves', in Lauren Bacall's words. And Taylor had no intention of allowing Burton to bow out. Meanwhile, down south, in Cuernavaca, Mexico, Huston was ready to shoot. He offered Burton the part. Burton declined, 'Could he [Huston] wait?' Huston told him that he had to do it now. Huston feared he would soon die. Ironically, Burton died first, prematurely, aged just 58, a year later.

Anthony Hopkins was then approached. But he was committed to *The Bounty*. In interviews at the time Hopkins said he preferred to play Captain Bligh because he thought he 'knew him better', perhaps a curious comment from a recovering alcoholic. Finney was third choice. Huston and Finney had collaborated well on *Annie* two years earlier. Although *Annie* had lost a lot of money and failed to wow the critics, there was reason to believe that this, altogether more ambitious venture, would restore Huston's reputation. Finney had read Lowry's novel before filming began. He admitted to finding it 'very complicated and very difficult to get into', but said that he had liked it. It all sounded promising enough.

Financing, however, had proved almost impossible. The great John Huston – the words naturally going together as they do with John Ford or Orson Welles – the director of such classics as *The Maltese Falcon*, *The Treasure of the Sierra Madre* and *The Misfits*, was simply not 'bankable', and movies like *Escape to Victory* and, indeed, *Annie*, hardly dispelled the image of a director past his prime. Huston was 77 in 1983. The same year, he was honoured with the American Film Institute's Lifetime Achievement Award. The director's reference to his increasing debility – 'I'm being dismembered bit by bit' – reminded the industry that he didn't have long left.

One of the eventual producers of *Under the Volcano*, Wieland Schulz-Keil, recalled the story behind the AFI tribute:

No one would back Huston. I was told he was too old, he had had too many flops. I couldn't believe it. He was one of the legends and we couldn't raise a nickel on his name. All the moguls who had been turning me down were up there singing his praises. It was quite disgusting. By the end of the evening I was so angry I actually physically attacked a couple of film executives as they left the hotel.[4]

But Huston had never been universally popular. (John Wayne, for example, fell out with Huston on the set of *The Conqueror*. 'Outside *Moulin Rouge* and *Asphalt Jungle* I don't think he's done anything worthwhile when Bogie or his dad weren't there to help him,' Wayne once said, conveniently disregarding a lot of films.)

Huston was by now bitter over his rejection and failing health – in particular emphysema – after a lifetime of heavy smoking and boozing. Ironically, his condition made him well-placed to direct such a tale. So too, in a way, was Finney, someone who clearly liked drinking. And here is as good a place as any to analyse Finney's relationship with alcohol.

Think of British hellraisers and Burton, Richard Harris, Peter O'Toole and Oliver Reed spring to mind. These were the four most famous imbibers of their generation. But the list is endless, Ian Hendry, Trevor Howard and, in the past, Robert Newton, as well as countless others. Finney is not mentioned in the same league but he had a 'reputation', as they say. Graham Lord's biography of Jeffrey Bernard tells a funny, ironic story. When Finney was courting Anouk Aimée they went to the cinema with Lauren Bacall. Bernard was Bacall's blind date. The writer was, as usual, pissed. Anouk turned to Bacall and said, 'be careful of that Jeffrey Bernard. I think he is a drinkeur [*sic*]' – clearly not aware of Finney's reputation. But Finney has always denied being a hard drinker. He has often said that wine is his favourite tipple.

We should be wary of quotes, misquotes and apocryphal anecdotes that are routinely bandied around. On the set of *Annie*, Huston said that Finney could drink a gallon of wine and hit his marks next morning, word perfect. Such routine hyperbole is the stuff of show business. A gallon is equivalent to 8 pints – not of beer, but of wine! Huston's comment evokes an image of Finney, almost in the manner of pulling up at the petrol station, ordering a gallon of wine in the evening. He would have died long ago had he so consumed. Finney's own account of his relationship with booze is more trustworthy:

As a youth, it seemed relatively attractive to be the roaring boy. You know, where you drank at the pub during lunchtime and then gave a performance. I found the idea of it appealing, playing that role, but my system in those days – it's got more hardened since – actually couldn't cope with it. I guess it's possible that it was a kind of escape hatch. If you're regarded as someone of talent, expected to be an achiever, perhaps if you screw yourself up, they'll say, 'Well, if only he hadn't become an alcoholic, he would have fulfilled the promise.' But it didn't happen for me because I simply couldn't do it. My digestive tract couldn't cope. After a few whiskeys I used to throw up – but I'd come back to the party and drink more Pernod anyway. Then my appendix burst. I got peritonitis and realised I couldn't take it. It was what I call 'the Barrymore syndrome'. You know – you're more interesting and romantic if you seem bent on self-destruction. There may even be some ladies drawn to you who suffer from 'the Florence Nightingale syndrome'. And then, you see, if you don't live up to their expectations, you have the get-out clause.

Finney is not an alcoholic. Friends often mention his drinking – and it's clear that he has sometimes imbibed more than was good for him – but he was never in the same league as O'Toole, Harris or David Hemmings. Yet a lifelong tee-totaler would have probably found it difficult to play the Consul.[5] In the words of Jeannine Dominy, Guy Gallo's widow, 'you didn't have to be a drunk to play the Consul but you had to know what it's like to be drunk.'[6] Likewise, Huston. A *Times* portrait captured the 'grizzled veteran', as he was frequently described, on set when filming started in August 1983:

> John Huston, grand old man of the American cinema, sits in a white golf cart from which he rarely stirs, his eyes focused keenly on its tiny video screen which monitors the images recorded by the camera. At 77, he is a shadow of a figure once so imposing. His legs are elongated and thinned out like a stork's, his chest is hollow, his belly droops. But the eyes still have wit and intelligence, and age has enforced a calm sobriety.

Lowry's novel was set on the Day of the Dead. It covers the final day in the Consul's life. Essentially, reduced to its simplest, a drunk mourns his wife's desertion. He prays for her return. She comes back, but seeing her again, and his half-brother Hugh with whom she has had an affair, stirs his feelings of rejection. He takes off and drinks himself into oblivion. His actual death comes from criminals' bullets in a clapped-out cantina.

We must also remember the date, November 1938, and the backdrop of rising tensions in Europe. Finney, as the drunken Consul, questions the German ambassador about whether a Nazi movement is being funded in Mexico. The sense of threat is a motif in Gallo's screenplay, further condemning Firmin. Later, when Firmin is cornered in the cantina by taunting bandits, he is accused of being a Jew. Firmin fends this off with the frequently cited comment that Jews are seldom '*borracho*'. He is surrounded by Nazis.

Jeannine Dominy, who shared many discussions with her late husband about the filming and had access to his notebooks, believed that Huston was approaching the story through the lens of his own life. It was the Consul's death that fascinated Huston – with the politics and the Consul's erstwhile passion for his wife, Yvonne (Jacqueline Bisset), on the backburner.

Dominy said:

> Huston was an opinionated man, a real sadist who liked to play power games with people. He had a history of smashed-up relationships. He had not shaken off his Irish Catholic sense of guilt. He was paying off his sins. Can you have redemption at the last minute? He would bristle at suggestions of passion between the consul and Yvonne.

So it seems that, for Huston at least, 'soused in Mexico' was a fair summary of the project. He saw the Consul as in some way an emissary from his own tempestuous life. 'So long as the Consul comes out heroic and true, that's all that matters,' said Huston. It was self-destruction but also the possibility of salvation – literally, as it were, arising from the ashes of the volcano – that fascinated him. And when he, Huston, died, which he believed was imminent, would he have redemption? (Huston's death was four years away.)

Unusually, Huston allocated several days' rehearsal to Finney. 'It was important that Finney and I discuss the significance of the book,' he said. Dominy believes that Huston devoted little time to Bisset or Anthony Andrews (Hugh). 'I don't direct actors. If I get the actor, I'm assuming he can do it,' Huston said at the time. Or, in Dominy's words, 'if Huston didn't trust an actor, he couldn't be bothered to fix him'. At the time Huston said of Finney:

> I think we do feel the same way about the character, more or less. In fact we had a rather long session and I don't normally do that with actors. Once I've made a decision in the casting I tend to leave it up to the actor and I tell them when they're going a little wrong on the set.

Finney later recalled that Huston would say, 'I like to see what the actor offers me'. It appears to be the only time that Huston ever sat down with one of his actors to discuss a role.

Finney approached the part determined not to be fazed by the portentous material. 'You can't say – my God – this film is profound and intensely personal and otherworldly. It is. But it's the same if you play Lear or Hamlet. If you think like that you can never do it.'

For Finney, however, the part was challenging; he was known for his carousing yet he was not a depressed individual, let alone a suicidal drunk:

> In no way have I ever been as self-destructive as the Consul. If I were to relate my own experiences to the state of the consul in the screenplay, I'd say that my depressions and highs are like mounds and hillocks compared to his mountain ranges. And therefore all I can do is extend imaginatively my own mediocre ups-and-downs and try to chart the extremities that are his.[7]

Finney's performance has many layers. The movie opens with the Consul, somewhat inebriated, meeting a friend. Finney always played drunks well, noting the person so afflicted walks with great precision in a bid to appear normal. (Peter O'Toole was equally skilled in *Jeffrey Bernard is Unwell*. O'Toole played the part as if he were a drunk trying to be sober – with sometimes explosive consequences. This was the correct approach. Tom Conti, by contrast, played Bernard as a blurry-eyed wreck when he inherited the part.)

We see the Consul bend down carefully, tenderly stroking a dog. At once we get the driving force behind Firmin's drinking – loneliness. He can't survive without his wife: 'Without love there is no life'. Later, at a reception, drinking furiously from an assortment of spirits, he insults the guests. A remarkable moment comes later in a cantina when he relates an episode from his service in the First World War. Finney, convincingly, does a double take when Yvonne returns. This was his best scene. It ends with him stumbling out of the bar, aided by Yvonne. 'How, unless you drink as I do, can you understand the beauty of an old Indian woman playing dominoes with a chicken?'

Finney's portrayal of drunkenness was convincing enough to make some wonder if he was sozzled during filming. What a cheek! Finney said that before a shot he would wet his finger with tequila and taste it to get a 'flavour' of the scene. But that was the limit of his daytime consumption. He didn't believe that to play a drunk you had to be soused, and it would not have worked if he had.

The trouble with films about alcoholism is that it's simply too harrowing a condition to depict convincingly. It's difficult to believe, for example, that Ray Milland's desperate drunk in *The Lost Weekend* is really that desperate because his appearance doesn't reflect his addiction. Jack Lemmon and Lee Remick were good, but somehow still too respectable in *Days of Wine and Roses* as a couple more besotted with the bottle than each other. Nicolas Cage's rendition in *Leaving Las Vegas* was more credible but underwater swimming and lovemaking are not really dying alcoholics' pursuits. Meg Ryan's sozzled act in *When a Man Loves a Woman*, taking surreptitious midnight trips to the garbage to down vodka, just didn't convince.

Finney's performance suffers in another sense. He looks like he has lived well rather than badly. There is nothing wrong with his actor's kit. Indeed he is superbly well equipped to play such a part. But somehow his ruddy cheeks and burly build make him seem too healthy. And here again we could draw a distinction with Burton, emaciated and worn down and drained of vigour by run-ins with the life-sucking bottle, who would have been more credible. (Finney's appearance, however, does match Lowry's description of the Consul.)

Another problem is that Firmin is treated rather like a horrific come-on by some of the other players. Only his friend and the barman recognise his tragedy. Otherwise we are treated to Firmin's neighbour, Quincy, taunting him about his cat and whether he's seeing pink elephants. Then there is the silly-arse Brit (played by Finney's old RADA pal, James Villiers)[8] who almost runs him over. But, rather than trying to figure out what the problem is, he merely offers him more booze. Similarly, Hugh (Andrews) never realises how far 'Geoff' has sunk. He enquires about his welfare rather like one would of a friend who goes on the occasional bender, not about someone drinking himself to death. And in the final scene, where Finney makes a reference to the earth revolving and him waiting for his house to come round, this sounds like an old Richard Harris joke.

Clearly a lot of thought went into Finney's portrayal, yet the pursed lips and rolling eyes – the sense that we are sometimes invited to laugh at this grotesque figure as he stumbles around his garden searching for hidden bottles – detracts from the tragedy. It's a sterling effort but one that perhaps Huston should have, at certain points, reined in. This Huston did not do; he referred to Finney's performance, again with a touch of hyperbole, as the greatest he had seen on film.

Huston's strength was a great eye for a telling image. The first day's shooting had Finney tottering around in his tuxedo, wearing sunglasses, surrounded by the festival and various skulls. Out of nowhere Huston suddenly got the idea to do a shot looking into Finney's face with a big skull reflecting perfectly in each lens of his mirror shades. Finney's sunglasses made for a great movie poster.

Ultimately, however, *Under the Volcano*'s shortcomings were more a failure of direction than acting. It was a valiant attempt to film a tragic story but perhaps finally brought down by unrealistic expectations and a director past his best. Dirk Bogarde, an actor who had longed to play Firmin, 'and nearly did three times, once with the Mexicans, once with Cukor who backed out, and once with Losey, who eventually dumped me', (but, of course, Losey did not end up making it either) wrote to Bertrand Tavernier that 'it breaks my heart that Huston made such a mess of *Under the Volcano*.'[9]

Tom Milne thought the film presented a different story to the novel:

Ultimately one is left not, as in the novel, with a man destroyed by the apocalypse of his own imagination but with little more than another world-weary
cuckold following in the wake of Greene's whisky priest and all those other
drunkards who have moored in Mexico.

Finney and Huston greatly enjoyed their second collaboration. Huston said:

> Finney has a wealth of invention. He would do things that were completely
> surprising to me and I would sit back in amazement. We spoke in a kind of
> codal communication. I mean, I would nod and he would look at me and
> smile and that's all there was to it. There was little or no directing required.
> All credit due to Finney.

Michael Fitzgerald, executive producer, noted the same rapport:

> Albert would do something, they would both look at each other and they
> would crack up in laughter. Both knew that whatever had happened was
> awful. And so they did it over. Hardly a word was exchanged. Sometimes,
> John would shake his head and Albert would change completely in the next
> take. Or John would nod affirmatively, and Albert would smile. That was their
> sign language. They got along just like that. They seldom talked about things.[10]

For Guy Gallo, Finney was the model of professionalism and played the part
perfectly: 'He delivers it as you wish to be delivered.' Finney would sit with the
crew at lunch, and Gallo was struck by his warmth and conviviality. 'He only
had lovely things to day about Albert,' said Gallo's widow.

Finney won some excellent reviews. *The Times*'s David Robinson said, 'it
provides Finney with an ideal part. He is perhaps the only British film actor
today still capable of the larger-than-life grand manner of Laughton. His consul
is a rich, colourful creation by turns proud, pathetic, dignified, absurd, touch-
ing, comic, brave.' Yet Robinson also noted, 'the manner of gripping the lips at
whatever is painful or angering is more noticeable and comes more often'. Leslie
Halliwell thought the film too heavy for cinemagoers: 'A subtle novel has on
film become a drunken monologue, fascinating as a tour de force but scarcely
tolerable after the first half hour.'

Sadly for Huston, who tried hard to promote the film at Cannes the following year, the film did not win the awards he hoped for. Many felt it was the old
warhorse's last stab at glory. Finney, however, secured another Oscar nomination,
his fourth in the leading actor category. The other nominees were Jeff Bridges
in *Starman*, Sam Waterston in *The Killing Fields* and Tom Hulce and F. Murray

Abraham (the eventual winner) in *Amadeus*. Speaking in February 1985, just before the Academy Awards, Finney said the only performance he had seen was Waterston's. 'I thought he was very good and I think that it's encouraging that a serious film such as that is doing so well, a serious film that didn't cost 50 or 60 million dollars'.

Finney was never concerned with awards and was a selective filmgoer (among his favourites were the *Godfather* films and *ET*), saying only that he liked to see smaller, independent productions breaking through. 'One of the big differences today – one of the attitudes I don't like – is that it has to be all or nothing. Nobody will take a chance on a relatively small little movie with a small budget. There's an insistence on having the big winner every time.'

As for his own movies, rather like grown-up children Finney always said that they made their own way in the world with a pat on the back and best wishes. David Warner once recalled Finney telling him, once they're in the can, you can only move on and hope for the best: 'One main hit, that's all you can hope for'.

By the time Huston was at Cannes, Finney had wooed critics in London by directing and starring in a stage production that was neither a play nor a transcript of a trial but somehow a combination of both. As ever, Finney was determined to break new ground. *The Biko Inquest* would shame the South African government.

BARING BIKO

I like to observe people rather than be observed.

Albert Finney.

Finney's reputation was running high, fresh on critical plaudits for *The Dresser* and *Under the Volcano*, when Andrew Eaton, chief press officer at Hammersmith's Riverside Theatre, took a call from a Sunday newspaper. A journalist was enquiring whether it was true that Finney was starring as Steve Biko in the new production entitled *The Biko Inquest.*[1]

Before we laugh too much, we must remember that Finney was once, back in the sixties, offered the part of Gandhi by Richard Attenborough.[2] When Barry Norman once put to him that he couldn't quite picture Finney as Gandhi, Finney replied, wryly, 'I couldn't see myself either, irrespective of how many years I spent at a health farm.' Anthony Hopkins felt similarly. When he was offered the part, his father apparently said, 'so it's going to be a comedy, is it?' Parents can bring you down to earth. There was, of course, no chance of Finney playing Biko because the production in question focused on events surrounding the inquiry into Biko's tragic death in custody in South Africa 1977.

Critics were rightly impressed by *The Biko Inquest.* They poured out of the Riverside Theatre in Hammersmith on opening night, heads bowed in deep contemplation, fascinated, yet appalled. What had they just seen? The word 'play' hardly applied here. Some of Britain's finest actors, including Finney, had staged an abridged reconstruction based on actual transcripts of the inquest into Biko's death. Biko, incarcerated under the notorious Section Six of the Terrorism Act, had been kept naked and chained in his cell and died three weeks later, the forty-sixth detainee to die in police custody. Although testimony in the two-week hearing was condensed into just two hours, a version 'written', or rather edited, by Jon Blair and Norman Fenton, every word heard at Riverside had been uttered at the inquest itself.

The Biko Inquest was the first venture of the newly formed United British Artists (UBA), a partnership of Finney, Glenda Jackson, Richard Johnson, Peter Shaw, John Hurt, Diana Rigg, Maggie Smith and producer Peter Wood, and backed by Lou Grade's Embassy Communications. The model was clearly the American film company United Artists, founded in 1919 by Mary Pickford, Charlie Chaplin, Douglas Fairbanks and D.W. Griffiths. UBA was formed with the aim of mounting West End stage shows and then adapting them for video, cable and television with the awareness that barriers between media were fast dissolving. It was the first time that exclusively British performers had banded together in this way.

Ever since UBA's creation in early 1983, a series of board meetings had been convened to discuss what to produce next. When Finney spoke to the press, clad in a neat transatlantic blue suit, looking rather like a CEO addressing his company, he said that UBA had unanimously agreed to produce *The Biko Inquest* and that Richard Johnson, its chairman and chief executive, had chosen him to direct and play the lead in it. 'I delightedly agreed to accept the dual engagement,' he said.

Finney played Sydney Kentridge, the barrister for the Biko family. He decided to play the proceedings straight, without attempting accents. Famous names were in support. John Standing was the prosecuting attorney, Van Rensburg; Nigel Davenport, he of the scowling countenance, was ideal to play the brutal chief of police, Colonel Goosen (Goosen even accused black suspects of inflicting brain injuries on themselves!). Michael Aldridge was especially good as Dr Tuckern, chief district surgeon, the embodiment of evasion and cunning – giving a false, sly smile to the judge to disguise his discomfort as Kentridge destroys his reputation.

The South African authorities were involved in a spectacular cover-up, their behaviour all the more abhorrent for their casual dismissal of Biko's horrific injuries. The play had a trickle of black humour. Davenport triggers laughter when he maintains that 'no assault charges have ever been brought against my assaulting team'. Kentridge's onslaught is forensic and relentless: 'Why don't you note it when you keep a man in chains?', 'What methods of "persuasion" did you use?', 'Why did you order that he be kept naked?' He was also a master of sarcasm: 'Surely he [Biko] had a pleasant and comfortable night?', 'Is there anyone else you would like to smear before I ask the next question?'

The official version, that Biko's death resulted from a self-inflicted injury and not a punishment beating, is shown to be absurd. The evasiveness of the witnesses, the deliberate concealment of barbarity, is clear. This makes the judge's verdict, which absolved the security services of any wrongdoing, all the more shocking. And we must stress again that all this actually happened. Blair and

Fenton's script contains no fiction – every word uttered on stage was heard at the inquest.

Finney analysed Kentridge's intention in the face of obvious establishment lies, 'I think he felt that over the period of thirteen days that after a few days it would be difficult to get a result and concentrated on how Biko was treated by the security branch and the studied lack of curiosity into his welfare'. Finney, sporting a red tie and handkerchief, scrutinising witnesses over half-moon spectacles, made you believe he was, if not Kentridge (who was physically dissimilar to Finney) then at least an incisive investigating lawyer. Indeed, the proceedings at the Riverside were so compelling that the real Kentridge, in the audience on the first night, kept wanting to intercede. 'I remember sitting behind him and every time the magistrate called for Mr Kentridge, I could see him virtually springing to his feet, then realising that it was, in fact, Albert who was being called,' said Jon Blair.[3]

Bernard Levin, also in the first-night audience, corroborated this story in *The Times*. He thought Finney was superb:

> A portrayal that hardly ever touches anger, let alone stridency or melodrama; even the forensic use of sarcasm, in which Kentridge is a master when defending South Africa's victims, is touched so lightly as to be almost indiscernible. And yet, Kentridge, the latest in that long line of lawyers from Cicero to Clarence Darrow, who have served truth against its enemies, comes to full life on the stage, indicting wickedness in words of fire that burn the more savagely for being so carefully doused.

Irving Wardle, also in *The Times*, praised the entire cast:

> Davenport's police colonel, John Standing's attorney general, Michael Aldridge's district surgeon and the rest are dignified servants of the state, conscious of being put in an unusual position, but utterly convinced of the rectitude of their case and blithely unaware of putting their foot in it.

The Biko Inquest made the South African regime, already unpopular, even more of a pariah. Yet Blair thought it had a more universal message. 'The play is just as much about how people are treated by security systems everywhere', a statement that resonates even more in 2017. As for Finney's performance, Blair encapsulates it in a word – 'Brilliant!'

For Finney it was a rare foray into a 'message' play. Yet he was not a political animal, 'I don't believe I could convince anybody that I completely believe anything,' he once said.[4] *The Biko Inquest* was subsequently filmed and shown on Channel 4. Jon Blair thought it a faithful rendition of the stage version (and it is the screen version on which I base my opinion of the production).

After *The Biko Inquest*, Finney had another successful stage outing in *Sergeant Musgrave's Dance*, John Arden's ballad play, with songs and dances galore, set in the 1880s during a pit strike in a northern town. Finney played Musgrave and also directed. The production also included Max Wall whom Finney had bumped into during the run of *The Biko Inquest* at the Riverside. He offered him the role of the bargee. Wall resisted, pointing out that he had just recovered from sciatica, but Finney insisted.

Irving Wardle liked the production. 'Finney, more than anyone, holds the fable on course with energy and smouldering resolve. It's a great moment when this ramrod figure finally unbends into the creaking dance of carnage on the market place, under a skeleton festooned granite obelisk,' he wrote in *The Times*.

Michael Ratcliffe in *The Observer* said that the production had opened before it was ready but paid tribute to 'a spectacular role for Finney once his directorial responsibilities are shed'. Finney, in sideburns and ruddy-cheeked, looking like a younger version of the Uncle Silas character he was to portray fifteen years later, was generally praised for his acting. Michael Billington, while not uncritical of the production, said it was 'held together by Finney's doughty performance'.

After a hectic schedule by Finney's standards, five movies and two stage productions, directing as well as starring, it was time for an extended break. Finney went skiing in Idaho but spent most of the time at racing venues. By 1985, Finney owned nine horses in America alone, as well as two brood mares in Ireland. Finney was a regular visitor to Ocala, northern Florida, to inspect his prize 3-year-old stallion, Yaw, who was being trained and stabled at Wooden Horse Stud Farm in Reddick. In Ocala he would stay with his good friends Mickey and Karen Taylor, owners of Seattle Slew (1974–2002) one of only eleven racehorses ever to win the Triple Crown, at Wooden Horse Stud Farm. By 1986, Finney owned nine foals by him. He came nearest to glory with Synastry, which was reckoned to have a chance in the Kentucky Derby until a knee gave way.

Local journalists found Finney modest and unassuming. When he gave interviews, he was always accommodating, yet he seldom granted them. 'I usually don't do interviews or anything unless it's related to some project I'm working on,' he told the *Ocala Star-Banner*.

> Between films I don't get involved in all that. I don't see myself as a marketable person, a commercial product. I see myself as simply an actor – sometimes I'm not even sure about that! I don't get recognised that much because the characters I've done tend to look very different from me –

either in make-up or disguised somehow. I like being anonymous, though. I like to observe people rather than be observed.

For all Finney's bonhomie and good humour, we sense that he was the watcher in the woods when off-duty. As he neared 50, he was about to score his biggest stage hit in years courtesy of a groundbreaking play, one that would see him hailed for capturing 'the baleful watchfulness of a cat-like outsider'.

ORPHANS

All you needed was a little encouragement.

Albert Finney as Harold in *Orphans*.

It was the final scene of Finney's performance as Harold at London's Hampstead Theatre, then a 173-seater hall[1] that looked like a more suitable setting for a school play than a venue for one of Britain's greatest actors. Finney, all shot-up and dying, was slumped on a sofa while Kevin Anderson, playing Phillip, nestled at his feet. Suddenly the tears rolled down my face; then I heard a gentle sobbing from some other theatregoers. That's when I knew – this was a true HIT!

Finney's old buddy Michael Medwin had first alerted Finney to a new play at New York's Manhattan Theatre Club. Lyle Kessler's *Orphans* was being staged by Steppenwolf, an innovative theatrical company set up in 1976 in Chicago. Its productions were marked by great verve and energy, often to thunderous musical accompaniment and acrobatics. Founding members included John Malkovich, Joan Allen and Gary Sinise.

Orphans was a simple play with great profundities. Or was it a complicated play masquerading as a simple one? That was one of the questions that preoccupied audiences and critics. Finney was entranced by it and set about negotiating a transfer to London. *Orphans* was duly brought to this small off-West End theatre in Swiss Cottage. Michael Attenborough was then artistic director at Hampstead Theatre. 'It wasn't unknown for commercial producers to bring a play to such a small theatre. It was a convenient thing from their point of view,' he said.[2]

Before that, Finney had also visited Steppenwolf in Chicago where, true to form, he soon proved a hit with everyone from the actors to the backstage crew. He even helped out at the box office, taking reservations and answering phones. It was this 'regular guy' persona, his sheer down-to-earthness, attested to in too many stories for it to be insincere, which always made Finney so popular.

Ellen Ross, a volunteer fundraiser for Steppenwolf, who won the accolade of sitting next to him at a special dinner in Chicago, recalled that Finney spoke a lot about the ladies – mentioning, jokingly, that he liked to look over his son Simon's girlfriends – and, especially, horses. She asked to keep his place card at the dinner as a souvenir. She still prizes it.

Kessler's play centred on two orphaned brothers living in a derelict house in Philadelphia. Phillip, an agoraphobic, is dominated by his bullying, violent, thieving older sibling, Treat. One day, Treat mugs and kidnaps a Chicago businessman, Harold, who turns out to be a wealthy mobster on the run. Finney played Harold, Jeff Fahey played Treat and Kevin Anderson played Phillip (Anderson had done the original Chicago and New York production of the play and won many awards), Gary Sinise directed. (Sinise later became famous for playing the lead in the TV series *CSI: New York* for many years.)

Rather as in Joseph Losey's film *The Servant*, the balance of power shifts, not gradually but rather rapidly in this case. Harold turns the tables first on Phillip and then Treat, becoming their mentor, master and a kind of surrogate father. The play's key theme is the transformation of Phillip, a shambling, cringing wreck living under his brother's fist, into a more assertive hoodlum under Harold's guidance.

London theatre, just like any business, is subject to the vagaries of the economic climate as well as the availability of box office names. The mid-eighties was boom time. In 1985, Anthony Hopkins had won over the critics at the National as the reptilian newspaper magnate Lambert Le Roux in *Pravda*, a performance which John Gielgud hailed as one of the best he had ever seen. The following year Hopkins gained more moderate reviews, but ones many actors would still aspire to, in *King Lear* and *Antony and Cleopatra*.

Around the same time Finney's buddy Martin Sheen was starring in a wonderful and informative play, *The Normal Heart*, at the Royal Court, one that brought discussion of AIDS out into the open. Charlton Heston played to full crowds in *The Caine Mutiny Court Martial*. Lauren Bacall was offering old-style star quality in Tennessee Williams's *Sweet Bird of Youth*. Derek Jacobi triumphed in *Breaking the Code* as Alan Turing (while Benedict Cumberbatch was still in short trousers!). Peter O'Toole was enjoying a renaissance of a sort (still restoring his reputation from his 1980 debacle in *Macbeth*) in George Bernard Shaw's *The Apple Cart*. Finney's old mucker, Colin Blakely, was in Alan Ayckbourn's *A Chorus of Disapproval*, a rollicking play within a play. Later that year, 1986, Jack Lemmon would win good reviews in *Long Day's Journey into Night* at the Haymarket, albeit straining to be heard at the back of the theatre.

These productions were popular with critics and theatregoers but – and this is perhaps the acid test, is it not? – with the possible exception of *A Chorus of Disapproval*, I'd be hard pressed to remember key lines or scenes from the productions. A mega-hit play is tangible from the beginning. It's partly a combination of a good script, fine actors and sharp direction. Yet even these elements combined do not guarantee a winner. The rest is that intangible electricity, a kind of energy that suffuses the theatre, a fusion between cast and audience in which spectators come to feel part of the proceedings. It's as though the audience is being led on to the stage by a caressing, invisible hand.

Such was the feeling at the Hampstead Theatre in March 1986. And, to the credit of the other actors, it was not just Finney. From the moment Fahey walked on, hectoring and tormenting his younger brother, *Orphans* felt special. *Orphans* marked the first time I had seen Finney so close up, and I was sitting at the front. What struck me was Finney's sheer size, his broad shoulders and barrel chest, the large leonine head, pink cheeks and challenging, mischievous eyes. Finney was looking quite plump by 1986 (and perhaps his tight gangster's suit accentuated it) but it did not diminish his power. He has one of those forceful faces, likened to 'a sensitive potato' by one of those critics who have the luxury of penning such unforgettable descriptions. Also 'a friendly face', as Phillip says in *Orphans*. Finney's voice was warm and penetrating but not forced. Anderson and Fahey were extremely good, but Finney was the person one noticed.

Perhaps the most charismatic actor on stage I saw was O'Toole. He had an intangible magic. With Finney, charismatic though he is, it is more *presence* that carries him through. *Orphans* was reminiscent of old-style gangster movies, and Finney's brisk movements, pugnaciousness and quick wit evoked Cagney.

Orphans's opening scene saw Finney perform an extended drunk act. As usual he played pissed well, reminiscing about his time in an orphanage with an extended monologue about meat and potatoes (the passage became a favourite audition piece for aspiring actors). Even when trussed up and gagged, alone with Phillip the morning after his kidnapping, Finney commanded the stage with a mere grunt. His Harold was kindly and benevolent but also dangerous – pulling a gun on Treat, berating him for not frisking him beforehand, or besting him in a fight.

Phillip's transformation, under Harold's tutelage, from punch bag to survivor, is handled touchingly. Harold shows him understanding and kindness, enticing him into the outside world by extolling everything from the convenience of loafers to the joy of women's breasts. The play's most memorable line – 'It's all right, Phillip, you just needed a little encouragement' – was particularly moving in Finney's hands as he gives his young protégé a tweak of the shoulder.

Orphans quickly sold out. At the time critics enthused more about Finney than they did the play. Michael Billington noted, 'The play itself may be only moderate shakes, but the Hampstead stage is currently vibrating with more

energy than any other theatre in London'. Billington hailed Finney's best performance in years, 'compact in Celtic roguishness, paternal love and the kind of
bull-like self-possession that bespeaks profound loneliness'. The *Daily Telegraph's*
John Barber also had praise for Finney but reservations about the play, 'Exciting,
marvellously acted and wholly meretricious … this is a typical transatlantic
exercise in the art of trivialising by exaggeration.'

The *Daily Mail's* Jack Tinker homed in on Finney's greatness:

> What gives the performance its stranglehold on the audience – and stamps
> the play with a hard credulity despite its soft centre – is the aura of bleak
> isolation in which he wraps himself. Behind his level, watchful gaze there is
> that strange sense of separation which sets the successful criminal or gambler
> apart from his fellow man.

For Michael Attenborough it was the contrast between the acrobatic Fahey
and Anderson, 'like two monkeys in a cage', and Finney, mostly sitting in a
chair – with his 'danger, magnetism and stillness' – that made the play. 'I felt
that the production was bound to lead to some awards.' It was, above all, what
Attenborough describes as 'the highly physical side of the production' that
would have shocked audiences thirty years ago.

Like others, Attenborough fell in love with Finney. 'He was there because he
wanted to be. He was fortunate enough, having made some money, to be able to
cherry-pick his roles. And he was fantastic in the play.' Attenborough remembers
Finney's special way with people:

> He was the perfect example of how a well-known actor should behave. He
> was just impeccable and completely delightful. He was just there to do some
> work. And he was as interested in the assistant electrician as he was in the other
> actors. There was nothing flash about him.

When Easter fell that year, a fortnight into the play's run, every staff member at
Hampstead Theatre received a large chocolate egg courtesy of Finney.

Finney was in a great mood that March. He had scored a big hit – in racing!
His horse, Synastry, son of Seattle Slew, had won his first major race as a 3-year-
old with victory at Hialeah Park in Florida on 13 March. And, oh yes, he had
triumphed in the Kessler play.

Orphans quickly gained a West End transfer to the Apollo. And, surprisingly,
Finney appeared on Terry Wogan's weeknight live talk show. He had generally
avoided the British chat show circuit, shunning even famous interviewers like
Parkinson and Aspel. His rationale was simple. 'If I'm trying to convince the

audience I might be Tom, Dick or Harry, the less they see of Albert the better,'
he would say. He liked to preserve what he called his 'scarcity value' (he even
declined an invitation to appear on *Desert Island Discs*). So he clearly intended
to give *Orphans* a plug, not that he really needed to gild the lily. But, as he told
Wogan, 'you either get involved in hype or you don't'. Cordial but a little cool,
Finney spoke about his love of horses and the appeal of *Orphans*. Prompted by
Wogan to utter a few lines in Harold's gangster drawl, Finney politely declined.
'Come and see the show,' he told his host, who liked to get a laugh by asking
a guest to do a funny voice. (In 1987, Wogan even asked Bette Davis to muster
her best cockney accent.)

Lyle Kessler, reflecting on the production thirty years later, thinks that only
a great actor like Finney could have done justice to Harold:

> I met Albert when he came to New York to see the Steppenwolf production
> of *Orphans*. The play has attracted some world-class actors to play Harold. Al
> Pacino did it in LA along with Jesse Eisenberg as Phillip. Alec Baldwin did
> the Broadway revival. Anthony Hopkins was going to do it in LA but couldn't
> because of the pending Broadway production. I did travel to London to see
> Albert in the play and I hung out with him at the time. He's a great guy, told
> stories about his dad who was a bookie in England.[3]

Kessler adored Finney's performance and this, we must stress, not from a
fellow backslapping 'luvvie' but from a seasoned writer who had seen Pacino
play Harold:

> He was absolutely wonderful in the production … I cherish what Albert
> brought to the role. His relationship with Phillip was especially touching and
> moving as he guides him to step out into the world. When you write large
> epic characters like Harold there are maybe a half dozen world-class actors
> who can play them and capture every nuance of the role. Finney and Pacino
> are, of course, at the top of the list. I have a new play called *The Great Divide*
> with another marvellous role that Finney and Pacino would be wonderful in.
> Unfortunately, 'time is the enemy of us all', as Tennessee Williams's character
> Chance Wayne says at the end of *Sweet Bird of Youth*. And the role needs to
> be played by a younger actor. But where are the Finneys and Pacinos of the
> younger generation?

Offstage, Finney was conscious of his role in luring this brigade of hungry
young talent to London. He was paterfamilias, a charming and generous host
as he led his cast around town. Set designer Kevin Rigdon remembers how

Finney secured Sinise's entry into the UK. Sinise had, according to Rigdon, 'just a one-way ticket with a pocketful of change,' but Finney introduced all the gang to some of London finest drinking establishments and restaurants. Rigdon reflects in the present tense on the events of thirty years ago:

> One night, we have dinner at some chic Italian restaurant [probably San Lorenzo] where he was chums with the owner, alongside Ronald Harwood, Robert Fox, Maggie Smith, Gary [Sinise], Kevin [Anderson], Jeff [Fahey] and several others. We are treated like royalty. My dinner partner happens to be Maggie Smith – I am in heaven! Like many night time excursions with Albert, the details begin to glaze over. Much merriment and fellowship takes place, stories are told between courses of food and drink – the next day and even thirty years later, the love of life, profession, and friends, remains. Kind, loving, generous, and yes, living life like this could be your last day.[4]

Rigdon also offered a behind-the-scenes insight into the problems facing a set designer:

> Walking to the Apollo one morning while the set is being loaded into the theatre, there is a crowd gathered outside the loading door staring into the theatre. I join them, they are looking into an empty stage, but we are hearing a Pat Metheny concert being played by an invisible Pat Metheny Group – it is sound check, First Circle at concert like sound level. The fire marshal makes his inspection touching flame to various pieces of scenery. The stage is littered with stash and copious amounts of wadded up newspaper, the accumulated mess that the orphans live in prior to Harold's influence. As the fire marshal approaches the papers, which will go up in a ball of fire if he touches it with his lighter – none of this has been treated with fire retardant – I ask him to please not light the stage on fire, that none of this trash can be treated because Albert will crawl around in it and we don't want him to break out in a rash from contact with the flame retardant chemicals. He accepts my explanation; we are permitted to go on. The truth is we had forgotten to treat the papers but the prospect of Albert Finney being covered in ash bought us the time to get everything treated.

Rigdon describes Finney's performance and the impact of his friendship:

> On stage Albert is a joy to watch. The love of life he shares offstage is chan-nelled on stage through his character – Albert is Harold is Albert. Through Albert, I had the opportunity to meet and work with some of the finest

artists and people in our business; Maggie Smith, Ronald Harwood, Michael
Medwin, Lenny Tucker [head of the National Theatre's lighting department],
Cyril Griffiths [technical director of Stoll Moss Theatres], Robert Fox, Edward
Fox – people I would work with again in my career. I owe a debt of gratitude
for bringing these people into my life. The kindness that they extended to me
helped to shape and informs the artist in me.

Nan Cibula-Jenkins, costume designer, remembered Finney's faith in her abilities and his professionalism, her inclusion of 'Mr' underlying her respect:

> We did all of our costume fittings in New York City, where there was a
> rehearsal period as well. My experience with Mr Finney resulted in an anec-
> dote that I still share with my students. In the US [and particularly in Chicago,
> which is notable for 'actor theatres'], the actor and the costume designer work
> closely as collaborators. Many actors have a significant say in the appropri-
> ateness of his or her costume. When working with Mr Finney, I asked him
> to indicate which of the suits he tried on at Barney's he preferred for the
> character. He said, 'Darling, you are the costume designer, so I trust you to
> make the right choice.' So I did! He wore the one with the more significant
> stripe in the material to help underscore the mobster in him. I enjoy my
> collaboration with actors, but I also relished the acknowledgement from Mr
> Finney that he didn't have to worry about making the choice because he had
> a professional to do it.[5]

The *Orphans* 'family' clearly owed a great debt to Finney and everyone stayed
friendly with him after the show ended. Finney deservedly won the Olivier
award for best actor that year. His award, rather charmingly, was bestowed on
him by the great Dame Athene Seyler, then 97 years old. He also won the
Evening Standard Theatre Award for best actor.

A solitary 'orphan' onstage he might have been, yet offstage Finney always
seemed to have an attractive lady on his arm. By 1986, Finney and Cathryn
Harrison had parted company and he was now seeing Susan Mason, his companion through to the end of the decade. In the mid-eighties Finney had also
dated singer Carly Simon. 'He makes you feel appreciated, even if you're one
woman among many,' said the singer. If you could have bottled Finney's sex
appeal, you would have been on to a nice little earner. But, perhaps along with
other men who are a hit with women, he appeared to be genuinely interested
in them.

Later the same year, 1986, a film was made of *Orphans*, wrapping in November.
Kessler recalls, 'A bunch of wonderful American actors were up for the role in

the movie but the director Alan Pakula saw the London production and chose
Finney.' Matthew Modine played Treat in the film. 'I just had such a great
time working with him … he is such a gentleman and such a great actor,' said
Modine, who admits that he went on to appear in the 1994 film of *The Browning
Version* solely because Finney starred in it.

Orphans *was essentially a theatrical experience. Perhaps its claustrophobia*

Orphans was essentially a theatrical experience. Perhaps its claustrophobia
was part of its appeal. So the decision to film it was always risky, yet valuable
for recording a great performance. Pakula's version added some exterior scenes,
notably Treat robbing a victim in the park. It also shows us how Treat entraps
Harold. Yet it added little to the play and slumped at the box office. Given the
acclaim surrounding the play, the reaction to the movie was surprising. Kevin
Anderson reflected, 'I received a lot of attention for *Orphans* onstage and really
wanted the movie to be special. I was very disappointed; the studio kind of
gave up on it.'[6]

Nevertheless, the part of Harold revitalised Finney's career. The 50-year-old
Finney was at the top of his profession. Finney marked his half century with a
magnificent party in May. He had come to enjoy the wealth offered by shrewd
business and artistic choices. 'One more *King Lear* won't make any difference,'
he once told a local newspaper. Talking to John Freeman back in 1962, Finney
had rather pooh-poohed talk of wealth. Perhaps Finney had simply changed.
But, then again, doesn't everyone between 25 and 50? It's a celebrity's misfor-
tune to have his pronouncements scrutinised and forever regurgitated. He is
not allowed the luxury of contradiction. This may explain why, although the
Face to Face Finney interview was repeated on the BBC in the late eighties, it
was excluded from a DVD compilation. Perhaps he no longer recognised the
person in the 1962 interview?

Around the mid-eighties he had sealed his reputation as a man about town –
whether that town was New York or London. But he was more *bon vivant* than
hell raiser, more of a restaurant man than a pub-goer, although the Star Tavern
in Belgravia was a watering hole he frequented a lot in the sixties and seventies.
Among his regular London restaurants – apart from San Lorenzo, which soon
came to be dubbed 'Trattoria Hysteria', perhaps on account of its popularity
with 'luvvies' – were Wilton's in St James, the Ivy in Covent Garden, Hilaire in
Kensington, the Wolseley on Piccadilly, 11 Park Walk in Chelsea and L'Escargot,
La Trattoria Terrazza and Elena's L'Etoile in Soho.

In the sixties, the White Elephant Club on Curzon Street was a particular
favourite, owned by television producer Stella Richman and her husband Victor
Brusa. The White Elephant was the home of many great stars, both homegrown
– the likes of Tony Newley and Stanley Baker – and American visitors such as
Sammy Davis Junior.

In New York Finney particularly liked Elaine's (the restaurant where he performed his tap-dance routine) and Fromagerie, where he and Huston consumed
some expensive wines. In the South of France he always visited La Columbe
d'Or, where he had met Anouk.

Finney always seemed to have a good life/work balance. And once he had
found a talented collaborator – Anderson, Reisz, Richardson and Lumet – he
tended to work with them more than once. Likewise, Finney's successful collaboration with Ronald Harwood on *The Dresser* led him to star in three plays
written by his new friend over the next five years.

The first was *JJ Farr*, about a Catholic priest who had just been released from
captivity and torture at the hands of Islamic fundamentalists in the Middle
East. Staying at a kind of halfway house in Buckinghamshire, Farr rediscovers
his faith, only to be goaded by another lapsed Catholic (played by Bob Peck).
Ronald Eyre directed. Finney's Farr brought to mind the then recent kidnapping of Terry Waite, but Finney dismissed the parallel:

> For a start Terry Waite is not Catholic and he is not a priest. He has nothing
> to do with the problems of JJ Farr. The similarities between the case of Terry
> Waite and JJ Farr are as strong as the physical similarity I have to Mickey Mouse.

Finney, looking slimmer than in *Orphans*, and with closer cropped hair, played
Farr to moderate reviews. As someone who saw the play – and I admit that
some of its complexities may have eluded my 20-year-old self – I found the
proceedings remote. *Orphans* and *The Biko Inquest* were plays that totally succeeded in bringing the audience into the experience; *JJ Farr* did not – one of
those occasions where the audience seems full of tired middle-aged businessmen
brought along by nagging wives to experience a little culture.

'Finney is certainly affecting as Farr, tortured in mind and body, but is rendered almost inarticulate by Harwood's illiterate script,' wrote Maureen Paton
in the *Daily Express*. Jack Tinker, who had loved *Orphans*, did not approve. 'Even
the sacrificed talents of Bob Peck and a hopelessly miscast Albert Finney cannot
perform the miracle of making *JJ Farr* believable.' Christopher Edwards in *The
Spectator* was more positive:

> Finney certainly lives up to our expectations, when, as JJ, he finally arrives,
> disorientated and horribly branded by his captors. Finney exudes a massive
> authority coupled, at the start, with a troubled, half-understood inner torment.
> He gives an obvious but powerful performance, full of hesitations, interrupted
> sequences of thought and barely contained recollections of horror. It as an
> often riveting, dignified and convincing study of the character. Finney's simple,

matter-of-fact account of the sensational circumstances of his experience is
beautifully delivered.

It was not difficult to see what had attracted Finney to the work of Kessler or
Harwood. Quite what he saw in Bryan Forbes's *The Endless Game* (from the
same film director's novel) is another question. A sub-espionage tale, it saw
Finney play a world-weary British agent caught up in European spying. An
uncharitable person would say that it only seemed 'endless' to the viewer.

Executive producer Graham Benson recalls the production as mediocre and
also remembers a lack of connection between Finney and Forbes. Not that there
were arguments or disagreements on set, but Finney expected more guidance
from Forbes. Benson remembered:

> Albert was a total delight on *The Endless Game* and his participation was a
> highlight in my career on what was, to be candid, a bit of a run of the-mill
> thriller nowhere near the class of Le Carré or other more recent examples.
> However, as well as Albert we had a wonderful cast – Kristin Scott Thomas,
> Ian Holm, John Standing and Derek de Lint among them. Albert and Forbes,
> the originator of the material and the director, really didn't gel from day one
> and although he kept his own counsel he used to confide in me after the wrap
> when a few of us used to congregate in the nearest pub. I think if you'd asked
> Forbes he'd have said he got on fine with Finney … which he did, there was
> absolutely zero problem on or off the set … but my feeling always was that
> Albert wanted more from the director.[7]

The story became convoluted and, at times, impenetrable. Finney, who usually
had a distant attitude to reviews and rarely sees either rushes or his own final
performance, became concerned that Forbes had chopped an important scene.
Benson recalls:

> I won't forget in a hurry the fine cut screening we all viewed at Shepperton.
> I knew he rarely looked at cuts but we invited him and he came readily.
> I travelled to the studio with Albert and afterwards he and I were concerned
> that a scene late on in the story had been cut resulting in a less than successful
> denouement. The executive from Rete Italia, our Italian partner, Riccardo
> Tozzi, agreed as did the producer, who had become a good friend, Fernando
> Ghia. Albert did feel strongly, though he put forward his view quite gently and
> he was right. It wasn't just an extra shot, it was an entire scene, and we went
> to Scandinavia to shoot it. There was money left in the budget to do so. The
> scene was shot a fortnight later, directed by Albert, and added to the final cut.

Benson remembers Finney fondly, 'I enjoyed his company, admired his utter professionalism and leadership of the company … a truly great British star who opened the door for so many other actors from outside the metropolis.'

Ray Loynd, in the *LA Times*, described the final production when it aired:

> Finney's intelligence agent draws up memories of Richard Burton's grainy portrayal in arguably the best spy movie ever made, *The Spy Who Came in From the Cold* (1965). TV has rarely presented a spy tale this devious. But beware: Forbes's Muse here isn't so much John le Carré as the game Scrabble. Fitting the pieces together will keep your head spinning for the length of this 120-minute movie. Even when it's over, ending in Moscow, you can't make sense of everything you saw.

The Endless Game was a bit of a yawn. Soon after, thankfully, a midnight telephone call supplied Finney with one of his most memorable film roles. It would shore up his credibility as an international star.

FINNEY IN A PINNY

I never heard him talk about acting.

Gabriel Byrne on Albert Finney.

A sudden death gave Finney the opportunity to give one of his best performances in cinema. Trey Wilson died tragically young, aged just 43, of a cerebral haemorrhage as he was about to start filming *Miller's Crossing*. The role had been specifically written for Wilson. But Finney, who had always admired the Coen brothers' work, quickly agreed to replace him.[1] The result was a marvellous mobster movie, aided by a memorable theme tune that seemed to evoke life's vicissitudes. Finney made the part so much his own that the Coen brothers now admit it's impossible to imagine anyone else as Leo. And perhaps that's the ultimate arbiter of success.

Finney played a gangland chief in an unnamed US city (the accents are definitely *not* New York) who dallies with the girlfriend of his best friend, Tommy (Gabriel Byrne). Tommy has also fallen in with rival Johnny Caspar, with whom Leo has fallen out over the influence of a manipulative bigshot, triggering a gang war.

The film captivates you with its images: big men in trench coats and massive machine guns strolling through an autumn forest, their hats floating in the wind. But it's the characterisation that makes the whole violent mayhem so enjoyable despite some sadism and pathos.

Great actors create a character in seconds, and the late Jon Polito (as Caspar) and Finney do so magnificently, albeit aided by a brilliant script. It's clear that Caspar is a nasty guy. He rues that if you can't fix a fight these days, what can you do? As if complaining that the trains are unreliable! Finney, as Leo, just sits there, eyeing him cynically. It's a brilliant first scene. Polito later recalled it with some irony. He had always admired Finney and was looking forward to working with him, yet in their opening dialogue Polito does all the talking while Finney just looks at him.

Finney and Byrne adopted Irish accents. 'The characters are of Irish extrac-
tion but their parts weren't planned to be spoken with an accent,' said Joel Coen.
'When Gabriel [Byrne] read the script he thought it had a style, a rhythm, that
was authentically Irish, and he suggested trying the lines with his accent. We
were sceptical at the start but his reading convinced us. So Finney took on the
accent too.'[2]

Finney plays one of the gangsters in the Bogart/Cagney films he saw as a
kid. This, though, is no Fatty Harold but an altogether fitter Finney, slim as a
razor blade, hair slicked back, a severe parting, the air of a no-nonsense crime
boss in a city that's got too big for two mobsters. Polito's gangster is a slouchy,
dopey grease ball, at one time lamenting that his fatso son is overeating and then
casually ordering the murder of 'the Jew' who's got into his way. A clash of egos
ensues but Caspar underestimates Leo, to his cost.

The Coens have a brilliant set-piece. Leo is lying in bed, smoking, bespectacled and bedecked in a silk red dressing gown. The idyllic scene, complemented
by the strains of Irish song 'Danny Boy' in the background, is shattered when
several of Caspar's henchmen launch a midnight assassination. Leo notices the
smoke rising up through the floorboards, dives under the beds, blows their
kneecaps off and then jumps down from the terrace to kill the remaining
mobsters in the bedroom. He then chases several others down the street amid
a flurry of machine-gun fire.

The Coens hired Irish tenor Frank Patterson to perform the song. After the
scene was edited, Patterson went into the studio with an orchestra and watched
the monitor so he could match the lyrics to the growing corpse count. When
Finney, smoking a cigar, sees all the assailants die in flames, you hear Patterson
sing, 'I will sleep in peace … until you come to me!'

The Coens shot the sequence over several weeks. Scenes were re-filmed
countless times because they felt that the characters' deaths were insufficiently
vivid or that the music was out of kilter. So much so that Finney became a
regular fixture in New Orleans, a copy of *The Sporting Life* close at hand.

Finney made a convincing tough-guy, likeable but with a steely stare, marking
him as a guy not to be crossed. His catlike grace and sangfroid, casually disposing
of opponents like pesky mosquitoes, all adds to the fun.

The Coens' career contains a few misfires, such as *Intolerable Cruelty* and
Ladykillers, but also wonderful films such as *Fargo* and *No Country for Old Men*.
All signature ingredients are served piping hot here – striking images, close-ups
of unpalatable characters and grisly humour. John Walker liked *Miller's Crossing*,
calling it a 'sombre, solidly made thriller, directed with a macabre skill'.

Gabriel Byrne found Finney a joy to work with, popular with the crews and
other actors alike:

We shot that in and around New Orleans, and I think if they'd had an election for Mayor that year, Albert would've won it, hands-down. He led the St Patrick's Day parade and was up and down Bourbon Street every night. The last thing you'd think of Albert after talking with him was that he was an actor, which is the greatest compliment I can give him. You'd talk with Albert about racehorses, football or politics, what was going on down the road. I never heard him talk about acting, and I'm not someone who likes talking about acting, either, or talking about the business. We had many great conversations. I remember after we shot that scene in the park, we were two hours from New Orleans, and myself and Albert came back together in the van. We didn't have separate cars in that film, everyone just went in the van together. It was great. Coming back, I just sat with Albert for two hours and he told me all about where he was born, and where he was brought up, what working in England was like in the fifties and sixties … he told me how he turned down the lead in *Lawrence of Arabia*. I said, 'Did you regret it?' He said, 'No Gabe, I didn't regret it, because the next year I won the Oscar for *Tom Jones*'.[3] [Finney probably meant this metaphorically. In fact, he was only nominated.]

Polito remembered Finney as 'a master on the set … and a total master to watch … he should have been nominated.' Marcia Gay Harden found him a great teacher. She remembered him coming up to her and saying, 'Darling, I don't want to be the old soldier but if you want to ask me something, do'. She said she learnt more from just watching him, both on- and off-screen, 'And it doesn't have to be about acting. Maybe it's how to conduct yourself in the business.'

Memory, however, can play tricks. You probably think *Miller's Crossing* was a box office hit, but it didn't make much money. The *New York Times* was full of pernickety criticisms. Now, as Polito commented in a recent interview, the same newspaper calls it a classic.

Finally, have you ever seen Finney in drag? If you have seen *Miller's Crossing*, then you have. He appears in the powder room scene where Tom (Byrne) barges in on Verna. 'Close your eyes, ladies, I'm coming through.' The dames make a hasty exit, including Finney, to Byrne's immediate left near the door, wearing a black and white pinafore.

From one great movie Finney went to another, one that became the most award-nominated show in HBO's history. Finney had read Brian Rehak's script, an indictment of modern trial by TV media, while shooting *Miller's Crossing*. *The Image* focused on a news anchorman, Jason Cromwell, played by Finney, who becomes bigger than the stories he exposes. As an investigative reporter and presenter, Cromwell is a kind of American Roger Cook – judge, jury and executioner – as he uncovers wrongdoing. There's also a touch of Peter

Jennings, Dan Rather or Walter Cronkite about Cromwell. He likes to think he's a Mr Clean, blowing the lid off the greedy and uncaring. But does he always get it right? Cromwell, in his eagerness to break the big story, to win the scoop that will keep his ratings high – a trend even more familiar in 2016 than in 1989 – is now sentencing 'suspects' on camera. 'Who set you up as God, Cromwell?' complains another suspect.

Cromwell, cheating on his wife (Marsha Mason) with a colleague (Kathy Baker), in between swooping on his targets, is a total narcissist – arrogant, unscrupulous and indiscreet. And yet, as often with a Finney character, he is perversely likeable, enhanced by a smidgen of self-loathing. 'I make a real nice living from other people's disaster,' sings Cromwell to himself one day in his dressing room. His reputation unravels when a suspect in another supposed scam, one unfairly vilified by Cromwell, commits suicide. The cynical reaction in the studio – 'Why would he do it? The show got good reviews.' – is all too believable.

Cromwell is confronted by the victim's widow and falls out with his long-standing producer friend Irv Nicholson (played by fellow Brit John Mahoney who, coincidentally, played the very first Harold in the Steppenwolf production of *Orphans*). It all ends with Cromwell delivering a live diatribe against scurrilous journalism.

The Image is particularly believable in its portrayal of backroom backstabbing, the endless quest for higher ratings and cost-cutting. The delight is the minimalist, naturalistic joshing between Mahoney and Finney. These two really seem like good friends and long-time collaborators. The story may not have been new – bigshot TV anchor suddenly gets conscience pangs – but it's all in the handling. Apart from a slight lurch into English at the beginning, Finney's portrayal of Cromwell is authentic. *The Image* received many awards.

(One question haunted me – why do Americans frequently call even close friends/lovers by their surname? Even his best friend and mistress both address him as 'Cromwell'. Answers in an email please …)

Actor Dennis Haskins, best known for his role in *Saved by the Bell* and its sequel, *Saved by the Bell: The New Class*, only had a couple of lines in *The Image*, but he has never forgotten Finney's warm welcome:

I took this part because I got to have one speech with Albert Finney … And Albert goes – 'Hi Dennis, nice to meet you. Watch out for this one, he's a scene stealer.' And he goes. Well, the person that was the scene stealer was John Mahoney, who ended up being the dad on *Frasier* and a lot of other wonderful roles. So, I had a scene with John Mahoney.

So, the director after the scene said, 'you know what – we want you to stay. We're gonna put you in a couple more scenes.' So, I had to stay that night.

I had only the clothes on my back. I was just gonna go back, you know, the next day. Wardrobe gave me shirts to wear the next day. So, I'm in this sleepy little train stop hotel.

I'm going down to eat dinner with whatever money I've got in my pocket, which wasn't much by the way. And down the stairs comes Albert Finney. Albert looks at me, remembered my name from many hours before, says, 'Dennis, mind if I join you?' And I said, 'Please!' And two hours later, I had the most wonderful evening that I can remember as an actor listening to Albert Finney tell me stories of all the wonderful actors in England and different things he'd done.

So, then we go to the wrap party for *The Image*, and Mr Finney is there. And I walk up to him, and I said, 'Albert, I just want to thank you for making me feel so welcome.' And he got serious, and he said, 'I see myself as the host of the party, and if you're having fun at my party, we're going to have a pretty good party.' And I took that with me.[4]

Kathy Baker, playing Finney's lover in *The Image*, was another fan of the actor. 'He's so down to earth. So incredibly … it's just hard to describe. You know what Finney does? He directs, he sets up the lights, he changes the words, he's in everybody's face and we all love it. He's magical.'

But, off-screen, Finney had another diversion in *The Image* – Marsha Mason. In her autobiography, Mason revealed that Finney crossed her path at a vulnerable time after her divorce from playwright Neil Simon:

Albert seems to have a great time with life; he's a flawless actor, a kind and terrific man who loves being social. He loves good food and great wine; he's deliciously funny, full of energy and a great flirt. His joie de vivre became enormously appealing to Marsha, the Couch Potato Celibate. His love of life was charmingly contagious. Dammit, I decided I want some of that! He made me laugh and I started to feel sexy again!

'I think it's time we try on a new pair of shoes, don't you?' I asked all my selves in the mirror one day. (I'm addicted to shoes too.) Surprisingly, everyone was in agreement. He was the perfect person to lose my virginity with. Again. I've sometimes been rather straightforward when it comes to asking for what I want in the romance department. 'Would you like to spend the Fourth of July weekend with me?' I asked straightforwardly, smiling all the while. If only I had some of that brazen quality when asking for what I needed in some other areas of my life.

'Why, I'd be charmed,' he answered, charmingly. 'You take my breath away,' he added, kissing my hand, being Tom Jones all over again. What a great adventure. I was definitely pleased. I told him I planned a big party on the Fourth for the whole cast and a bunch of my friends, that I had arranged everything and that he could sit by the pool and relax.

'Nonsense, I'll help,' he replied. And help he definitely did. He brought coffee, juice and toast to bed in the morning and patiently answered the zillion questions I asked him about his personal and professional life. I was way too earnest but he was forever gracious. We spent the next day picking up food and drink and setting up table by the portale by the pool.

Then, mysteriously, even to me, I became withdrawn. Personal growth, hitting walls, celibacy, and sudden intimacy were a bit too much for me, even though men and sex still made me a bit frivolous. Frivolous. Withdrawn. Poor guy. I was hard to figure.

We finished all the preparations for the next day's party as the sun was setting and twilight was creating magic. Albert decided he wanted to water the grass and the hill so that everything looked perfect. I came down the hill, where I am now, and cut flowers for the table. Looking back and seeing him watering everything so intently, I was struck by the domesticity of the scene and how nomadic an actor's life was, and how important it was to have some creature comforts in our lives when we're on the road, working hard. He was having as pleasurable a time watering the lawn at twilight as I was having surreptitiously watching him.

The following morning after coffee and more fun in bed, Albert left to return to his hotel, dress and then come to the party with John Mahoney and a couple of guests. When he arrived we greeted each other as if he'd never been here. It was delicious having this secret together. Albert was the hit of the day as twilight darkened the sky, everyone stood at the edge of this hill and watched the various fireworks displays in Malibu, Long Beach, and a huge one right in front of us at eye level. Watching the colourful explosions, I thought that this celebration was a gorgeous 'stepping out', celebrating the end of celibacy with a grand display of fireworks no less.[5]

Mason was right; Finney was a vagabond player who had spent most of 1989 living out of a suitcase. He needed to have a little luxury around him while on the road. By the time *The Image* wrapped in the summer of that year, he was preparing a return to the London stage after several months in America.

Finney's second West End collaboration with Ronald Harwood, after the faltering *JJ Farr*, was altogether more successful. *Another Time*, which opened in September, had an intriguing way of handling the story of two generations of a South African family. The first act takes place in the fifties in South Africa. Finney plays a poverty stricken, sickly salesman who cadges cigarettes and spare change off his son (Christien Anholt), a promising concert pianist.

Finney was wonderful – the grimacing, whining self-pity and self-loathing as he fumbled through empty pockets. At just 53 he impersonated an older man extraordinarily well. In the second act, flash forward thirty years, he played the son, now London-based, who has become an internationally famous concert pianist.

The play examined a theme familiar to liberal South African exiles. Should he perform in apartheid South Africa? Being a Jewish family only compounded the dilemma. (We quickly gather that this, in some way, is Harwood's autobiography.) Yet the second act was perhaps less interesting if only because the emotional soul-searching and the 'our boy made good' story is a bit clichéd. One day, a dramatist may write about a riches-to-rags family and the difficulty of adjusting to reduced circumstances.

Changing fortunes, however, were not really at the heart of *Another Time*. It was essentially about South Africa, the wistfulness of estrangement from one's own country and the difficulty of facing up to a regime that you loathe but are powerless to challenge. Overall, it was thought-provoking and thoroughly enjoyable, a well-deserved hit.

Something I remember from the performance I saw, a couple of weeks after opening night, was the final curtain call amid a rapturous ovation. Christien Anholt sought guidance from Finney on how to handle it – whether he should come back for a further bow. Finney kept eye contact with him throughout, leading him through his paces, as if to say 'I'm here for you'.[6]

Finney also took *Another Time* to the Steppenwolf Theatre Company in Chicago in 1991. Molly Regan and Terry Kinney co-starred in a production that launched a new multi-million dollar theatre in Halsted Street. 'Finney is a master actor, and anyone who finds himself in Chicago should consider spending the couple of hours of *Another Time* with him,' said *The Washington Post*'s Lloyd Rose. Rose noted, somewhat dryly, that Finney:

> Could have been a movie star. He had the looks. He had the force. He had the sexiness. And, oh yeah, the talent. When Albert Finney played the lead in the film of *Tom Jones* back in 1963, it looked as if he were on his way to becoming an international star and sex symbol. Then it turned out that he wanted to act.

This backhanded compliment – the reverse of those who said that Finney had forsaken the classics for an easy life – proved that a celebrity simply can't win whatever path he chooses. Someone will always censure you when you are in the public arena.

Finney's 'idol', Laurence Olivier, had died in July 1989, the mentor who had handed Finney a poisoned chalice by describing him as 'the greatest actor of his generation'. Finney attended a star-studded memorial service in Westminster Abbey on 20 October. Among the celebrities were Michael Caine, Peter O'Toole, Frank Finlay, Peggy Ashcroft, Alec Guinness, Jack Lemmon, Richard Attenborough, Jill Bennett, Gordon Jackson, Dorothy Tutin and John Gielgud. Finney read from Ecclesiastes, 'There is a time for everything, and a season for every activity under the heavens, a time to be born and a time to die ...'

Even at memorial services theatrical people judge each other. Lindsay Anderson wrote that Finney read the lesson 'very badly, in a plummy, upper crust Shakespearean manner'. Anderson also disliked the whole affair, describing the train of celebrities carrying souvenirs from Olivier's performances as a 'po-faced procession of notables'. He thought, perhaps correctly, that Gielgud was the most eloquent performer, giving a moving rendition of Donne's sonnet 'Death Be Not Proud'. (Gielgud also read the same poem at Richard Burton's memorial service.)

Gielgud's voice carried with it a kind of lyricism and musicality, once likened to an A-string on a violin by Robert Hardy. For all Finney's outstanding talents as an actor – his facility for transformation, his gift to inhabit a character completely, the sheer power he summons on stage – his is not, essentially, a finely tuned classical voice in the tradition of Olivier, Gielgud or Burton. He is, rather, a brilliant modern actor but speaking verse is not his forte.

So who was the obvious successor to Olivier? There was no obvious answer; Finney was determined to go his own way.

DIGGING DEEP

They don't keep asking De Niro when he's going to play Lear, do they?

Albert Finney.

Finney became pudgier and redder-faced with each outing as he entered his fifties. It didn't detract from his appeal. Nevertheless the actor who entertained BBC viewers on Sunday nights in the autumn of 1990 in Kingsley Amis's *The Green Man* (directed by Elijah Moshinsky who had also directed *Another Time*) was a long way from Tom Jones. This was true dirty old man territory. Yet Finney, as a hysterical hotelier with penchant for rich food, good whisky and three-in-a-bed romps, was charm personified.

Amis incited madness in his devotees. In the early nineties, fans used to wait outside his home in Regent's Park Road, hoping for a glimpse as he hauled his great bulk down the steps. Young writers would follow him to his local pub to beg him to read their jottings. Those who did were given short shrift.

'I know it would be an imposition to …'

'Yes, it is!' Amis would bellow back.

Or, 'I know it's rude to interrupt you …'

'So why are you doing it then?'

But perhaps this was all part of the fun, to then slouch home knowing that the irascible literary giant had deigned to scream at them. (I had a friend who would visit a wine emporium in Regent's Park Road, ostensibly for tastings, but really because the store lay directly opposite Amis's home. When Amis passed away, in 1995, my friend said that trips to the premises would never be the same.)

Amis, like many writers, tended to repeat his favourite themes. The middle-aged male protagonist would be a heavy drinker and womaniser, usually undergoing some kind of crisis. And so it was with Maurice Allington in *The Green Man*, a novel of sex and the supernatural to which Finney had purchased the rights twenty years earlier. But Finney was then too young to play Allington. By 1990 the time was right.

Allington is visited by ghosts and beds the wife (Sarah Berger) of a doctor friend (Nicky Henson) who orders him to lay off the hard stuff. Yet Allington's main preoccupation is sex. 'When are you going to let me make love to you?' Finney asks Berger before they take a romp in the fields.

Nicky Henson, one of Finney's co-stars, remembers Finney's helpfulness during filming:

> As in my time at the National 10 years before, Albert was particularly helpful to me, and in fact he's always been a bit of a guiding influence professionally to me. On *The Green Man* I was doing a very difficult scene with him, just a two-hander, and about half way through I was getting in quite a state about it. But Albert felt it. After about a third take, when I'd messed up again, Albert put a hand on my elbow. 'Calm down; it's OK.' It was a sensitive thing to do and helped me a lot.[1]

The Green Man proved diverting, if perhaps not ultra-compelling entertainment. Finney's lovable old lecher was the whole show.

Moshinsky also directed *Reflected Glory*,[2] a curio play about sibling rivalry, again scripted by Harwood but not as successful as *Another Time*. Finney and Stephen Moore were bickering brothers. Finney said that an encounter with his sister reminded him of problems between siblings:

> What can happen in one's mid-50s is one can be bugged by something they [siblings] say that makes you react as if you were six. I was reminded of this a year ago when I was spending some time with one of my sisters. What she said and how she said it made me feel like a child. It may have been totally accidental on her part. That's the thing. It's hard to pull the wool over their eyes because they have seen you go through all sorts of things when you are growing up.

In 1992, during the run of *Reflected Glory*, Finney made his second appearance on the *Wogan Show*. This time Finney appeared friendlier, perhaps because he appeared alongside *Coronation Street*'s Barbara Knox. Wogan broached a subject which probably irked Finney and his many admirers. Had he fulfilled his promise? Interviewers, perhaps mindful of sounding pompous, often couched the question to make it sound like the view of a (nameless) third party. It goes like this: 'The trouble with being hailed as the next Olivier is that, in the view of certain people, you have not quite …' A wordy euphemism for: 'When will you be carrying Cordelia at the Old Vic?'

Finney explained his attitude to Wogan, 'I've done a lot of new plays in my career. I like doing classics from time to time but if you wear tights all your life you walk funny. I like to do modern things.' He subsequently developed a stock answer, 'They don't keep asking De Niro when he's going to play Lear, do they?'

Finney said that he was deliberately pacing himself, hence his penchant for taking time off. 'I want to be acting when I'm 90. I don't have to do it all this week.' He also told Wogan – with a nod to the tough times in 1992 – that the recession had forced him to sell a racehorse or two.

Reflected Glory opened to respectable reviews. It was the usual Harwood mix of family banter, unresolved jealousies and cheerful disharmony. None of it could be taken too seriously. And that perhaps was part of the problem; audiences paying hefty prices expected more than froth.

The run ended prematurely with Finney claiming that the producers, the Mark Furness Company, had not paid him, so he simply withdrew from the role. An article in the *Independent* which had earlier alleged that Finney had refused to go on despite a suitcase of money being delivered to his door, was later corrected. 'Finney left the show when substantial sums due to him and other principals remained unpaid. There was no suitcase of money,' reported the newspaper. This seems to have been the definitive version.

Finney was usually generous. Sporadic acts of largesse were one thing; being unpaid for services rendered was different. And Finney had an eye for business. In 1990, he had written to John Osborne to inform him that he was taking legal action against Woodfall Films for royalties still owed from *Tom Jones*. The sum, owed jointly by Osborne and Richardson, was about £75,000. Finney's letter explained that he was 'writing for old time's sake' and ended, 'Hope you are busy, well and heading towards the year 2000 in good heart'. Osborne, although debt-ridden by then, did not dispute the sum. Richardson, however, was appalled. 'He's had enough already,' he reportedly said,[3] referring to the share of profits that had made Finney so rich.

Approached by a mutual friend to forgive the debt, Finney refused. Unsurprisingly, Osborne, the master of vituperation, had some choice words for Finney. Reportedly, he sent him a note, headed 'with the compliments of John Osborne', adding, 'I only hope one of your fucking racehorse tramples you to death'.[4] Finney, in a letter to Osborne's biographer, John Heilpern, denied any bad feeling between them. In his view, it was all 'my eye and Betty Martin', i.e. nonsense. However, Osborne's widow, Helen, banned Finney, along with Peter Hall, theatre critic Nicholas de Jongh and playwright Arnold Wesker from attending Osborne's memorial service in June 1995 (Osborne had died in December 1994).

Finney, throughout his career, always conveyed the sense of being a jobbing actor. The size of the role was usually immaterial. So was – that awful word – the 'commercial' appeal of a project. What mattered was that a part was meaty. Sometimes that led him to appear in seldom-seen films. *The Playboys* was one such, but who wouldn't want to act alongside the beautiful and talented Robin Wright?

The Playboys was a rich period piece, filmed in Redhills, near Cavan in Northern Ireland, and directed by Gillies MacKinnon, in which Finney played an embittered policeman unhinged by his unrequited love for Tara (Robin Wright). Wright starred as an unwed mother whose charms even drove one suitor to suicide. She excited the entire male population, especially Aidan Quinn, playing Tom Casey, a member of a troupe of travelling players who offered some broad farce that included scenes from *Gone with the Wind*. Veteran actor Milo O'Shea played Freddie, the leader of the players, a part that had originally been offered to Finney. Finney declined what was a peripheral role, the light relief to a sombre story. So MacKinnon offered him Sergeant Hegarty, a dour, dried-out drunkard determined to marry Wright by whom he has fathered a baby after a roll in the hay.

When Quinn appears, a charming younger suitor who wins over Tara after some typically headstrong 'Oirish' recalcitrance, Hegarty cracks. Nothing, and nobody, will stop him marrying Tara. He has even fashioned a crib for the baby. 'Don't drive another soul to drink and despair,' the priest warns Tara, but it's too late. There is a touch of Lear about Hegarty. 'Marry me or I'll go mad,' he tells her.

Back on the booze, and even baby-snatching, Hegarty takes a predictable beating from Casey. And Finney again displays his ability to play a drunk 'straight' without bleary-eyed vagueness. Looking fierce and determined, yet with the vacant look of a demented bull, moving steadily but losing accuracy with each swing, the defeat prompts his (self)-expulsion from the town.

Although over-the-hill for the part, perhaps even by fifteen years, Finney brings a stone-faced, rocklike quality to Hegarty. He suggests a man without self-knowledge, driven by animal-like grief. Yet that is not the whole story. It's his baby, after all, and we feel he's entitled to be bitter. It's an underrated film and Finney's policeman is a sad, wretched character. Carolyn Seymour, who had appeared with Finney in *Gumshoe*, thinks it was one of his finest screen performances. 'That was him at his best, a real lesson in film acting. My heart moved.'[5]

Finney's part took just three weeks but, as usual, the locals found him a generous host. MacKinnon remembers:

Albert Finney is a true gentleman. Before we started he took me to one side and offered some advice. I thanked him. He said 'That's okay. It's your first feature film and you need all the help you can get.' And he meant it, it was a generous gesture. Albert had the amazing ability to memorise the names of the whole crew and all the local villagers. This ability to treat everyone with respect and consideration earned him great affection. One Sunday he hired a coach and took the whole crew to the races. I slept through that event unfortunately. Our night off on the borders of Ireland usually sparked off a party which lasted until dawn. When we wrapped, Albert Finney was arrested by Shaun, the local policeman. He was arrested for impersonating a policeman and for drinking on duty. The joke ran all the way to the prison cells, where Albert finally put his foot down and demanded an unconditional release.

MacKinnon said he owed a lot to Finney:

Whenever he came to the set to start a scene he would always ask the continuity girl: 'What time is it?' By this, he meant the time in the actual story. He very quickly had a nuts-and-bolts grasp of the part. I was under a lot of pressure and often had to settle for just one or two takes and he was always very co-operative.

It was the first time Finney had played a policeman. 'I'm at the sort of age where I'm not going to get the girl, so it seemed an attractive possibility, really,' he said at the time. Some locals got so used to seeing him dressed as a policeman that they mistook him for one. Finney recalled, 'One old fella, who'd been in the pub all day, came tiptoeing past me while we were shooting, and whispered, "Is it all right if I go and talk to me mate over there?".' Another time, cars coming from two directions had converged and caused a jam in the village; Finney, in his sergeant's stripes, directed traffic and eased the bottleneck. No one challenged his authority. All in all, it was a fun experience for Finney. 'I like films about a family or community in a defined area, and you get to know that world,' he said.

Janet Maslin, reviewing the film for the *New York Times*, thought Finney brought gravitas to the part. 'Finney, looking puffy and ravaged in the role of a policeman who has lost much of himself to drink (and whose obsessive interest in Tara somehow offers the chance of redemption) brings a furious buried intensity to Hegarty's longing.' John Walker called it 'a soap opera-style narrative of thwarted love, of interest mainly for its performances'. Alexander Walker described it as 'a heartbreak tragedy wrapped up inside an ingratiating comedy'. That it was.

Finney told Barry Norman on *Film '92* a funny story about coverage of the filming. The local Cavan newspaper, aside from reporting on the presence of distinguished actors such as O'Shea and Finney, also commented that 'the star of the film was Robin Wright who's now married to Sean Penn who used to be married to Maradona [*sic*]'.

In the same interview Finney said that he was unbothered by praise or damnation:

I'm a working guy. I just want to go on working. I hope to remain promising until I stop. If you believe the good things people say, you must also believe the bad things people say. It's best to believe none of it and go your own way and don't ever take it as a sort of burden.

Referring, yet again, to the Olivier mantle, Finney told Norman, 'it's nonsense, just one person's response … it's only a point of view, entirely subjective. You must never believe what people say about you, good, bad or indifferent.'

Finney, who once, perhaps with tongue in cheek, had told Norman to mind his own business when the critic had advised him to do more films, ignored perceptions. Doubtless he would have agreed with Charlton Heston who, reacting to some grudging reviews when he starred in *A Man for all Seasons* in London in 1988, told Terry Wogan:

I was once doing a play with Laurence Olivier and we got – and maybe deserved – very bad notices. As we shared a bottle of brandy, I said to Olivier. 'I guess you learn to ignore the bad notices.' Olivier took my hand and said 'Chuck, it's just as important to ignore the good ones.'

Finney's next film, Bruce Beresford's *Rich in Love*, was a story that may have looked interesting on the page, yet it was unspeakably bland in the final cut. A slender story of marital desertion, adaptation and acceptance (by the team who directed and wrote *Driving Miss Daisy*) it teamed Finney, as wealthy retiree Warren Odom, with Jill Clayburgh as his wife, Helen. At the outset she abandons the family's seaside home in South Carolina and disappears. After his wife's desertion, Warren spends his days doing little household chores, moping around the garden and munching mayonnaise and crisp sandwiches.

It comes as no surprise that Clayburgh has left him. There are few surprises in *Rich in Love* at all. We somehow know that Warren, after the initial shock, will pull himself together, stop whining and start living. Predictably, the attention of an attractive neighbour (Piper Laurie) makes him clean up his act. He even starts pulling the hairs of out his nostrils. Homemade cake, trips to bookshops, some nostalgic video rentals and he starts to adjust. Meanwhile, his wife turns out to be living in a nearby beach hut. 'Being married to him was killing me. When he retired he was always there. It was all so permanent. We carried love to its conclusion,' she explains to their daughter. Doubtless this would have chimed with Finney's real life credo!

Finney equips himself well in the role, with a sleepy, soothing southern drawl that draws you in. There are nice shots of the water and the film wins points on atmosphere. You can feel the humidity, the swampy, lush vegetation, the relaxed, old-style charm of Charleston life. As a story, however, it is pleasant but utterly forgettable. 'A meandering domestic drama, an attempt at a character study, which fails because its participants distinctly lack character, cleaving only to the obvious and expected,' wrote John Walker. 'It could play on television tomorrow and nobody would find anything amiss, save perhaps the ratings dropping precipitously as the audience drifted away in search of something more than genteel good taste,' wrote John Harkness in *Sight and Sound*.

Finney's co-star Piper Laurie admitted that whenever she looked at him she still got goosebumps, 'I've seen all his movies and I saw him in the theatre a lot and, well, I had a crush on him. It's hard to get over that, you know.'

Finney was the first actor approached by Beresford to play the father:

Generally, when you're looking for actors in their 50s, just about all the ones working are pretty good or they wouldn't have been working so long. But you get some actors who can't convey what the others can. We needed an actor with an emotional range. Albert had it … I think, of all the actors I've worked with, he's the most aware of what's necessary for film. Because you get a lot of actors who, when you're fiddling with the focus and you're measuring distances, and they've got to lean this way or that, a lot of them seem to have an attitude that it's all some kind of a trick to make things difficult for them. They think you're not doing it in fact to make them look good. But Albert understands everything you're doing and you don't have to explain.[6]

The movie, however, was no great shakes. Much better was Mike Figgis's remake of the Terence Rattigan classic *The Browning Version*, about an unpopular, unloved classics master at a boys' boarding school. Ill health has forced Andrew Crocker-Harris into early retirement, and his wife is cheating on him with a younger teacher. Just when all seems lost, he is buoyed by an unexpected act of kindness.

Some great actors had played Crocker-Harris, not only Michael Redgrave (in the 1951 film), Nigel Stock (in the 1976 King's Head stage production) but also John Gielgud in an American TV version. Crocker-Harris is an introverted, weary corpse, spiritually and emotionally broken, and a dull, pedantic teacher. Redgrave, in particular, seemed the perfect choice for the part. Something about him suggested repression and trauma. Finney was an odd fit to play such a man, 'a double first-class wimp' to his wife (Greta Scacchi) and yet 'Hitler of the lower fifth' to the children.

Ronald Harwood's script explains this inherent contradiction. Crocker-Harris retains perfect discipline in his classes, a fact acknowledged by his replacement teacher (Julian Sands) at his final lesson. But when the headmaster tells him that he will not get a full pension, even though an exception was made for another teacher, he is too dejected to reply. Similarly, when his wife tells him that Taplow's gift was merely a ploy to gain the promotion the boy craves, Crocker-Harris just disappears, tail 'tween legs. All very unlike Finney, one can guess ...

Perhaps Anthony Hopkins, Derek Jacobi, Corin Redgrave or Ian Holm would have been more obvious choices for the part, yet Figgis wanted Finney. When the film came out some felt that Finney, whose larger-than-life persona was so different from Crocker-Harris, was miscast. To which one should reply that perhaps Finney *was*, technically, miscast. Yet sometimes casting against type can be rewarding. One thinks of Robert Mitchum as the shy, subdued school-master in *Ryan's Daughter*. Finney's portrayal of Crocker-Harris is interesting because it's a surprise.

Figgis tells how he became interested in a modern version, 'I was in LA getting ready to go to dinner when the old black and white version of *The Browning Version* came on TV. I wanted to do a remake and I always wanted Finney right from the beginning.' (He had originally wanted Finney to play – yes – the part of Finney in his film, *Stormy Monday*, but Sting played him instead.) 'Ridley Scott owned the rights to the remake but he immediately offered it to me.'[7]

Figgis believes that Crocker-Harris's character was misunderstood. 'In the early days he might have even been seen as a hip sort of guy,' he said. But with time he changed. Crocker-Harris may be a sad sack but he's all too believable. Perhaps only British audiences, and especially those who have endured the luxurious, lonely lock-up of a boarding school, can understand the stifling atmosphere. You feel that the staff only exists in the confines of the school and that long-serving teachers can be emotionally stunted.

On the first day of filming in the early summer of 1993 (Bryanston and Sherborne schools in Dorset were used) Figgis saw Finney standing by with a big marker pen, seemingly amending the script. Figgis, curious to see if Finney was changing Harwood's words, approached him. Finney told him that the lines were 'perfect'. He was just deleting some stage directions, psychological notes and prompts – presumably along the lines of 'he gazes wistfully into the distance' – that peppered the script. He just wanted the dialogue straight – no nonsense. Figgis noted Finney's shrewd instincts. At one point the headmaster (Michael Gambon) tells Crocker-Harris to make his farewell speech at the beginning, rather than go last as tradition dictates, because the other departing master is 'adored' by the boys. Figgis suggested that perhaps Finney should cry. Finney, probably correctly, replied that he would be crying when Taplow gives him the book. Was it wise to bring on the tears too soon?

The 'Crock's' old-fashioned classes are shown up by the younger, trendy chemistry teacher Frank Hunter (Matthew Modine from *Orphans*) who is having an affair with Crock's wife. Figgis handles the story movingly. Pained resignation, humiliation and an aura of quiet defeat do not come easily to Finney; they are not natural components of his personality, but he projects a melancholy that makes him credible. Above all, it is his fundamental stillness, his titanic, immovable presence, which sustains interest. Finney's emotions spring loose in the final class when he injects some passion into the proceedings. By the time Taplow hands him the book, the audience starts to empathise with him.

Harwood's script adds some unusual touches, including bullied boys extracting revenge on an older pupil. It also injects some four-letter words to make it all more modern. Hitler is substituted for Himmler in the new version, presumably allowing for modern audiences' unfamiliarity with Nazi tyrants. It keeps the original ending and here, one had to say, the address at the final assembly does strain credibility. It seems unthinkable that a schoolmaster, even one stricken by guilt, would readily admit so many failings. 'I have deserved the epithet Hitler of the lower fifth,' says Finney as Crocker-Harris. 'I have degraded the noblest calling a man can follow. I hope you can find it in your heart to forgive me for having let you down.'

It all sounds rather like a post-torture confession at some state-sponsored show trial. Somehow one feels that the 'Crock', even when the floodgates have opened, would never go this far. It's also difficult to believe that such a statement would win a standing ovation from the boys. What, after all, are they applauding? Crocker-Harris's admission of failure? This seems like an odd reaction. It's as though they are agreeing that he *is* useless.

Figgis sometimes lingers too long over certain scenes – the way Crocker-Harris stares at the book from Taplow (a winning performance from Ben Silverstone) has a touch of melodrama to it. Yet, on the whole, it's a thoughtful, provocative remake of a moving story, of how transformative little acts of kindness can be. And Finney's unusual casting has its rewards. Perhaps the only comment would be that, rather like Burton's failed, seedy university lecturer in *Who's Afraid of Virginia Woolf?* it's difficult to see Finney as a failed anything.

Such an unorthodox choice of lead was bound to draw strong reactions. And Figgis, although he enjoyed the shooting, recalled an unpleasant fallout involving producer Ridley Scott:

I delivered the film. I knew that Ridley [Scott] didn't like the film, and he made no bones about it. He didn't like Finney's performance. He didn't like the way I directed it … I ended up back in LA with the film because I had to show it to the studio. Sherry Lansing from Paramount pictures was there, and Ridley was there, along with some others … I was being somewhat shocked by what appeared to be their favourable reaction. I remember catching the word 'Oscar' and Sherry saying, 'it's just the most beautiful film. Albert Finney is going to get an Oscar.' It was kind of an odd situation because I knew Ridley really didn't like the film and suddenly Sherry loved the film. She was the head of Paramount.[8]

As it turned out, there were no Oscars or raspberries. The critics disagreed. Here was Quentin Curtis in the *Independent*:

If, like me, you admire Rattigan's work, watching the film will be like seeing a close friend being mugged. Ronald Harwood has adapted the play with distressing crudity. I also feel Finney is badly miscast. Think of Finney – of his fondness for wine, women and racehorses and you think of a *bon viveur* rather than a corpse. When we watch him overseeing his class he does not have a schoolmaster's rigidity, borne of study and supervising, but the coiled stillness of a heroic actor. He is still outstandingly attractive, a magnificent physical specimen – a real problem since Crocker-Harris is supposed to have failed his wife in physical love.

Doubtless, Finney would have smiled at that. As for the miscasting, one can only repeat the original point about interesting miscasting and downright stupid miscasting.

Caryn James in the *New York Times*, while praising Finney, thought the subject should have been consigned to the past:

Albert Finney, who has given some over-the-top performances in his time, is wonderfully restrained here, terse and not afraid to be unlikeable … [but] … it carries the unmistakable whiff of a musty tale dragged into the nineties, where it seems conspicuously out of place.

John Walker called it 'a remake of no particular distinction or point, cut adrift from its original period setting and losing in credibility because of it.' Terrence Rafferty in *The New Yorker*, on the other hand, liked it: 'Strong and affecting – perhaps because neither the director nor the star has worked with this sort of material before.'

Figgis loved working with Finney and puts him at the top of the pantheon of British acting greats. Like many before and since, he noted Finney's generosity as well as his fondness for fine food, wine, Cuban cigars and good company. He was staying at a large manor house in Dorset. 'We had an idyllic summer making the film in the most beautiful part of England,' recalls Figgis. 'Every evening cast and crew would have magnificent dinners. On the last night everyone was treated to a jug of wine at Albert's expense.'

The director recalls an interesting conversation with Finney about Figgis's upcoming film, *Leaving Las Vegas*, then at planning stage. Figgis repeated what was presumably a bit of a joke by Nicolas Cage, who said, since he was to play a severe alcoholic, he may as well stay drunk throughout filming. Finney reacted with consternation, reminding him that this would spell disaster. He told him it was impossible for an actor to play a drunk if he really was sloshed.

Figgis also revealed that, on the final day of shooting, Finney said he had rarely enjoyed making a film so much but that he 'probably wouldn't see it', which says a lot about Finney's detached attitude towards his work. He was always the perfect professional but, once completed, it was on to something else. Another bonus for Finney was that his son, Simon, then 35, was assistant cameraman on the film. 'Get me out of focus and I'll cut you out of my will,' he'd quip to Simon.

Some critics pondered the reasons for reworking a classic. Perhaps Mike Figgis should have the final word, 'The play is done all the time but who under the age of 30 knows of it? Doing it in period would have no bearing on younger audiences and I wanted to attract them.'

Soon after *The Browning Version* wrapped, Finney found himself in another unlikely part. He was playing a character called Alfie, but this was as far removed from Michael Caine's Alfie as could be imagined. Virgin territory … yes, that's right, from a guy like Finney, a veritable 'lifer' as far as women are concerned!

A WALK ON THE WILDE SIDE

I was so touched by his childlike fascination for the machine that I bought it from the museum and gave it to him as a present at the end of shooting.

Suri Krishnamma.

Finney as a gay man may seem about as likely as Jack Nicholson playing Quentin Crisp. *A Man of No Importance* contains Finney's most complete transformation in films.

Dublin, 1963. The Profumo scandal is breaking; Kennedy is in the White House; and Finney is Alfie Byrne, a closet gay bus conductor and Oscar Wilde aficionado who delights in singsongs on the bus and staging his idol's plays with local amateur actors. Meanwhile, he lusts after a handsome bus driver (Rufus Sewell). Barry Devlin's screenplay even asks us to believe that his character is a virgin. But, somehow, thanks to the skill of Finney and director Suri Krishnamma, it all seems credible.

Alfie lives with his sister Lily (Brenda Fricker) over the butcher's shop run by Carney (Michael Gambon), who seems surprised that Alfie had never married. Has he, or more to the point perhaps, his sister, never guessed Alfie's true inclinations?

Krishnamma answered my question:

So as far as Lily is concerned, her brother is simply a little behind everyone else. I don't think it could occur to her that he is gay, given the context of the time and that homosexuality was illegal. It just wouldn't be something she would think about, until of course it becomes evident in his behaviour and when the wider society around him gets to know.[1]

Lily even tries to set him up on a date with the beautiful young Adele (Tara Fitzgerald) who Alfie casts in his local production of *Salome*, a staging that arouses suspicions among locals on account of its blasphemy. We quickly learn, however, that Alfie's heart is not with Tara. It lies with his bus driver, Robbie, whom Alfie calls 'Bosie' (Wilde's nickname for his lover). But still no one suspects that Alfie – who quietly kisses a photograph of Robbie he keeps at home – is sublimating his true passion.

Finney's Alfie is a revelation. This is a pudgy Finney with a red, cuddly cardigan, delicately placed spectacles, boyishly pink cheeks and a lyrical Dublin accent. Alfie, as played by Finney, is not effeminate as such, but rather a gentle tenderfoot. An air of bemusement surrounds everything he does. Even playing snooker with a few young lads (including Jonathan Rhys Meyers in his first role) seems audacious. Alfie is an innocent in his fifties who believes that Adele must be ill when he hears lovemaking coming from her bedroom.

Yet Alfie, a stranger to the joys of the flesh, is a bit incorrigible in other ways, what with his tendency to stage Wilde plays. In the end he succumbs to temptation and seeks out 'a cuddle' in a pub. Predictably, he is mugged. It looks like he is finished. Yet somehow we know that it will work out, notwithstanding his tarnished reputation, because Alfie's such a good-natured soul, and so kind to cash-strapped passengers on his bus. So his friends (including the wonderful David Kelly) will stand by him in spite of his wanderings.

Finney's achievement is massive. He is a totally different creature from Arthur Seaton. Easy to do, you may say, considering it was thirty-four years earlier. But I talk not of the passage of time. Seaton had a hard face whereas Alfie is one big softie.

Krishnamma offered some perceptive comments on Finney. He had originally considered a younger actor, David Thewlis, then a rising star, to play Alfie:

> But when Albert was suggested it occurred to me that an older man might be more interesting and actually more appropriate for the role of someone who had spent his life struggling with his sexuality, bereft of any sexual experience himself. An older man might add a further dimension to a character wrestling with the distinct difficulties of repressed sexual desire that play out against the backdrop of sixties Dublin, where homosexuality was, of course, illegal.

Just like *The Browning Version*, but for entirely different reasons, Finney was an unusual choice to play the lead. Finney has cultivated the off-screen image of being a great sensualist. And Alfie is not only gay but, and this is perhaps a key point, his hands are 'innocent of affection', as he tells his sister.

Krishnamma, however, was not particularly aware of casting against type:

I only really see actors in two groups – good actors and bad ones – and a good actor should be capable of performing any role they are physically suited to. I have often cast 'comedy' actors in serious roles, such as Richard Briers in the BBC's *A Respectable Trade* [1997] based on the novel by Philippa Gregory. In that drama, Richard played a dark, vicious and aggressive slave-trader, but was at the time better known for comedy roles. So when Albert was suggested it never occurred to me to consider whether he was capable of playing the part of Alfie Byrne given his towering talent. That said, 'casting against type' can help stretch an actor and encourage him or her to go to places they might be less familiar with. It may help release some hidden energy that has been constrained by stereotypical roles in the past. This approach to casting can extend into cross-gender casting too where new dimensions to characters can sometimes be revealed.

Krishnamma, just 33 at the time and a relative novice, was understandably nervous at the prospect of working with such theatrical giants as Finney and Gambon, as well as Brenda Fricker, who had just won an Oscar for *My Left Foot*. The first time he met Gambon and Finney together was a hilariously bungled encounter:

It was quite a disastrous start to our relationship. I'd already met Albert in London, had instantly fallen in love with him for the role, and then spent an agonising couple of weeks praying that the deal would be done to secure him on the film. That took longer than we'd expected, and the producer [Jonathan Cavendish] was being pushed to the brink by Finney's people, whose unreal-istic expectations simply couldn't be met. On the day the deal was finalised, Jonathan and I were holed up in his office, aware that if we didn't clinch it by the close of play, the production would be shut down and we'd all pack our bags and go home. So securing Finney was the single reason the film, ultimately, got made. So once Michael had agreed to join [as well as Brenda Fricker, Tara Fitzgerald, Rufus Sewell and many other brilliant local Dublin actors] we were flying with a truly great ensemble cast.

The main cast arrived in Dublin and I arranged a dinner with Michael, Albert and Tara in their hotel for that evening. I'd spent the day putting together detailed notes on all their characters. This was my first theatrical feature film and I was nervous as hell, so I wanted to be as fully prepared as possible. I shut myself away in my Dublin apartment, cut off all television and radio contact, and got to work. The hotel was a short walk from where I was staying, so I left for the dinner in good time – or so I'd thought. When I arrived I could see from a distance Albert, Michael and Tara sitting at a table in the corner. I could also see that they were eating. I was confused, and a little disappointed – why would they meet early and then order their meal without me? As I approached I heard Albert say, 'ah … here he is'. 'Am I late?' I said, knowing (or believing) that I was not. 'Only an hour' said Michael, 'but no matter, come and join us'. I looked at them utterly confused. 'But we said 7 p.m.' I said, 'and it's just five to seven now'. 'Five to eight' said Tara. 'The clocks went forward last night'. 'The clocks …' I looked at them in disbelief, reddening with embarrassment. I'd been shut away for the day and had absolutely no idea that the clocks had changed.

After the initial awkwardness, filming went well. Gambon told Krishnamma beforehand that he could say anything he wanted to Finney who always welcomed suggestions. And so indeed it proved, according to the director:

Attitudes often trickle down from the top and spread – and so it was with Albert being at the top of the acting tree. His warm reception to me as a fledgling director, quiet understanding and respect of my method and unobtrusive approach was evident in the way that he behaved on set and, scene by scene, building his character. He was as generous to me as I could have expected and set the tone for all others to follow.

Krishnamma remembers Finney's wide-eyed appreciation of little things:

Finney is a sensitive, shy, unassuming man in real life. He has a great curiosity and fascination for all new experiences – something that was much on display during the shooting. I remember how he took to his little ticket machine that had to be draped around his neck while he rode the bus and recited Oscar Wilde. He was enchanted by its simple functions, his eyes widening as he turned the handle and issued the tickets. I was so touched by his childlike fascination for the machine that I bought it from the museum and gave it to him as a present at the end of shooting.

For Gambon, the Irish accent was second nature; he soon slipped back into the Dublin brogue of his childhood. Krishnamma recalls that for Finney the process was more intense:

We employed a voice coach for him to work with along with other actors such as Rufus Sewell and Tara Fitzgerald. It's a big task to take on board a 'foreign' accent as well as deliver a memorable performance – because to do the latter you have to work, at times, unconsciously, so being conscious of the accent can be a barrier. This is one reason, I suspect, why actors such as

Daniel Day-Lewis fully immerse themselves in their roles – speaking in the accent of their characters at all times during pre-production and shooting – so that the accent becomes second nature. Albert's 'method' is different. He wears the evidence of the character like familiar clothes, but never fully 'becomes' the person he is playing. So, beat-by-beat, the technical requirements of the character (such as accent) are likely to be more conscious to him. From my point of view, the performance must come first – and if at times the accent meanders (which, to native Dublin ears, it perhaps does) that is less important. Much more alarming would be if Albert's performance meandered – and that it most definitely does not.

A Man of No Importance received international distribution, albeit only a limited run. But in the end it made a modest profit. Expectations that it would break through and become a kind of *succès d'estime* were perhaps unrealistic. *Screen International* even suggested on its front page that Finney may get an Oscar nod. Yet it didn't happen. Such a film needed publicity. This, Krishnamma records, was always a contentious issue for Finney:

Albert has in his contracts the option not to do publicity if he so chooses. To this day, he remains stubbornly resistant, but the pressure on me from the distributors to convince him otherwise became too great, and so I took the unusual step of calling him myself to ask if he would change his mind. He gave me short shrift on the phone and followed this up with a blunt and to the point letter. He made it clear that I should not do the dirty work of others – that it was their job to publicise the film and not ours. In many ways, he was right – but in the harsh reality of a market where such 'art-house' films struggle to be seen, every little helps. Generous as always, Albert, of course, forgave me and understood – but I do regret being used in this way and have never repeated that mistake since.

Krishnamma said that Finney was easily the most popular man on the set:

The women on the crew of *A Man of No Importance*, led by a brilliant female first assistant director, had a vote for the sexiest man on the unit. I was hugely disappointed to discover I came second, but rather flattered when I learnt that I'd only been beaten by Albert himself!

Finney was always loved by actors and crew alike – no tantrums, no side and having a healthy interest in the people around him. Yet he could withdraw if he had to play an emotional scene. 'Please advise people on the set that I won't be particularly social today. I need to be in my own private thoughts,' he would sometimes tell a director. 'You may have a pause in the shooting but you must guard your emotions carefully,' he once told Melvyn Bragg.

On the whole, reviews were quite flattering for *A Man of No Importance*, especially for Finney's performance. Caryn James reflected in the *New York Times*:

> At certain points throughout the film, though, Alfie is clobbered by reality. When he goes to Adele's rooming house and hears moaning coming from behind her door, only a naif like Alfie would think she was ill. And, when he opens the door, only an actor as profoundly talented as Albert Finney could register all the emotions behind his horrified face.

And Michael Wilmington in the *Chicago Tribune* caught the full scale of Finney's transformation:

> Albert Finney pulls off a moving virtuoso acting feat. This charismatic, ultra-masculine actor, with his cool eyes and his rasping voice (as harsh and rich as a slab of beef), transforms himself into his seeming opposite, a gentle, effeminate, ageing Irish bus conductor.

John Walker, however, was unimpressed, calling it 'a pointless and virtually witless exercise that resembles a timidly gay reworking of a third rate Ealing comedy. It is heavy handed whimsy weighed down by some broad acting.'

Most people disagreed with Walker. I would rather sit through several viewings of *A Man of No Importance* than most Hollywood blockbusters. The film was subsequently made into a Broadway musical and Krishnamma said he was flattered that a movie he had directed was 'elevated to such theatrical heights'.

After the film's release an American journalist asked if Finney would put a rainbow flag on his car's bumper. 'I said I don't "do" bumper stickers, but if I did, I'd be pleased to use that one. After all, everyone's included in the rainbow, aren't they?' he replied.

The mid-nineties was a good period for Finney. Actors come into their own once they hit their late 50s. And that was especially true for Finney. He had lost the handsome 'beefcake' look that made women swoon. But he was now a versatile character star capable of conveying everything from toughness to vulnerability. Apart from a smoker's pouch under the eyes, he had aged well, far better than the likes of O'Toole or Harris. He was still handsome, almost leonine, with his full head of ginger hair and pinkish face. But it was the rugged good looks of a labourer or seaman. There was a touch of salt and spit about him. It was small wonder that he was still in demand for earthy character roles or that associates, once they had worked with Finney, felt that any other actor was second best.

The Run of the Country, adapted by Shane Connaughton from his novel and directed by Peter Yates, could be seen as a sort of follow-up to Finney's *The Playboys*. Not only is *Run of the Country* set in the same place as *The Playboys* but Connaughton also wrote the screenplay for both films.

Finney stars as a bored widower policeman in a small County Cavan village battling to save his relationship with his teenage son, Danny (Matt Keeslar), who blames him for his mother's death after a domestic quarrel. Though a Catholic, Danny falls for a well-heeled Protestant girl, Annagh Lee (Victoria Smurfit), who lives north of the border. The relationship ends painfully after she miscarries and father and son are eventually reconciled. The film is best described as a coming-of-age tale.

'Mr Finney fixes his crusty, demanding, sometimes mawkishly emotional character right on the line between lovable and impossible,' said Stephen Holden in the *New York Times*. Roger Ebert said he thought Yates had not really decided whether he was making a tragedy or a comedy:

> As written by Shane Connaughton and played by Finney, he seems made out of two different versions of the same character. At times, he comes across as a hard-drinking bully, mean-spirited and closed-minded. At other times, he relaxes into the role of a sunny philosopher. We never know where we stand with him, and I'm not sure that's the film's intention.

Peter Travers in *Rolling Stone* thought that 'the formidable Finney, one of the finest actors on the planet, is wasted in a role that calls for him to bluster and break down at predictable intervals'. Michael Wilmington, *Chicago Tribune* film critic, noted, 'Finney's outstanding trait as an actor is the solidity he gives his parts – his growly voice and bulldog chin pulling the audience one way, his yearning eyes pulling them another'.

As Finney neared 60, there was no sign of him slowing down. He was still much in demand. Yet Finney's own statements – his *bon vivant* act and self-deprecating humour – sometimes deceived people into thinking he was lazier than he was. Filmmaker Robert Gardner recalled a meeting with Finney in early 1995, at the behest of producer Michael Fitzgerald, who was thinking of filming John Coetzee's novel *Waiting for the Barbarians*. Gardner was casting the central character of an unnamed magistrate of a small colonial town that borders an empire.

Gardner recorded that he thought Finney would be unsuitable:

My feeling about Albert Finney was that he was not, contrary to Michael Fitzgerald's view, all that interested. I felt he was wary of an inexperienced director and, possibly, of a production more or less in the wild, away from comforts he seems to require as he rapidly goes to seed. Albert is by now pretty soft, and more than a little boozy. As seen in his recent performances, he is even more flamboyant. So it would have been problematic had he wanted the part. I'm not sure he could have been contained in the way he would have to have been to be a reasonable magistrate.[2]

Yet Finney was about to enter a golden period, courtesy of a droll deathbed drama from Dennis Potter. That year, 1995, saw him spend twenty weeks in Colombia filming a Joseph Conrad novel.[3] Eat your heart out, Mr Gardner.

HAVING A FEELD DAY

It's important to live as you want to. Which I have, you know.

Albert Finney.

Dennis Potter's terminal illness in the spring of 1994 not only highlighted his work but brought one of television's most memorable and moving interviews. The 59-year-old writer, suffering chronic pain from pancreatic cancer and sipping a cocktail of morphine and champagne, reviewed his work and spoke frankly about his diagnosis to Melvyn Bragg.

Whatever view you took of Potter's private (well, perhaps not so private!) views – his disdain for creeping commercialism in film and society, his hatred of Rupert Murdoch (he took pleasure in calling his tumour 'Rupert' and said he'd like to 'kill the bugger') – there was no denying the stoicism, painstaking self-appraisal and quiet dignity with which he faced his end. Then there was Potter's reference to the 'whitest, frothiest, blossimest blossom', a phrase which stuck as representing the clarity with which the condemned man surveys the world.

Potter's illness, tragic though it was, also gave the playwright a reservoir of goodwill, as he must have been only too aware. Potter told Bragg that he was working on two separate stories. One was about the last days of a dying writer who believes that events in the real world are mirroring his final work. The other was a kind of fantasy, but one floated more often in the twenty years or more since Potter's passing, that a corpse could be subject to cryopreservation and then somehow resuscitated in the future once a cure has been found for whatever ailment proved fatal. The two screenplays were later christened *Karaoke* and *Cold Lazarus*. And, said Potter, in that gentle, charming bucolic burr, he felt he would 'go out with a fitting memorial' if the BBC and Channel 4 would agree to co-produce the two works. Such a proposal from a dying man could hardly be refused. One feels that, even if Murdoch had been in the studio alongside Potter, he would have been forced to, if not offer his own disembodied head on a platter, then at least run a respectful interview in the *Sun*, the newspaper Potter so abhorred. It was impossible to refuse and Potter knew it.

Two years later and Bragg was again interviewing another chain-smoking 59-year-old. But this time it was Albert Finney who had agreed to be filmed over lunch at London's L'Escargot restaurant, ostensibly to discuss *Cold Lazarus* and his role as Daniel Feeld in *Karaoke*.

Potter is not to everyone's taste and I was surprised when surveying people that *Karaoke* seemed to have slipped through the radar. The four-part series has all the usual Potter touches, nostalgia for the past, a lead character with a penchant for singing and the sense of broken, discarded memories returning to haunt you. Daniel Feeld, the writer in *Karaoke*, is manifestly not Potter, and Finney made it clear he was not out to impersonate him. Yet there were certain similarities, not least the writer's determination to complete his final work before he dies. And Roy Hudd, playing Feeld's literary agent, was unnerved to find that Finney, on their first meeting, was wearing an identical corduroy suite to the one favoured by Potter – whether intentional or not is unclear.

Finney's character, Daniel Feeld, is drinking heavily, even straying into dipso territory. He becomes convinced that conversations and events around him are duplicating the screenplay he's working on, that his words are literally coming to life. Meanwhile, the director of the television play of Feeld's work (Richard E. Grant) has problems of his own. Yet it's Feeld's drama, the story of his last few days as he faces up to his fatal tumour, which grips you. The fallen writer rediscovers a meaning to his final act as he stumbles upon a sadistic club owner, Arthur 'Pig' Mailion (Hywel Bennett) who has 'glassed' the mother of a karaoke dancer, Sandra, (Saffron Burrows), leaving her scarred for life. If all this sounds grim, it's leavened by healthy doses of graveyard humour and the sheer force of Finney's personality. Whether running around the rain-swept seedy streets of Soho, smoking slyly in his hospital bed, or imitating Bing Crosby in the final karaoke song, Feeld, alias Finney, is the whole show.

Also in the mix were autobiographical elements common to Feeld and Potter, in particular an aversion to anti-smoking fanatics and 'moderate' drinking campaigners (something that Finney, doubtless, would have shared). It's easy to see why Finney was drawn to Feeld. And there's the voice of Potter speaking through Finney's Feeld, 'I'm not the sort of writer who thinks that his words are some sort of holy tablet of stone!' Not arf! It was Potter's way of saying goodbye.

This was a Finney who makes even Maurice Allington look healthy – pushing 60, heavyweight, blustery, irritable, pugnacious, chain-smoking and sweating as he fights to get his affairs in order and disentangle the mess surrounding Burrows. The subplots in *Karaoke* – the likeable but loopy agent forever mouthing spoonerisms, the cheating television director, the emergence of the still delectable Julie Christie, the ubiquitous silly Japanese tourists in the karaoke club – all pale beside the main event, which is Feeld's, or should we say Finney's, or Potter's, story. Getting confused?

Finney projects considerable charm as Feeld, guffawing with laughter in between stabbing stomach pain as he is offered a hand job by Sandra, the cockney girl who evokes passions he had long since suppressed (the script makes clear that Feeld's last love was forty years earlier). *Karaoke* was also in the capable hands of Renny Rye, who was familiar to Potter territory having directed *Lipstick on my Collar*.

As ever, Finney was a delightful colleague. Roy Hudd recalls:

They always say the bigger the star, the nicer they are. I think so too but perhaps I've just been lucky. Albert was a diamond: a superlative pro and a funny, generous and thoughtful workmate. His knowledge of the technicalities of filming was amazing and he certainly helped me to understand all the bits I needed to know … I love to act with people who give you the truth. If they can make you believe the situation, and that they, as characters, are real, the work is an absolute joy. I immediately think of Sue Nicholls, Albert Finney, Stephen Lord, Neil Dudgeon, Billy Dainty and Jack Tripp.[1]

Ironically, although in *Karaoke* it was Daniel Feeld (Finney) who couldn't drive and he is chauffeured by his agent (Hudd), the reality was just the opposite. Hudd could not drive. This presented a problem because one scene called for Hudd's character to take Feeld home in a Jag. Hudd recalls Finney's dexterity: '"You just steer the thing," he said. "I'll handle the rest." I did and he did. With his right foot across mine, he accelerated, braked and changed gear while doing all his dialogue – he could have been doing a tap routine with his left foot!'

Hudd cites another example of Finney's generosity. During filming Hudd heard that a burglar had broken into his wife's home and stolen her jewellery. When he returned home that evening he found that his wife had received flowers from Finney, accompanied by a message – 'nil desperandum – love Albert'. Finney had never met Roy's wife. It was just a typical spontaneous gesture.

It was a strange fusion of Potter, Feeld and Finney on Melvyn Bragg's *The South Bank Show*. The programme offers us a fascinating insight not so much into Potter as into Finney. Firstly, as often repeated by Finney, he 'likes to have lunch', the sentence uttered with some relish. Finney and Bragg banter about booze. Bragg tells Finney he has just survived sixty-six 'dry' days. Finney eyes him suspiciously. The actor has no such compunction, ordering a Negroni cocktail and a French white wine while settling down to enjoy what he calls, with a touch of irony, 'a light lunch' of carpaccio and then braised lamb shank. By the end of the meal Finney has moved on to red wine, calvados and coffee and is happily blowing cigar smoke in Bragg's face.

'When I'm working on a film then during lunch I don't drink – and I just have cheese and crackers,' Finney tells Bragg as if it were a surprise to himself. 'Half of the time I sleep [at lunchtime] … I believe in the sensuality of the ambience of food and drink. I love that, not having to work in the afternoon.'

Asked about *Karaoke* and his approach to the part, Finney stressed that he was not trying to imitate Potter. 'We were not saying that Daniel Feeld is Dennis Potter. I never met Dennis and I'm not trying to impersonate him and neither am I trying to imitate his Ross and Wye burr.' Rather, said Finney, playing a part and studying a script is a bit like being a detective:

> You're looking for clues as to why he's doing this and that. When you're film-ing you try to get the sense of it being freshly minted, the spontaneity. It's a bit like playing jazz. There's no point in saying I glanced at him last time so I must do it the same way again. When you're recording it, immortalising it, it's a case of you've done the homework, you just go out and do it.

Bragg managed to coax some private revelations from Finney. 'Travelling and horses are very important to me,' he told Bragg:

> In the horse trade I meet people from a totally different world. I think that's invaluable. Life is more important than art. I like talking to my butcher, baker and candle-stick maker. I don't know where my life is going to lead. I reserve the right to make my own road. And hopefully I have some time left.

When Bragg mentions that there's a lot of drinking in *Karaoke*, Finney wryly remarks, referring to himself, 'there's a lot of drinking on *The South Bank Show*'.

Karaoke went down well with the critics and even the carpers liked Finney's roustabout performance. 'This is a television event like no other. And to make it even more so, both films [*Karaoke* and *Cold Lazarus*] star Albert Finney, one of the greatest actors on the planet,' noted *The Washington Post*:

> The riddles are fascinating and you're kept deliriously off-balance for most of the film. Even if you didn't buy a word of it otherwise, Finney's perfor-mance would win you over – he's roguish, robust, ferocious, desperate, a magnificent crank railing against evils and conspiracies that may be actual or fanciful. In the last analysis, which he himself is facing – what's the dif-ference? … The high point is when Finney himself does a karaoke number

in the final hour, a tune with heavenly resonance for even casual fans of Potter's. Finney, with an assist from Bing Crosby, makes this a triumphant, exhilarating, mystical moment.

We should add that Bragg's film, which has shots of Finney and director Renny Rye in the recording studio, show Finney having a rip-roaring time as Feeld. When Finney sees himself doing the Bing Crosby number, his eyes mist over. The only brickbats were reserved for the other subplots, notably 'Roy Hudd's spoonerizing literary agent, a running gag in search of a decent punchline,' according to Stuart Jefferies in *The Guardian*.

In *Cold Lazarus*, altogether a more sombre affair, a Potterish dystopian vision of a future commercial hell, Finney only appears either in flashback or as a disembodied head. Hence, it's rather out of our remit.

Finney's performances in *Karaoke* and *A Man of No Importance*, enjoyable though they were, were not especially subtle. Rather, they were full-on, red-blooded assaults on convention in which Finney appeared to be having as much fun as his audience. This brought the occasional accusation that he was overacting; a little broad in his impersonations. In *Karaoke*, Finney had little choice but to take him where the script led him; Daniel Feeld was never going to be less than exuberant.

Finney's style of acting *is* starry. He likes to let rip and show the full range of his talent. Many times, even in his sixties, Finney said that he couldn't wait to tackle a certain part. His enthusiasm and professionalism are undiminished. He loves acting and isn't too self-effacing. He likes to make an entrance. It's a grand flourish that is increasingly unfashionable in an era of mumbling soap actors, often without theatrical training, who probably couldn't project beyond the fourth row of a theatre.

The director John Dove categorises actors as either red or white wines. Michael Gambon and Finney, according to Dove, are full-blooded reds, while Derek Jacobi and Nigel Hawthorne are examples of vintage whites. To the list of reds – but this is a far from complete list, merely some notable examples – we could add O'Toole, Harris, Burton, Nicol Williamson and Trevor Howard. To the whites we could add Tom Courtenay and Ian McKellen. Anthony Hopkins, for all his relish in playing Hannibal Lecter, is not naturally extroverted or full-bloodied. He is perhaps a white? Or maybe, taking this a little further, a rosé? Another rosé could be John Hurt and, I think, Ian Hendry, the subject of a previous biography. These are two actors whose brilliance is sometimes unobtrusive. This is a superficial summary of some great actors but perhaps not entirely unsubstantiated. (And I have it on good authority that Finney's favourite wine is indeed red – an Italian wine called Barolo!)

Not only is Finney's style of acting a definite 'red' but his voice – commanding, rich and fruity, at times even extravagant in such a way that could lead to the accusation that he is overacting, even when he isn't – is that of a smoker. We would not wish to recommend the benefits of smoking but Michael Gambon, another transgressor, believes that the weed lends the actor's voice an extra dimension. 'I think that [smoking] helps, I think it makes the voice. Olivier smoked quite heavily. And Gielgud always had a fag in his mouth. Alan Howard is a chimney. Ron Pickup, my good friend Ron Pickup, is a chimney,' said Gambon.

The new naturalistic style of acting perhaps lends itself more to white than red. You are not supposed to make an entrance but, rather, sink unobtrusively into character. You must conform to the director's vision. Richard Harris, on a chat show in 1988, said he believed we were suffering from 'a plague of good taste', by which he meant that many modern actors were too bland. He cited an incident from an Olivier play in which Sir Laurence swung from a rope on to the stage, making an entrance that made the audience gasp (probably *Coriolanus*). The new breed of actors struck him as 'bank managers'. One suspects that Burton and O'Toole would have agreed. And almost certainly Finney.

Finney always said that he didn't want to become a prisoner of a lifestyle which forced him to run faster and faster simply to pay the bills. As Finney turned 60, and his earning power had peaked, his life had become a little quieter. He was still living in Chelsea but not quite in the grand style of old when a plate of venison would appear on command. 'I used to have a couple living in, and there was a button under the carpet you could press with your foot so they'd come in with the next course. Everybody thought it was a miracle.'

He also told a reporter that he had once had a Rolls-Royce Phantom which could take five in the back – 'great for going to the races,' he added. But Finney couldn't get insurance to drive it, had to have a chauffeur, and sold it. Then he bought a Mercedes convertible. But he did only 3,000 miles a year, so he sold that too. By 1996, Finney, rather like Daniel Feeld, was without a car and dependent on taxis:

> As this wonderful Jewish fellow once told me in New York, 'If it flies, floats or fucks, rent it.' He was right. He was against buying planes, boats and all those silly things people do with their money. So here I am – servantless and carless, but not horseless … It's important to live as you want to. Which I have, you know.[2]

A chauffeured limousine also came in handy when Finney visited his elderly mother in Davyhulme. By then Alice was living with her daughter, Marie.

Apparently Finney was revered by all the chauffeurs in his employ because he never put on 'airs and graces' and he was always a generous tipper. Finney continued visiting his mother regularly right up until her death.

Carless and servantless perhaps, yet Finney, more importantly, was not womanless. By now he was living, since 1989, with travel agent Pene Delmage, eighteen years his junior. They would eventually marry in 2006 and she would nurse him through a period of ill health. The late Lynda Bellingham described Pene as (like Finney) 'just gorgeous' (Pene and Lynda shared a mutual friend, the late Sally Bulloch, the entertainments manager and lavish hostess of the Athenaeum Hotel). Julia Goodman was another admirer of Pene, although she only met her once, at her Uncle Gordon Smyth's 70th birthday in 1996 in a country hotel. 'I liked her a lot. She was very warm, down to earth, funny, rather diffident and shy,' Julia recalled.

Finney continued to charm the ladies, but that was it. 'I'm exceptionally happy with Pene,' Finney said in 2003. 'I'm a born flirt and that will never stop but I would take things no further. I'm loyal and content.' Womanising may have been behind him by the nineties but the love of horses and travel remained. He believed that he 'travelled well'. He was happy to get a free plane ticket, take off somewhere new for a few weeks and immerse himself in different, albeit temporary, surroundings.

Washington Square, filmed in Baltimore in 1996 by Agnieszka Holland, was a world away from *Karaoke*. A screen version of Henry James's novella of the same name about a plain, rich girl courted by a handsome fortune hunter in New York in the 1890s, it had been previously filmed in 1949 with Montgomery Clift and Olivia de Havilland as *The Heiress*. Holland thought *The Heiress* was 'a beautiful film', but she 'found it different from Jamesian philosophy; it was very much a revenge story, whereas I was more interested in identity issues'.[3]

Finney was the prickly Dr Sloper who had nursed a grudge against his daughter, Catherine, ever since his wife died during childbirth. The novel seemed to indicate that the doctor, while aware of his daughter's shortcomings, her lack of good looks and charm, had a residue of affection for her. In the film he seems to have little or no time for his daughter at all, regarding her clumsy affections as irritating. Dr Sloper, as played by Finney, views her with a condescending sneer throughout. 'I never thought of her as delightful and charming,' he says of her at one point. He dismisses her suitor, Maurice Townsend (Ben Chaplin), as a calculating mercenary. 'He's altogether too familiar, too self-assured,' he says of him. He's convinced that Townsend is just after her money. 'He thinks she has 80,000 dollars a year'. The book, although retaining the same themes, is a little vaguer about Townsend's motives and marginally more sympathetic towards Sloper.

Dr Sloper is a control freak and distinctly cool to everyone around him. Although he is vindicated, in the sense that Townsend turns out to be every bit as mercenary as he predicted, he evokes little sympathy. 'She [Catherine] didn't fulfill his expectations and he [the doctor] loved himself too much to love somebody so imperfect,' said Holland. Chaplin does a good job as Townsend and Jennifer Jason Leigh conveys the heroine's awkwardness and diffidence.

Holland loved working with Maggie Smith, playing Catherine's meddling aunt, Lavinia, in their second film together. (They had previously teamed up on *The Secret Garden*.) Smith would advise the younger actresses on how to wear their corsets. She found Finney not so involved in collaborating with the younger actors but remembers him as 'a fine actor'. She also recalls that he enjoyed exploring Baltimore. Holland related how Jennifer Jason Leigh had read the entire works of Henry James in critical editions and several other books about the period, 'Her knowledge was even greater than mine!'

Washington Square is delightfully quaint and visually pleasing, but doesn't quite gel as a whole. Somehow the characterisations are a little forced and starchy. The finest touches are the period feel and the little clues sprinkled throughout – for example, when Townsend surreptitiously opens a silver cigarette case or seems overcome by Dr Sloper's lavish home. Jamesian fans may take note that Holland believed that Townsend was not just motivated by money, although he craved the good life, but 'he loved also the image of himself fighting over the woman with somebody like Dr Sloper. When Catherine decided to leave her father (and his money) – Maurice lost his interest in her. She ceased to be the object of desire'.

Washington Square failed at the box office. Holland believes that Disney simply didn't know how to market it, 'You also need some momentum. Sometimes more complex period movies can find a larger audience. But frankly, one doesn't know how to make a successful movie. It's better just to try to make the good one.'

John Walker found the film 'a clumsily routine adaptation, with generally unconvincing performances, and given a feminist slant that confuses the point of James's world'. Michael Coveney, in his biography of Maggie Smith, thought that Finney 'didn't really seem austere or frightening enough in the role, his out-bursts sounding like those of someone in a bad temper after too good a lunch'. Janet Maslin, by contrast, praised Finney for his 'caustic authority' as the father.

By 1996, the year of his sixtieth birthday, Finney had not trod the boards for four years. By his standards that was a long time. His next production was to be his last stage hurrah. But, in the best traditions of show business, he was to go out on top.

ART AND MARRIAGE

He's not tormented in real life. He's a tremendous lover of life.
                                        Michael Wearing on Albert Finney.

'Nobody can have expected a play for three male characters by an obscure French Iranian to have run for more than seven years in the West End, getting through twenty-six cast changes,' reflected *The Times*'s theatre critic, Benedict Nightingale. But that was just what had happened to Yasmina Reza's *Art* by 2003 in London.

By then, stars as diverse as Richard Thomas, Nigel Havers, Anthony Valentine, Barry Foster, Patrick Duffy, George Segal, Roger Lloyd-Pack, Ben Cross, Jack Dee and Richard Griffiths had appeared in the play. But the first cast, and by far the most esteemed, teamed Finney with Tom Courtenay and Ken Stott.[1]

I mentioned that a hit play is a fusion of many ingredients but, above all, a feeling that suffuses the theatre. *Orphans* was such a play; *A Chorus of Disapproval* and *Jeffrey Bernard is Unwell* were others. But *Art*, which opened in London in October 1996, of all these, was perhaps the least likely. At first sight it seemed rather lightweight, even frivolous. The plot is deceptively simple. Serge spends a fortune on a blank canvas and is ridiculed by his best friend, Marc, a hearty, extrovert aeronautical engineer whose first reaction is to call it 'shit'. The friendship starts to disentangle before our eyes. And it's only a mediator, Yvan (Stott) who seems capable of resolving their differences.

Reza's play is manifestly *not* about art. It is how a friendship can be tested and even destroyed by an argument. We want to trust a friend's judgement. If we disagree too violently about anything – politics, a film, even a new purchase – then we can feel betrayed. Mundane arguments can even lead us to reappraise the friendship. Reza's later play, *God of Carnage*, although on a different theme, shows how a spat involving two children exposed simmering anger among their parents.

Tom Courtenay and Finney were now firm friends, so their teaming seemed natural. Courtenay had always been, as he cheerfully admitted, 'in awe of Albert', to which, as Courtenay acknowledges, Finney would (jokingly) reply, 'he still is.' Their friendship has flourished despite their differences. Tom is an introvert; Finney, tangibly, is not. Courtenay admits finding Finney's youthful ebullience, and tendency to tease, a bit overwhelming.

By the time they did *Art*, however, Courtenay could stand his ground and bite back. The two men, then both around 60, traded stories about their medical complaints. Courtenay, in particular, seemed health-obsessed, so much so that Finney gave him a medical encyclopedia during the run. Tom would rib Finney about his love of food. Their relationship was playful and 'unluvvie'. The previous year, when Courtenay scored a hit with his off-Broadway production of a one-man show, *Moscow Stations*, Finney had burst into his dressing room with the immortal words – 'You little fucker!' Courtenay knew that this, coming from his friend, was high praise indeed!

Tom, perhaps influenced by Finney, also developed a love for a little flutter on the horses. When, in 2010, he won £626 after placing £20 on Great Endeavour at Cheltenham to win the Byrne Group Plate, his first reaction was, 'wait 'til I tell Albert'.

They'd also tease each other about awards. 'I had won the Volpi Cup [acting award at the Venice Film Festival] in 1964, for *King & Country*,' Courtenay says:

> Albert had won it the year before, for *Tom Jones*. Then Albert won the Silver Bear for *The Dresser*, over me. But I got the Golden Globe. So Albert sent me a telegram saying, 'The score is Manchester United, 1, Hull City, 1. The scorer for Manchester, S. Bear; for Hull City, G. Globe'.

Matthew Warchus, later to become artistic director of the Old Vic, directed *Art*. Stott eventually won most critical plaudits just as, five years later, Richard Griffiths stole the notices in the same role. Ironically, Stott had serious reservations about the play:

> I thought it was a shallow little comedy and it would be enormously successful. But I thought it would be purgatory doing a load of old shite with two actors like Albert and Tom, whom I really admire. But Matthew wouldn't take no for an answer and told me to read it again and I decided it was probably a deep play masquerading as a shallow one.[2]

Even so, doubts persisted. About a week before the first preview, Stott was in despair:

I went to Matthew and said, 'This is going very badly. Yvan is useless, hopeless, nothing like as interesting as I'd hoped he'd be.' Matthew just smiled and said, 'I had Tom telling me the same about Serge yesterday and I'm looking forward to Albert telling me the same about Marc tomorrow.' [Actually Albert said he liked the script immediately.]

All three actors proved amenable to advice, according to Warchus. 'Good actors like these three aren't egomaniacs in rehearsal. They start from scratch. They're groping uncertainly. However strong their technique, they're always suggestible: they want to collaborate and be challenged.'

Art proved a huge success, a kind of runaway train that never stopped, although the choice cast grew progressively less starry and compelling as the years passed. Matt Woolf in *Variety* paid tribute to Finney's performance, 'The Marc who ends *Art* is a different person from the one who began it, and Finney's strength is to suggest the imaginative rebirth of someone able to permit colour into a black and white life that had been defined by bluster.' Benedict Nightingale thought the evening was the West End's highlight:

> Yasmina Reza's *Art*, at Wyndham's, is the play of the moment. It has already attracted attention all over mainland Europe. In London, it has been acclaimed in the conservative *Daily Telegraph* as 'smart, sharp and wonderfully funny' and attacked in the liberal *Guardian* as 'old-style Fascist theatre, sly, slick, self-indulgent and passionately anti-intellectual'. As eloquently translated by Christopher Hampton, it is one of the hottest tickets in town and, in my view, by far the most satisfying entertainment.

The theatrical establishment, perhaps best personified by Richard Eyre, Peter Hall's successor as National Theatre director, was sniffy. Eyre noted in his diaries:

> I saw *Art*, which is a bewildering phenomenon. I'd heard it described in apocalyptic tones as crass, pernicious and philistine, but it seemed to me a slight, bland but good-natured after dinner sketch.[3]

That could be said to be a classic case of damning with faint praise!

Perhaps the most famous person to see *Art* was Manchester United manager Alex Ferguson. He tells how he was desperate for a pair of tickets and only got them by paying well over the odds:

> When Cathy [Ferguson's wife] and I turned up at the theatre we were surprised to be met by the manager and told that Albert Finney's girlfriend,

Pene, would like us to join her for a drink. How could she possibly know we were coming? Pene's explanation was amusing. That morning Albert had answered the doorbell at his apartment and found himself facing his newsagent, a big United fan. The man was extremely agitated because he had picked up word that Alex Ferguson had been trying unsuccessfully to locate tickets for the play. 'You must get them for him,' he told the actor. Albert was as helpless as I have often been when landed with a similar request but the newsagent's intervention brought Cathy and me the bonus of being asked round to the star's dressing room at the end of the evening. Finney had always been one of my favourite actors and although I had never met him until then, I had heard enough about him, from his close friend Harold Riley, the Salford artist, to know that being in his company was likely to be a pleasure. It was indeed. Cathy and I both enjoyed *Art* but, to be honest, that little gathering in the dressing room was the highlight of our stay in London. Albert opened a bottle of Dom Pérignon to celebrate my ten years with United. We were joined by Tom Courtenay and Ken Stott and a surprise guest was Joan Plowright, who looked fantastic. What impressed me about all of them was how easily they dispelled the notion that people in their profession are forever calling one another 'love' and 'darling' and generally indulging in over-the-top behaviour. They were just down to earth.[4]

An acquaintance of Finney's tells another story that illustrates the actor's no-nonsense approach to art and indeed *Art*. He also went to see Finney backstage post-performance. The visitor recalls the conversation:

'Can I ask you something?' I asked tentatively. 'Where did you meet Yvan?'
   'Who?' asked Albert.
   'The Kenny Stott character. I mean, he's a salesman. And you don't like him very much.'
   'That's correct.'
   'So I wondered where you met him.'
   'No idea,' said Albert. 'In a bar, perhaps?'
   'You've never thought about where you met him?'
   'No.'
   'So,' I ventured, 'you didn't think about it when you first read the script?'
   'No,' he replied. 'I just thought it was a wonderful script. And when we started rehearsing it, it just got better and better.'[5]

So, none of this motivational nonsense for Finney![6]

Finney was 60 when his run in *Art* ended in March 1997. It turned out to be his final stage appearance. At the time he told an interviewer he was reluctant to take the play to New York. 'I don't feel New York's a theatre town anymore. It's a show town, like Las Vegas … So I'll take things easy for a while. Maybe I'll go racing.' Richard Eyre recalled a similar conversation with Finney and notes that Finney added, 'I did all that in the sixties.'

If Finney, at this point, still had designs on a major classical role, especially Lear, then 60 would have been an ideal age. By 70, let alone older, such a colossal part usually proves too much. Not that it can never be a success at a great age – Brian Blessed, at 78, was a recent example – but the demands of the part mean that 60 is about right. Even Burton, in his late 50s, baulked at Lear because, he said, his bad back would prevent him lifting Cordelia. Anthony Hopkins played Lear when he was only 48. He has not appeared on the West End stage since *M. Butterfly* in 1989 when he was just 51. O'Toole dodged Lear, perhaps mindful of his *Macbeth* fiasco. His final stage appearance was when he was 67 in a revival of *Jeffrey Bernard is Unwell*. Berkoff may have still been treading the boards at 78, Angela Lansbury at 88; yet these are exceptions. Michael Gambon, 75 at the time of writing, recently announced that he would no longer do stage work.

In subsequent interviews Finney said that he doubted he would return to the stage, 'prancing around like an ageing juvenile'. All actors' fears – forgetting whole sections of dialogue and simply lacking the stamina to deliver – become more pronounced after 60. It might simply have been too exhausting for Finney, an actor averse to long runs.[9] Latterly, health considerations have ruled him out. And Finney likes to go his own way, a motif throughout all his public pronouncements.

But, even in 1996, Finney implied to Terry Coleman that Lear was beyond him:

Charles Laughton was 60 when he played Lear. I'm not saying I'm in peak condition, but Charles certainly wasn't, and it wasn't a great success. He's got to pick up Cordelia at the end. I think it was Charles who called John [Gielgud] for a tip, and he said, 'Get a very light Cordelia.'

And Oliver Ford Davies, while filming *My Uncle Silas* in 2000, recalled asking Finney if he would ever be doing *Lear*. 'Oh God,' he replied, 'eight shows a week doing *Lear* – no, no, no.'

Perhaps Finney's effective retirement from the stage reinforced the accusation that he had frittered away his career. Yet Finney, although discriminating, worked prodigiously and steadily until he was 75. And the flack comes from critics, not the public or other performers. Fellow actors are more understanding, perhaps mindful of the pressures involved. Take Anthony Hopkins, who said on Burton's death in 1984 that he 'didn't agree with all the self-righteous pundits who said he should have done more things on stage'. Likewise, Richard Harris, who, also referring to Burton, asked the rhetorical question, 'Why should he have lived his life for you? [The critics or the public]. Richard lived his life for himself.' Doubtless this could apply to Finney too. He felt he was entitled to tread his own path. And, unlike Burton, who died aged 58, Finney was to prove durable.

Finney also made it clear that he disliked the auditoriums at the National Theatre, a likely venue for a production of *Lear*. Not that this had prevented him attempting some great classical roles at the South Bank. Yet experience had taught him that the Olivier's acoustics were untrustworthy. He also believed that the Lyttelton stage was too wide, cutting the actors off from the audience. 'It's like reaching with your arm into a paper bag without ever being sure you get to the bottom,' he said. He disliked all the concrete. 'Not a natural sound box, is it? You don't make musical instruments out of it, do you?' Finney would say.

Richard Eyre's diaries from 1988 recall a similar putdown from Finney about the National:

> Met Maggie Smith and Albert Finney last week. Neither has much fondness for the building. They both want to work outside the West End and yet not get institutionalised. I tell Albert that Peter Brook says that a theatre should be like a violin; its tone comes from its period and age, and tone is the most important quality. 'Yes,' said Albert. 'And who'd build a violin out of fucking concrete?'

In 1996, Finney was still busy. During the run of *Art*, he could be seen on the small screen as the alcoholic Doctor Monygham in a four-part adaptation of Joseph Conrad's novel *Nostromo*, about the corrupting effects of a local silver mine. Set in a fictional South American country, it had a sterling cast, including Colin Firth, Brian Dennehy and Serena Scott-Thomas.

David Lean had originally set his heart on making a movie of *Nostromo*. But he had died (in 1991) before he could begin. In the end, the international television co-production was just as much work as a full-scale film. Six months of shooting began in May 1995, using sixty European technicians, mainly Italian and British, and 120 Colombians, as well as 15,000 acting extras.

Finney accepted what was quite a gruelling venture – and for less than his normal rate – because of his friendship with producer Fernando Ghia. 'I liked the idea of going back to South America and being paid for it. And it's a lovely character,' he said at the time.

The *Independent*'s Terry Coleman noted how Finney nearly stole the whole production from the nominal stars:

Such is Finney's power that the central thread of a complex story very nearly becomes Monygham's devotion to the young wife of the Englishman who has come to reopen the silver mine. Dr Monygham shambles in to warn her and her husband to go home. She receives him alone, gives him tea in a shaded courtyard, and his adoration is instant.

Peter Kemp agreed: 'One of its high spots is Albert Finney's pained, bitterly sardonic rendering of Monygham, the doctor crippled and psychologically maimed during Gruzman Bento's reign of terror.'

Journalist James Rampton describes one particular drunk scene involving Finney's Monygham:

An Irish doctor who has seen better days sits dressed in a pith helmet, dinner jacket and a towel. Pathetically singing, slurring his words and swigging from a bottle, he hails a returning war hero by throwing his arms up in the air. The scabbard flies off the regimental sword he is holding and clatters across the room. This is a bravura boozer.

Executive producer Michael Wearing, in the same *Independent* profile, noted Finney's skill in acting drunk:

It's a masterclass in how to act drunk. But it's just one scene. Albert has caught that mad English quality of those people who went all over the world and landed in the most inappropriate places, but still contributed something. Albert manages to understand that. He gives me the impression that he's in control professionally of what he needs to do. He's not at war with himself – the way most actors and indeed the rest of us are.

Finney said the heat during filming in Colombia made him lose weight, but joked that he was doing his best to put it back on: 'I don't feel I'm a masochist. I don't want to put myself through the wringer. I just felt he was an interesting fellow and his problems were worth having a crack at.'

Wearing reckoned that Finney conveyed anguish so well because, ironically, he's so much the opposite off-screen: 'He's not tormented in real life. He's a tremendous lover of life. He's not self-important, and he doesn't hide behind a whole intellectual cage of nonsense, which some actors do. What he's got is an endless curiosity about people and places.'

Writer John Hale, who adapted *Nostromo* and had first met Finney at the 1961 Edinburgh Festival, commented in a 1996 newspaper profile that he was 'the most convivial of men … he allows nothing to divert him. He'll always turn up on his mark, rock steady and DLP – dead letter perfect.'

'Concentration is the secret,' Finney said at the time. 'You try to be there. When you do a scene, you're there and nothing else is going on.' Reportedly, Finney was in the habit of getting up to rehearse two hours before filming. 'I like to go on set with the engine running,' he said. 'I like to be ready, it's an explosive event.'

Yet Finney never took preparation to an extreme:

> I think about the part but on *Nostromo* I didn't walk into a bar in the evening with crippled feet and a hunchback. One does like to be obsessed, though, that's one of the attractions of the work. But sometimes you get more ideas when you're not poring over the script with a clenched forehead. When I played Scrooge I was switching lights off a lot because I was thinking about the part, but I didn't become completely mean.

Rich character roles continued to come Finney's way. There was perhaps a hint of eccentricity to Finney as he 'matured'. He was rather like Trevor Howard yet somehow more intrinsically likeable. Ever since *The Dresser*, fans of Finney and Courtenay had looked forward to a screen rematch. It wasn't just that they were good friends. Somehow their different acting styles complemented each other. Angela Lambert's novel *A Rather English Marriage* proved a delightful 'sequel' to *The Dresser*, a kind of British version of *The Odd Couple*. Despite his working-class credentials, and role in *Saturday Night and Sunday Morning*, Finney also plays 'posh' convincingly. Perhaps it's his natural gravitas and author-ity. Courtenay tends to play more subservient characters. So it was in *A Rather English Marriage*, in which Finney, playing at least ten years older than his age, was a widowed RAF veteran, Squadron Leader Reggie Conyngham-Jarvis. (American readers should note that a double-barrelled name usually signifies 'upper-class' in the UK!)

Courtenay played a widowed milkman, Roy Southgate. Roy was also ex-armed forces but a humble non-commissioned officer. Because they were both bereaved on the same day, Roy, heeding a social worker's advice, moves in with Reggie. Roy becomes housekeeper to Reggie until he starts to tire of his master's domineering manner. Matters get complicated, however, when Reggie courts a younger woman, Liz Franks (Joanna Lumley).

Finney's Conyngham-Jarvis is a truculent taskmaster, a bit of a bounder. He even calls his new companion 'Southgate'. Finney plays him with the effort-less authority of those who think they are born to rule. A pompous old poop, perhaps, but Andrew Davies's sassy dialogue sustains the interest. 'You are a prissy tight-ass aren't you,' he tells Southgate. Or, after being cut off in traffic by another driver, 'may your balls wither and drop like rotten figs, my friend'. (If only one encountered such inventiveness of expression on the road in real life!)

Although 'squadron leader' does not wear his emotions easily, there are poignant moments, as when he returns home and summons his wife, momentarily forgetting that she's dead. And the scene where Reggie tries to bed Liz, suffering a stroke at orgasm, complete with flashbacks to his past as an RAF pilot, is a gem.

Joanna Lumley reflected on the production and, in particular, *that* love scene:

> He [Finney] couldn't have made it easier or more natural. Finney is loved by everyone who comes near him and I think it's because he loves them back. He adores women and women, me included, adore him. Women were jealous of me for my scene with Albert. Tom Courtenay and Finney were the stars of that film; it had taken ages to get it off the ground as the powers that be couldn't see the value of a story involving two widowers and a middle-aged woman. It got all sorts of prizes and has been shown and reshown here and all over the world … When you play tennis with Tim Henman your game goes up and if you're working with Finney and Courtenay the same thing happens. They were almost the reason I went into the business. You watch Albert Finney in *Tom Jones* or Tom in *The Loneliness of the Long Distance Runner* and think 'if only'. You think you'll never meet, let alone work with these people.[28] [Try with Andy Murray, Joanna!]

She later wrote that she cried when she saw it on transmission.

Finney also loved working with Lumley: 'I have admired Joanna's work for ages but I had no idea what to expect from working with her. In the event she was delightful, great fun and larky. I felt immediately relaxed and easy working with her. What more can you ask for?'

Reggie's wooing of Liz is ultimately doomed and he is left, frail and lonely, with only Roy to look after him. As the film ends, the two dance to *I'm Going to Get You on a Slow Boat to China* – theatrical but a delight. The class-consciousness may be puzzling to non-British viewers, but it was a great actors' piece. Predictably, *A Rather English Marriage* was rewarded at the Baftas, winning best actor for Courtenay and a nomination for Finney. 'A Tony cast, led by Albert Finney on overdrive, chews up the scenery to entertaining – and finally moving – effect in this true-Brit comedy of manners,' said *Variety*.

After success on stage and TV, Finney's movie career now took a little dip. *Breakfast of Champions*, based on Kurt Vonnegut's tale of American disillusionment, in which Bruce Willis played an ostensibly successful, but suicidal, car dealer, was dismally unfunny. It's a (very) broad satire, taking aim at the American dream, clearly more of a nightmare to Vonnegut. Watching the film is like being in a rattling cage full of shrieking monkeys. Even the 'rainforest' opening credits are too busy and noisy and, just like the ensuing drama, fly in too many directions. For satire to work well, it has to be taken seriously. Director Alan Rudolph had no such plan.

Willis's desperate car dealer is too demented to make us care. Finney plays Kildore Trout, an impoverished, unsuccessful pulp fiction writer. A solitary tramp-like figure, with only a budgie for a companion, he receives a fan letter and a cheque inviting him to be the star guest at an arts convention. What ensues, for Finney at least, is mostly a muttered monologue as he hitchhikes cross-country.

The film was not a success. 'Muddled and meandering satire on the American dream that misses most of its targets,' said John Walker. Derek Elley in *Variety* described it as 'a hearty meal that starts off tickling the taste buds but ends up smothering them'.

(Talking of food, the restaurant critic Ruth Reichl remembered seeing Vonnegut and Finney queuing outside the famous Sparks Steak House in New York in 1998. She recalled that, after about twenty minutes, the famous pair simply gave up and walked away, proving that, in some establishments, not even the world's most celebrated authors or actors can bag a table!)

Nick Nolte was another talented actor wasted in *Breakfast of Champions*. He played a demented transvestite. Coincidentally, Nolte was also in Finney's next film, an altogether more successful one, from Matthew Warchus, the director of *Art*. *Simpatico*, by Sam Shepard, tells of two old friends, Vinnie (Nick Nolte) and Carter (Jeff Bridges) who perpetrated a horse racing scam. Twenty years on and one is a multi-millionaire businessman, the other an alcoholic dropout. Vinnie flies to Kentucky, carrying a box full of incriminating, explicit photographs they had used to blackmail a racing official, Sims (Finney), into taking the fall from the scam. Now Vinnie hopes to persuade him to pay for the material.

The Sims who appears in flashback was a sleazy, violent lecher, operating on the margins of the racing world. Yet the Sims that Vinnie meets in the present is totally uninterested in the box and philosophical about the past. He's lost his family and been slandered but he's willing to let sleeping horses lie. Finney is excellent as Sims, a world-weary survivor with a gift for reinvention. He is the most sharply drawn character and, ironically, the most attractive despite his past.

It's no wonder that Finney was drawn to the part. Not only was he working with Bridges, Nolte, and Warchus, but also the backdrop of racing – Finney's milieu. The film perhaps doesn't quite succeed, lacking as it does a strong narrative drive. But Finney's character makes one think about the nature of redemption and self-forgiveness. He is also quite the charmer as he invites

Cecilia (Katherine Keener) to the Kentucky Derby, something we know Finney enjoys too.

'In the play's master stroke, it's this repulsive world-weary lout, reminiscent of Sidney Greenstreet stripped of grandiosity, who emerges as the film's only character to have made peace with the past,' wrote Stephen Holden in the *New York Times*. John Walker described it as 'a muted, melancholy drama of men being overtaken and destroyed by unnecessary guilt; the acting is a pleasure to watch'.

Sadly, *Simpatico* was little seen and totally eclipsed by that year's smash hit, *American Beauty*, which marked the cinematic debut of another British stage director, Sam Mendes. Yet Finney's next film was a blockbuster and one that would introduce him to a whole new generation of filmgoers.

AN ATTRACTIVE ATTORNEY

I make a lawyer appealing. That is something.

Albert Finney

Finney had notched up some multimedia successes in the late nineties, notably *Art* and *Karaoke* and *A Rather English Marriage*, but also some movies, such as *Simpatico* and *Breakfast of Champions*, and the TV series *Nostromo*, best described as curios. Although Finney's name still carried a lot of prestige, he was never in the Connery or Caine league of fame. Neither had he ever aspired to be. Independently wealthy, Finney had forged his own path. Commercial appeal was never his sole reason for accepting a part. Hence Finney was now a kind of quasi-celebrity to filmgoers. Few people, after all, would have seen *The Browning Version* or *Run of the Country* or *A Man of No Importance*. But Steven Soderbergh's *Erin Brockovich* was seen by almost everyone.

Julia Roberts was the queen of cinema at the turn of the century. *Pretty Woman*, *Sleeping with the Enemy* and *Notting Hill* were all box office bonanzas. Yet she was looking for that elusive vehicle to give her critical respect. The part of Erin Brockovich – a bold, brassy, broke, single mother who exposes the tragedies behind a corrupt energy company – was a dream.

Brockovich was one tough cookie. Audiences just loved the story of a feisty female, an unmarried single mother of three, fighting her way out of poverty. A good script has to present some mighty obstacles for our hero or heroine. And Erin sure is up against it, not only her personal bad luck but also the corrupt Pacific Gas & Electric Company and an old-school lawyer rattled by her impulsiveness. Finney played Ed Masry, the real-life American attorney who loses what was expected to be an easy case involving Brockovich and another driver. Masry is depicted as a jaded, cynical figure – a survivor of cancer, diabetes and a quadruple bypass – battling against the big, bullyboy corporations. He and Erin develop a mutual respect and affection but only after early tussles.

It's the tennis match between Finney's prickly attorney and his confrontational sidekick that provides the on-screen fireworks. Somehow you just know that they liked each other off-screen too. If Roberts's Erin is a bit too pushy, even over-articulate and almost Superwoman (how the hell does she remember all those phone numbers?), then Finney is a great foil.

Watch the film again and you will notice that Finney always reacts well to her outbursts even when he says nothing. Given that acting is essentially reacting – it's what you give the other actor that counts – then Roberts couldn't have wished for a better co-star. Thanks to Finney, this careworn, crumpled, coffee-stained lawyer becomes something noble.

Finney loved Julia and indeed the whole experience:

Julia's commitment to the part really touched me. When I read the script I thought, terrific part for her – slightly different from what I've seen her do and a great opportunity to show what she's made of. After three weeks I told her how great she was in the role … working with her was enjoyable because it was volatile and unpredictable. I was proud of her as a fellow professional. That's how a fellow trouper should be.

I thought the script was terrific, and I enjoyed the task of playing an American lawyer. He was a guy who was thinking about retirement. He was a bit jaded about his practice, and he'd had a bypass, all those things. Then this damned woman kind of comes into his life and gradually rekindles his enthusiasm for life. He still hasn't gotten to Palm Springs.

Julia reciprocated, 'I feel the same way about Albert as Erin does about Ed. I could not have achieved what I've achieved in this movie without him by my side, without his friendship and support, and he's a man I respect and really love.'[1]

Masry liked Finney too:

He's just a super guy. I can't say enough about him. Albert Finney is the type of a guy you'd want to have a bottle of beer or a glass of wine with. He's laid back, very intelligent and a great conversationalist. [As for Finney's portrayal] all in all, the movie was quite on, and I have no problem with his portrayal. I thought he did a good job portraying what was going on, although there was a tremendous amount going on that couldn't be portrayed.

Actor Michael Harney, playing a small part in *Erin Brockovich*, recalled Finney's unique way of making every scene seem spontaneous:

We were doing this scene where Steven [Soderbergh] set the camera up in the middle of this town hall, which was like a school, and Albert was going to come in and explain the case, and explain the suit, and what would happen, how the money would be paid, and all this kind of stuff, and what the potential of that was, and all of this. And he had this long-ass speech that he was going to go in and do, and I was sitting there in the second row, and I thought to myself, okay, well, I'm doing this totally in character, and then trying to break in thinking to myself wow, this is like a master class watching this guy give a speech, right?

So we start. Steven said, 'Okay, let's just rehearse it,' and he rehearsed it, and I thought to myself, 'oh my God'. It didn't look like he had it, and I was like, 'Oh shit'. And that was just my ignorance, see, because then Steven said, 'Okay, whenever you're ready,' and Albert starts going, and what I realised, his speech was beautiful, and I literally felt that he didn't know what he was going to say before he said it. So it was fresh. The whole damn thing was fresh. It was like a page-and-a-half, two pages, and what I realised was that during the rehearsal process, I think what he was doing was he was just getting rid of everything. He was throwing everything away so that he could just be there and just deliver it.

Harney believed that Finney was one of the best: 'Albert would just hang out. He was just a regular guy. To me, I think he's the best around, or I should say one of the best around, but he's up there with Bob De Niro. He's up there with Pacino.'[2]

Erin Brockovich, which raked in more than $256 million worldwide, earned Finney nominations for a Golden Globe, Oscar and Bafta as best supporting actor. Finney won the coveted Screen Actors Guild award, usually a sure sign of an Oscar victory. So much so that the *Daily Telegraph* forecast that he (and Judi Dench for *Chocolat*) would be lifting statuettes. 'His role as a curmudgeonly lawyer in *Erin Brockovich* makes him the clear favourite for an Oscar, according to the guild's own Oscar rankings issued last night,' said the newspaper in an article on 13 March 2001, entitled 'Oscars written in stars for Finney and Dench'.[3]

Sadly, for Finney's fans at least, Benicio Del Toro, who starred in *Traffic*, triumphed in all three awards. This, Finney's fifth Oscar nomination, was probably his best chance, so perhaps he was entitled to feel peeved. But, if he did, he kept it to himself. Finney had never even attended the Oscars. 'It seems to me a long way to go just to sit in a non-drinking, non-smoking environment on the off-chance your name is called,' he'd say.[4]

That same year, 2001, Finney was also given the Bafta Fellowship. Finney did a little dance as he made his way to the podium. 'If in years to come you cannot say he's a jolly good fellow, I hope at least you'll be able to say he's not a bad old fellow,' he said. Yet, although always gracious when honoured, awards left him cold:

> All the hoops you have to jump through on those occasions. It's not my favourite occupation. I'm basically relieved that we're able to do our job and go back into the woodwork. Walking around in the spotlight having to be me is not something I'm particularly comfortable with or desire. I'd sooner pretend to be someone else.

In 1999, Finney turned down a knighthood, having previously refused a CBE in 1980. Although not identified with radical politics – usually the reason for 'refuseniks' – Finney declined:

> Call me Sir if you like! Maybe people in America think being a Sir is a big deal. But I think we should all be misters together. I think the 'Sir' thing slightly perpetuates one of our diseases in England, which is snobbery. And it also helps keep us 'quaint,' which I'm not a great fan of. You don't get much with the title anymore. That was all carved up by the robber barons in the Middle Ages.

So no 'Sir Albert Finney' – even though it would have had a nice ring to it. Michael Gambon thought so too, 'I lament Albert Finney not being Sir Albert and running the National Theatre, being what everyone thought he would be. He obviously didn't want it. That's all there is to it.'[5]

Finney's part in *Erin Brockovich* and his admiration for Steven Soderbergh[6] – 'he is absolutely obsessed with filmmaking; he can be persuaded to take a lunch break, but he doesn't like to leave the set' – led him to agree to a cameo in the same director's film *Traffic*. Finney's involvement was withheld from the cast. According to Finney, the daily call sheet for the scenes between drug czar Robert Wakefield (Michael Douglas) and his unnamed chief of staff (Finney's role) listed Douglas's name and Giles Archer, a reference to Sam Spade's slain partner Miles Archer in *The Maltese Falcon*.

Douglas was kept in the dark to the end. The ruse worked, according to Finney:

> My hair was severely cut and they had me in full costume and make-up. They brought me to the house where they were shooting, and I knew most of the crew from *Erin Brockovich*. Then, from across the room I heard, 'Michael, I don't believe you've met Giles.'

Douglas started to introduce himself to 'Archer' …

Then he stopped. He couldn't quite figure it out. Then the penny dropped, he swore at us, and laughed hugely. We then proceeded to try to work.

Finney was on set for one day. His chief of staff is a stern piece of work.[7]

Meanwhile, a sudden death handed Finney another great part on TV. Oliver Reed's fatal heart attack on the set of *Gladiator* in May 1999 brought a flood of tributes, even meriting an ITN newsflash. The coverage made one reflect on the bizarre nature of modern celebrity. Reed, two years younger than Finney, had not accomplished anything near as much as Finney. He never had an Oscar nomination, let alone five. Few would have put him in the same league as Finney. And Reed was a totally different animal. He was in love with stardom, not acting. Even in his thirties, Reed was talking about retiring. Only financial constraints kept him working. In interviews he likened acting to prostitution, claiming he was forced to act in any old rubbish to stay a millionaire.

Most big stars – and here we undertake a little diversion – are more like Reed than Finney. It seems to be fashionable to belittle acting. Take another fallen legend, Richard Burton. His diaries are filled with diatribes against the tedium of filmmaking and acting, along with threats to quit altogether. Marlon Brando, another 'great', was adamant in his derision for his profession. 'There's no such thing as a great performance or a great film,' he told Connie Chung in a rare interview in 1989. He hated acting, hence an almost blank sheet in the eighties. It seemed at some point that deriding their craft was almost obligatory for the Burtons, Harrises and others of their generation. Finney is the opposite; even by 2000 his enthusiasm for acting was undiminished. Fame was never a lure. We remember the young Finney telling David Lean that he simply wasn't interested in becoming a star.

Reed's death jeopardised a television adaptation of H.E. Bates's classic short stories, *My Uncle Silas*, about a turn of the century Bedfordshire rascal. It was by the same team who had triumphed with *The Darling Buds of May*. Reed had died before he could sign up. Had he lived, the part would have been his. In a phone call to Michael Winner, just two days before he died, Reed told the director, 'they've offered me a great role on television'. Winner recalled that 'he was so thrilled because he thought he was all washed up and now he was back'.[8]

Superficially, Reed would have made a fine Silas, especially given the actor's notorious love of 'wenching' and drinking. Yet Finney turned out to be ideal casting, perhaps better able to express Silas's warmth and good nature. Reed's screen persona was becoming more sinister and malevolent – to say nothing of his aggressive off-screen behaviour. Somehow, an actor like Finney, rather like his contemporary John Stride, exudes a likeability that Reed could never muster.

Filming was set to begin in the summer of 1999. (The series had to be made during good weather.) But Reed's death delayed filming by another year as they searched for another actor. Philip Saville, who directed most of the episodes, was surprised that a star of Finney's stature would accept it. But he jumped at it and even, at Saville's request, agreed to gain weight for the part. Getting Finney was a triumph, agreed Robert Banks Stewart, who adapted the series. 'Albert has a kind of humanity and, being the sort of actor he is, he moves from being sort of a rambunctious, bucolic poacher, gravedigger, womaniser and boozer, and he suddenly changes gear and becomes a nice human being.'

Finney was hooked instantly:

I felt that it was rich material. I just had to do it. As I read I was almost salivating at the prospect of getting to grips with the character. The story harks back to the days where we were all more in tune with the seasons and nature. Silas is a man of the earth and he knows how to live life to the utmost.

Finney embodied the character so well that it's now difficult to see anyone else as Silas. Just as with *Scrooge* or *Miller's Crossing*, he might not have been first choice but he made the part his own.

My Uncle Silas is a pleasant, rewarding, if totally undemanding, canter through a vanished era. Sue Johnston likened the series to 'putting on very comfortable slippers. You sit down and enjoy it and let the warmth run over you.' View the episodes again and you notice some period detail and slices of rural life that you might have missed first time round. Silas's enjoyment of life's little pleasures – from Bedfordshire potatoes, whose creamy velvety skins he caresses, through to elderberry wine – is infectious. Finney's fleshy, pink face, double chin and long sideburns make him just right. By 2000, Finney was portly but it's very much the 60-year-old Silas, a life-affirming character and, again, a bit of a lecher as he dallies with the likes of Lynda Bellingham and Charlotte Rampling. He certainly nails the accent, a kind of tamed rustic roar.

Audiences were drawn in as the lovable layabout teaches his nephew, young Joe Prospero, how to spit long distance and regales him with stories about his youth. Bates's stories are light on substance. Not a lot actually happens. Silas calls on an old flame when he's supposed to visit his lawyer. He whisks the overworked wife of a temperance inn's landlord off to the coast (he converts the establishment into a proper hostelry before he's through). He irritates his housekeeper Mrs Betts (Sue Johnston) with his feckless ways but not enough to stop her cooking rabbit stew and apple dumplings. It all seems rather idyllic.

Doubtless, Finney shares Silas's love of food, reflected in his girth which, in one episode, is shown in all its splendour as he luxuriates in a hot tub. It's all gentle, harmless stuff, apart from one episode in which Silas battles an old foe. Finney somehow makes himself a believable fighter – no mean feat. 'Tom Jones with a bus pass,' was Finney's own description of the character. 'Silas is an old country rogue, a bit of a poacher who drinks homemade wines and tries to grab every passing female he can.'

Critics generally took the series on its own terms. John Carman in his review for *SFGATE* said:

There's so little to *My Uncle Silas* except for Finney's bawdy romp as a mischief-making senior, and a pleasant feel for rural England in the early 1900s, it's worth hanging around just to see Albert Finney gorge himself on the script to the point of bursting. Though not what you'd call a fine figure of a man, Silas manages to charm females of all sorts, from the overburdened wife [Annabelle Apsion] of a teetotalist hotelkeeper to an upper-class lady [Charlotte Rampling] who invites him into her bed under unlikely circumstances. There's not a great deal of meat in the script, but Finney feasts on whatever's available.

'The script is light and simple and tailor-made for Finney,' said David Stanners. 'He is brilliant as Silas. Perfectly cast, his rosy red cheeks, white surfboard sidies and hip flask full of homemade wine are every bit the happy country bumpkin.'

As ever, Finney was popular on and off the set. Lynda Bellingham recalled in her autobiography, 'I make no bones about my admiration for this amazing actor and I was so thrilled to get to work with him. He is just a lovely man.' One episode had Bellingham, as a wicked widow, being chased around her orchard in her petticoats by Silas. Unfortunately, Lynda fell over and pulled a muscle in her back. The next day, she had to play a love scene in which Finney was to untie her shoelaces and throw her on the bed. Bellingham was in agony throughout but she remembered Finney's kindness and understanding. So much so that she decided to throw a big lunch party at her house to which Sally Bulloch and Lynda La Plante were invited. The party lasted twelve hours. Bellingham, who tragically died in 2014, wrote that we could all learn something from Finney: 'He works to live. Too many of us live to work.'

Finney could still charm ladies of all ages. Sue Johnston recalls taking her 90-year-old aunt, a long-time Finney fan, to the set. (The actress, it will be remembered, had been in the audience in Stratford when Finney replaced Olivier in *Coriolanus*.) Johnston mumbled something about being tired, and her aunt turned to Finney and said, 'Wait until she reaches our age, Albert.' Finney, then 64, twenty-six years younger than Johnston's aunt, just laughed, 'How old do you think I am?'[9] But he didn't take himself seriously. (Johnston later reported that she showed the finished series to her mother, 'The look of delight on her face … She said it was like being back to her grandmother's time. It was exactly how it was for her as a child – horse-drawn carriages, the countryside.')

At least people saw *My Uncle Silas*, so much so that it stretched to two series. And everyone agreed that it was a pleasant diversion from modern life. The same cannot be said for *Delivering Milo*, a movie so obscure that few have heard of it. It is not a good film but perhaps a guilty pleasure for the bored on a rainy day if only for Finney's expansive turn as (yet another) old rascal, Elmore Dahl. It's essentially a one-joke movie. Dahl is dead but is summoned back to the world by an earnest-looking committee 'on the other side' that entrusts him with a special mission. A baby – who we are to understand is named Milo and who, inexplicably, seems to be an 11-year-old boy (the late Anton Yelchin) – does not want to be born. Dahl's job is to take him round New York, show him the joys of living and, hopefully, change his mind. That way his mother (Bridget Fonda) can finally give birth. No babies can be born unless Milo agrees to come out. Heavy stuff!

Finney must have been attracted by the idea of a free trip to New York. It can't have been the prospect of playing this 'real class-A jerk', as another character describes him. Yet, as ever, he's a likeable class-A jerk. We first see Finney emerging breezily from a lift (he rises from the basement, implying he's in hell) about to be briefed on his mission to 'save' Milo. We know what's coming. Finney is determinedly cheerful, brimming with avuncular charm. He will show Milo a good time, whether munching on a pastrami sandwich, walking around Central Park, taking a boat ride on the Hudson or feeding slot machines.

Sadly, the gulf between Finney's fun-loving self and the dour, introspective child is too great. Finney is in the attic and Yelchin is in the basement. It's painful seeing such a great actor caught up in this cartoon-strip, one-dimensional drivel. Olivier probably turned in his grave. Perhaps only Woody Allen could have salvaged this script from utter banality.

The other problem is that it's set in the New York of late 2000, with the Twin Towers still visible in the background. Its release date in America could not have been worse, just a few weeks after 9/11. Americans simply weren't in the mood for a feel-good walkabout in New York.

'Without Fonda's performance of bare-deep conviction or Finney's turn as an older but still ribald Tom Jones (albeit with a growly Bronx accent) helmer Nick Castle's fantasy would be pretty dreary,' said *Variety*. Fortunately, hardly anybody has ever heard of this film, let alone seen it. Yelchin, however, said he learnt a lot from Finney. He also has another memory. When Finney discovered his young co-star was an avid Beatles fan, he went out and bought him a complete set of their classic CDs.

By the time of *My Uncle Silas and Delivering Milo*, Finney, in spite of his loath-
ing of typecasting, was usually seen as a kind of incorrigible (larger than) life
force. What was needed was a role that made the most of Finney's gargantuan
presence but without lurching into self-parody. Britain's greatest wartime leader
gave him just that chance.

A CHURCHILLIAN TRIUMPH

Finney gives one of the performances of his career.

Nigel Kendall in *The Times*.

Portraits of Hitler and Churchill, superficially attractive for an actor, can spell trouble, prone as they are to caricature. Playing Hitler as a monster overlooks his dark, hypnotic charisma. Playing Churchill as a hero is just as wrong. Churchill is, for one thing, not universally popular. Some of his wartime decisions have since been subject to 'revisionist' re-evaluations, usually for political point-scoring.

Richard Burton's portrayal of Churchill in a 1974 movie proved controversial, not because of Burton's impersonation but because of his subsequent comments, perhaps prompted by an attack of class-based bile, in which he said he 'hated Churchill and all his kind'. Burton's friend, Robert Hardy, subsequently cornered the market in Churchill impersonations from the eighties, playing him in a wonderful television series, *The Wilderness Years*, followed by a West End musical, *Winnie*, through to the TV series *Bomber Harris* and *War and Remembrance*.

More recent Churchills have included Timothy Spall in *The King's Speech* (dismissed by the *Daily Telegraph* as akin to 'a distended bulldog who's been chewing wasps') and Rod Taylor (essentially a cameo) in *Inglourious Basterds* (Taylor had originally recommended Finney to Tarantino). Brendan Gleeson played him rather well in the HBO production *Into the Storm* and then there was Ian McNeice in an episode of *Doctor Who* and the late Warren Clarke in a stage play, *Three Days In May*. Yet, on film at least, the definitive portrayal is now Finney's in *The Gathering Storm*. (But, doubtless, Finney's old friend Michael Gambon will give him stiff competition in *Churchill's Secret*.)[1]

Finney took some convincing before he would accept the part, 'It's difficult playing a historical figure because you might get bogged down in impersonations. I was very loath to do it at first. But I suddenly thought, oh, bugger it, just play it!'

The Gathering Storm was successful because it managed to make Churchill a hero in spite of his personal flaws. Hugh Whitemore's script does not gloss over his shortcomings. It shows Churchill as a pre-war parliamentary pariah involved in a lonely, but righteous crusade against appeasement. Yet it's not afraid to show us where Churchill was wrong, for example in his irrational hatred of Gandhi. Brendan Gleeson, when he played Churchill, said, 'I had to get the idea of him as a hero out of my head. In fact, I couldn't sleep properly until I had made that decision.' Thankfully, it appears Finney reached a similar conclusion in the earlier film.

Whitemore's Churchill is extravagant, greedy, impetuous, self-obsessed, vainglorious and, occasionally, outrageously rude to underlings. And, so the screenplay hints, he has a romantic vision of war. He is also prone to savage self-pity and depression. 'I'm finished, a ghost witnessing my own demise,' he says at the beginning. Whitemore's skill is to show Churchill's shortcomings and eccentricity with illuminating little episodes. He dictates to his secretary while lying naked in the bath, even giving us a glimpse of his bare behind.

The funniest scenes come when he bickers with his butler, Inches (Ronnie Barker), in his final role. The film's PR spun it that Finney had somehow lured Barker out of retirement. Actually they had never met. But Barker enjoyed working with Finney, 'He's lovely, very professional, very nice, very easy. He knew his lines, did it well, didn't do many takes and was very nice to me. He seemed to respect me as a performer.'[2]

Celia Imrie was pleased to get a role as Churchill's secretary. She met one of the great man's real-life secretaries who pointed out some unlikely dialogue, notably Winston swearing in her presence. Celia emerged from these encounters brimming with creativity, 'I would come on to the set in the morning and barely manage to say "I've got an id …" before Albert Finney, who played Churchill, shouted, "Oh Christ, not another bloody idea!".'[3]

Finney's Churchill is cavalier about household expenditures and frets over the absence of Dundee cake. He is sometimes aggressive and unreasonable. Then he becomes like a wounded, chastened puppy after a row with Clemmie (Vanessa Redgrave), a scene which Max Hastings described as 'one of the most moving in the film'. The vulnerability just makes this great figure all the more human.

Finney gets the rhythm of Churchill's speech, that undulating style of oratory. At 65, he was a similar age to Winston in the thirties. Finney, with a little help from make-up, also looks and sounds uncannily like him, overweight, heavy-jowelled and with a thick, foghorn growl very like the cigar-chewing, brandy-swilling Churchill. Most importantly, Finney has that indefinable gravitas.

Michael Dobbs, creator of *House of Cards*, said such a part is not easy:

It's very difficult, actually, to portray Churchill because if you listen to the recordings of him, he does have a voice which is incredibly slurred. What you should try to do is to capture the heart and soul of a character. Which, of course, is much more than a simple accent.[4]

Vanessa Redgrave got on well with Finney, having worked with him several times before, notably in *A Midsummer Night's Dream* at Stratford in 1959, and in *Murder on the Orient Express*. 'I said I'd do it, and then heard that Albie had come on board. That was a great day,' said Redgrave. And Finney and Redgrave played off each other beautifully, even though she admitted finding it difficult not smoking (Clemmie never smoked whereas Redgrave does) while acting opposite 'Albie puffing on a cigar all the time in the most wonderful way'.

Phil Gallo, in *Variety*, hailed the excellent lead performances:

Physically, Finney makes for a great Churchill, and the mannerisms, not to mention the deep, authoritative tone in his voice, all suggest tremendous character study on Finney's part … Redgrave gives Finney a run for his money on the acting front. She is consistently dignified, and her two mood shifts – one to anger, the other to reflection – are startlingly affecting.

Ron Wertheimer, in the *New York Times*, focused on the eccentric depiction:

How did Winston Churchill prepare for the rigours of leading Britain through World War Two? He moped about the countryside, smoking fat cigars, even during meals. He drank prodigious quantities of champagne, although he could barely afford beer. He kept telling anyone within earshot what a great man he was. And he acted selfishly toward everyone from his wife to his butler, all of whom responded to his boorishness with devotion.

'With a larger-than-life personality like Churchill there is an insidious temptation to hope that exaggeration will cover imprecision. Finney repulses it, and gives as exact a rendering as we are ever likely to see,' said Paul Smith in the *Sunday Times*. Nigel Kendall in *The Times* said:

Finney gives one of the performances of his career. Shambling, determined, sentimental and devoted to his country, Finney gives us a rare glimpse behind the myth of the indomitable bulldog to reveal a vulnerable man whose career was effectively over until war was declared.

Max Hastings thought that the production reminded us 'how marvellous television can be when it is skilful and intelligent, when the medium does not seek to cheapen and diminish human affairs as it does for, say, 350 days of any calendar year'.

Finney deservedly won best actor at the Baftas for what was his greatest screen performance since *Miller's Crossing*. His Churchill was simply magnificent.

Finney looked quite heavy as Churchill. And somehow when I saw him in *Big Fish* I was reminded of a great beached whale, albeit an ultra-loquacious one. And he had one thing in common with the character; many who know Finney well mention that he is a great raconteur. Interviewers have come away charmed by Finney's anecdote-a-minute stuff, everything from working with old greats like Wilfred Lawson and Olivier through to tales of his latest film. It's possible that a well-told story is Finney's way of fobbing off interviewers lest they penetrate the 'hard top' that he carefully guards.

Theatrical anecdotes are repeated down the ages, sometimes apocryphal, or the names are interchangeable. The audience is advised to treat them with caution. In the case of Richard Burton, another scintillating storyteller, his daughter felt that his addiction to spinning a yarn came partially from nervousness, a way of avoiding real conversation. Perhaps, then, Finney identified with the character of Ed Bloom, a compulsive storyteller – but of fact or fiction? – who is visited on his Alabama deathbed by his son (Billy Crudup) in Tim Burton's enjoyable fantasy, *Big Fish*. Bloom has told so many anecdotes that in the end he has fallen out with his son – until that is, his illness raises the prospect of reconciliation. Finney's scenes, mostly bedbound, were shot at the beginning. He plays Bloom with a luxuriant southern drawl, almost lingering over his dialogue. (To have to listen to these oft-repeated tales in that slow voice must have been torture for Bloom's family!)

Rising star Ewan McGregor, who had a bit part in *Karaoke*, played Bloom as a younger man. 'It was a huge honour to meet Albert Finney because he's a legend, you know, and when you do meet him, he's a beautiful man. He's a really sweet guy,' said McGregor. And McGregor does bear a striking resemblance to the young Finney. (Once I caught myself looking at the Finney character in *Charlie Bubbles* and could have sworn it was McGregor.)

But what are we watching? It's a charming, picturesque, *Forrest Gump*-ish stroll as Finney recounts his misadventures. Whether the stories are real is perhaps not all that important. By the end, when characters from Bloom's past appear at his funeral, we are inclined to believe they are based on some truth, albeit embroidered into elaborate mythologies. A mixture of Santa Claus and the Easter Bunny perhaps, all heightened by a fantasy sequence at the end.

Burton thought Finney's larger-than-life, zestful image was ideal for Bloom:

Albert's got that real passion for life, very much like the character, and he brought a lot of himself to the role, while Ewan captured that heightened reality and open-heartedness – it's beautiful when actors can be open-hearted … The stuff with Albert was so intense and then we did the Ewan stuff which had a completely different energy. Ewan still came at the beginning but we didn't shoot much but he still came by. He was a quiet observer at times. We discussed things and Albert and Ewan spent a little time together, and we had a couple of dinners. With Ewan I sense he thinks a lot and does his own quiet study and research, and then he doesn't want to talk about it too much but he'll go for it. I sense that with him. I always sensed when he was ready to start shooting. I could see him quietly watching Albert and soaking it all in.[5]

Finney was initially surprised that Burton chose two Brits to play the old and younger Bloom, 'But I've played Americans before and so had Ewan and so, I don't think that Tim thought it was a problem. I enjoyed it too. I like playing accents, and doing things like that.'

Finney soon settled into what he called a 'lovely' set:

I didn't know any of the actors before but it felt almost like a family within the first few days. From the beginning of the film, I thought that I was somehow in safe, good hands with Tim. I think that all the actors did. You just feel comfortable with him, and he certainly makes sure that you're comfortable. He makes sure that you feel good and that you're happy with what you're doing.

Finney said he was struck by Burton's 'sweetness and niceness':

That continued to surprise because the project seems to be huge, the film, and yet, he seemed to have time for everyone and as Jessica [Lange] said, the way he ran about was funny. He'd just run, run all the time, and he walks about, doesn't he, he never stops. I think that they put an odometer on him one day and he walked miles.

Like many fine directors, Finney found that Burton was not so much directing as suggesting. He allowed the actors to fly with it:

He just lets you go, really. When we were kind of supposed to rehearse, I don't remember rehearsing at all. We just sort of gossiped and chatted. There was no specific rehearsal. All we did in Alabama was have a read through with the script, but there was no, 'well, it needs more. You've got to do this, Albert. You've got to do that, Jessica.' It didn't feel like that at all. He very much lets you be. You offer things up, I suppose, and he probably gently maybe changes it a little bit one way or another, but you don't feel directed as it were … I think that one of Tim's great qualities and abilities is in what seems like a thumbnail sketch to get something quite telling, very simply, when you're doing it or being in that thumbnail sketch, you don't feel that it's important. You just feel what the scene is, what it's about, be it a minute scene or a two minute scene, or a five minute scene, the scene in the bathtub that we had together, someone was talking about that before, but it didn't feel that we were doing anything sort of significant or dramatic, but we just got on with it. I think that Tim can do that in the film and he does it quite often. He has a very simple stroke.[6]

Finney and Pene rented a house on the river, staying for just over two months, just outside Alabama. 'I hardly got to see Alabama. You can't when you're filming, you're just busy,' he recalled. 'I used to come home and my girl would make me dinner and it was lovely. We lived on the river floating by and the world going by on the river was nice.'

He liked McGregor but said they didn't actually liaise that often:

The only thing that Ewan and I conferred on was how we cast a fishing line. We said we'd do it round arm rather than over, and that was the only time that we conferred, really. So, we didn't actually … I thought that I'd leave it to the young fellow to copy me, to lessen my workload.

Finney said he sympathised with the son in the story and that the father's endless storytelling must prove tiresome:

It's difficult, really, I suppose for the boy when you have a father who doesn't quite talk to you. He tells you stories, but then, after a while, when you want more, he doesn't give you more. He insists on this old elaboration, the old stories that never change. It's very difficult to have a father like that. I understand the angst of the son and the frustration of the son. His father's not there.

Finney said that his relationship with his son Simon, 45, at the time of *Big Fish*, was good:

Sometimes you feel more at ease with a nephew and he with you. It's not as complicated or as genetic or as responsible as the matter of being an elder to your own son … if you ask me how my relationship with my son may have flavoured my performance here, I'll tell you that's a question for Simon … Of course, I always think my relationship with my son is perfectly fine.

When Finney did *Annie*, a magazine article noted that he was the last person one would associate with children. And one can see why. Finney's whole life indicates a man who believes in moving, one suspicious of permanence. Even when his first two marriages failed, Finney seemed philosophical, oddly disengaged about the whole process. When Simon was growing up Finney admitted he didn't see him much. But, later, father and son grew closer. 'I took quite an objective view of this little fellow,' Finney said in 1982, shortly after Simon had graduated in modern English history from Oxford:

> And, of course, a certain conventional pride in achievement, that I helped make it. And perhaps what I was more conscious of was the surprise that it was not the all-embracing, grasping, illuminating moment of auteur that perhaps one had been led to believe. I became aware of the practicality of birth. I guess I kind of felt Simon would only be interesting to me if he were interesting. Or, if you will, that one's offspring are possibly interesting or not – I don't see that there's any rule that they have to be. When we were together in California, it became sort of a confirmation that we got on, that he was a pal and buddy. I enjoyed being with him; I hope he enjoyed being with me.

The final scene called for Finney to make himself light – if it were possible – so that his son could carry him to the pond:

> In ballet, when you kind of lift yourself here, it's all up in the head. So, you can try it when you're going up stairs next time. Instead of plodding upstairs, think of yourself as going up with your head, and it's amazing what you can do. There were wires, and I was in a sort of bucket moulded to my body. So long as the wires don't cross your face … I never thought that it would look like it did because with the crane, it's an extraordinary contraption. They're everything.

Critiques of *Big Fish* were generally favourable even though some tired of Bloom's hot air. Roger Eberts said:

> Because Burton is the director, *Big Fish* of course is a great-looking film, with a fantastical visual style that could be called Felliniesque if Burton had not by now earned the right to the adjective Burtonesque. Yet there is no denying that Will has a point: The old man is a blowhard. There is a point at which his stories stop working as entertainment and segue into sadism.

O.A. Scott, in the *New York Times*, also found Bloom a bit much:

The film insists on viewing its hero as an affectionate, irrepressible raconteur.
From where I sat, he looked more like an incorrigible narcissist and also, perhaps, a compulsive liar, whose love for others is little more than overflowing
self-infatuation. But all this might be forgivable – everyone else in the picture
thinks so – if Edward were not also a bit of a bore.

Scott added, however, that both McGregor's and Finney's accent were 'not bad
at all'.

Big Fish is pleasant whimsy if you like that sort of thing. Some of us have had
bad experiences with inveterate storytellers and, unless they are exceptionally
witty, find them off-putting. For Finney, however, it was another enjoyable
experience, so much so that, a couple of years later, he agreed to voice Finis
Everglot in Burton's animated feature, *Corpse Bride*, a part that reunited him
with Joanna Lumley.

Big Fish marked Finney's progression into (early) old age. At moments of
repose, lying on his deathbed, Finney, not just the character, seems a little tired.
Smaller character parts awaited him but ones Finney could still imbue with
greatness. As his friend Peter O'Toole once remarked, 'there is no such thing as
a small part, only small actors'.

SLOWING DOWN

Keep your head down and work hard.

                Albert Finney to actor Lloyd Owen.

Finney was all set to reprise his Churchill, this time taking him through to the war years. Whitemore was working on a script in 2004 but, in the end, it took several years to complete. When it was finally made in 2009, Brendan Gleeson inherited the part. Finney's agent said he 'lost interest' because he felt 'the script wasn't quite right'. However, Tracy Scoffield, one of the producers of the BBC-HBO drama, stated that Finney 'bowed out gracefully' only because he didn't like the idea of playing the same part twice.

Finney was now entering a quieter period. He told an interviewer that he tried to be selective when picking a part:

> That doesn't mean that I make the right selections. I'd like to be that selective. It's true that old actors don't die, their parts get smaller. You're less likely to get the part, many parts, if you're playing people your age as opposed to people who are younger. There are fewer parts around.

A gentle part was as Uncle Henry in Ridley Scott's *A Good Year*, starring Russell Crowe, filmed in the South of France in 2005. It's a story about rediscovering the innocence of childhood and self-appraisal. Uncle Henry appears in the flashback scenes with young Max, played by Freddie Highmore. Scott cast Finney, in spite of his alleged misgivings over the actor's performance in *The Browning Version*, after the screenwriter Marc Klein said that Henry, in his mind, sounded like Albert Finney. And this was a wine connoisseur, after all! 'A good wine never lies,' he tells Max.

Uncle Henry was no great stretch for an actor of Finney's skill. Yet his role is pivotal, as Crowe said at the time:

Once Max returns to the place where he spent his childhood summers the echo of what Henry said to him starts resonating in him more and he realises there's another way of taking those things Henry told him and taking them to a different sum total.

Scott had been aching to get away from the action genre:

As I go on, I'm very attracted to comedy. At the end of the day, because you've been having a good old laugh, you go home laughing – as opposed to dealing with blood all day and you go home and want to cut your wrists.

Unfortunately, *A Good Year* did not engender quite the laughter intended. Somehow the plot – successful, unscrupulous London-based bond trader discovers the meaning of life in the sun after falling for local girl – is rather clichéd. The film is too clearly a bid to replicate the success of Peter Mayle's *A Year in Provence*, on which *A Good Year* was based. Finney is fine but Crowe is not suited to light comedy; his appearance, manner and voice rather convey masculine authority – as in *Gladiator*.

The script is at its best in its incidental details, for example when Max, revisiting the house after thirty-odd years, sees marks on the wall where he used to play cricket. Suddenly the decades tumble away. A childhood home rockets you back quicker than a time machine.

Aside from producing *The Browning Version*, Scott had been executive producer of *The Gathering Storm*. He had also directed Finney's cameo in *The Duellists*. So this marked their fourth collaboration. Scott said at the time:

I know him pretty well. What you see on-screen in this film really is Albert. Uncle Henry is Albert Finney. He's as jolly as that character, he's full of joie de vivre and I couldn't think of anybody who could play the part better. Freddie Highmore, who plays young Max and spent a lot of time with Albert, adored him too.[1]

The critics generally thought it predictable stuff. Kenneth Turan of the *Los Angeles Times* observed:

The scenery may be attractive and the cast likewise, but something vital is missing in this all-too-leisurely film … The fact that we know exactly what will happen to Max from the moment he appears on-screen is not what's wrong with *A Good Year*. After all, we go to films like this precisely because the satisfaction of emotional certainty is what we're looking for.

Todd McCarthy called the film 'a simple repast consisting of sometimes strained slapsticky comedy, a sweet romance and a life lesson learnt, this little picnic doesn't amount to much but goes down easily enough'. The film went down all right. It made a slender profit but was viewed as a box office bomb in the industry.

In *Amazing Grace*, the story of William Wilberforce's campaign against the slave trade, Finney played a real-life figure, John Newton,[2] the former trader who undergoes an epiphany and backs the abolitionists. Finney, first seen in flashback sweeping a church floor, dressed in a sackcloth, brings dignity, depth and a kind of unusual (for him) asceticism to the part. He is, he says, living in the company of 20,000 ghosts, and adds, 'I'm not strong enough to hear my own confession.' Finney, as Newton, is almost spitting with rage when he urges Wilberforce (Ioan Gruffudd) to 'throw their dirty, filthy [slave] ships out of the water'.

Newton, by now blind, appears at the end to hear the House of Commons pass the Slave Trade Act in 1807 – actually shot at a church within Chatham Historic Dockyard. And Finney portrays blindness convincingly. As he listens to the final vote in favour of abolition his whole face brightens. His eyes stare ahead, locked and vacant, but somehow his face is monumentally expressive. Technically, Finney was always the master of his craft and his performance here is every bit as naturalistic as in *Saturday Night and Sunday Morning*.

The film, directed by Michael Apted, who had delivered some taut, fast-moving atmospheric thrillers like *The Squeeze* and *Gorky Park* and the Bond movie *The World is not Enough*, is well-meaning and earnest. Yet it feels like one of those old Sunday night BBC plays. The acting, however, is a joy. Alex von Tunzelmann, in *The Guardian*, said, '*Amazing Grace*'s strong performances sometimes lift its plodding pace but it's a stodgy and old-fashioned historical drama'. For Peter Bradshaw, 'a decent cast under Michael Apted's direction does its best, but it's dull, naïve and dramatically inert'.

As Finney turned 70, the parts were getting smaller. He enjoyed a pleasant reunion with Sidney Lumet, his old pal from *Murder on the Orient Express* in *Before the Devil Knows You're Dead*. Finney played a widower whose wife is inadvertently killed in a bungled jewellery shop robbery, one planned by their own sons. The film, which repeatedly jumped back and forth in time, was compelling yet not quite credible. The late Philip Seymour Hoffman and Ethan Hawke were excellent as scheming brothers. For Finney it was a breeze, until the ending which had him murdering his own son!

The Bourne Ultimatum was a part that Finney could normally have done with his eyes closed. The film itself is a fast-moving thriller, complete with dizzying camera angles, and quite a nice tour of various capital cities. Finney, bespectacled and ruddy-faced, could still command a scene. 'We didn't pick you. You picked us,' Finney, as Dr Albert Hirsch, tells Bourne in a rumbling deep voice.

Finney looked a bit rough in *The Bourne Ultimatum*, betraying his declining health. Up until now, the odd minor gripe notwithstanding, his health had been fine. But in 2007 he faced serious illness. He developed cancer of the kidney and needed an operation and six rounds of chemotherapy. Like many of his generation, when he spoke of illness it was simple, matter-of-fact, no bullshitting or self-pity. 'I didn't feel anything on the first two, then the third one, I thought, that's funny, I feel bad,' he said. 'That got worse. It took me about a year or a year-and-a-half to feel it was out of my system. But it saved me.'

It must have been a depressing time, but Finney seemed remarkably sanguine. In (rare) interviews – such as one for the *Manchester Evening News* when he visited his sister's home in Davyhulme – he reminisced fondly but without sentimentality. He told Paul Taylor that he accepted change:

> The Lowry painting of the industrial north with the factory chimneys and smoke … that was going to be forever. It looked eternal, and yet it's all gone. Now when you see the test match from Old Trafford on the television, you can actually see the Pennines, which you couldn't before. It's change for the better in some ways.

Finney was mostly out of action between 2007 and 2011. He had a minor role in *The Bourne Legacy*, his puffy, bloated appearance reflecting his illness. By now Finney and Pene spent most of their time in West Sussex. Emsworth, not far from Chichester, is a beautiful seaside town near the affluent yachting fraternity that formed the backdrop to the popular TV series *Howard's Way*. Lynda Bellingham described an idyllic trip to see the Finneys:

> Albert and Pene have the perfect home within walking distance of the sea and, as Albie pointed out, the town boasts over thirty pubs. Their house has a walled garden and herb patch, and it was full of gorgeous flowers. It had that wonderful calm about it which I always associated with walled gardens, as the old brickwork seems to absorb all outside noise except the birds and the bees. We sat and had a lovely glass of something cool and fizzy while awaiting the arrival of [Finney's close friend] Julian Holloway. It was good to see him again and remember old times. We then adjourned to Albert's local, the Bluebell, and had a glorious boozy lunch. It was bliss.[3]

As a lifelong supporter of Manchester United, Finney narrated the documentary *Munich*, about the 1958 air crash that killed twenty-three passengers, including eight United footballers, known as the Busby Babes in honour of manager Sir Matt Busby. Finney donated his fee for the voiceover to the Manchester

United Foundation. The programme aired on United's TV channel MUTV in February 2008.

Finney explained why he did the narration:

Being a Salford lad, the Munich disaster meant a lot to me at the time. Although I was away from Salford then, I was in the theatre working at a matinee and in the evening that day.[4] I was very hurt by it, shattered by the loss of such potential … We talk about the Swinging Sixties, but the seeds of change were happening earlier and I suppose Matt Busby was instrumental in that, to focus so accurately and smartly on youth. He saw what was happening and what could happen and should happen. And therefore in a way, the Busby Babes were the forerunners of that social revolution. They were certainly in the vanguard.[5]

Finney also spoke of his excitement at seeing United win the European Cup in 1968, beating Benfica 4–1 in the final:

I was there. We couldn't believe it. I mean, that victory was, it seems an odd word to say, almost justification of everything. But truly, it really justified Matt's insistence on going into Europe. I mean he was quite right. The old farts at the FA couldn't see their noses, couldn't see a yard in front of their faces and he was saying this is the way the future is. This is the way the game will go. And he's absolutely right. Look at the size of the game. But it was an incredible night. And I was very lucky to be there. I was glad I wasn't working at that time so I could go out at night instead of being stuck in a theatre saying some silly lines.

'Silly lines?' In a theatre? Surely not!

By now, Finney could afford to be extremely selective with the parts sent his way. His lawyer, Nigel Bennett, speaking in 2011, made clear that his client was careful about roles, 'Mr Finney is at the time of life when he can be extra choosy about the roles that he accepts. These are difficult times for film producers and he won't even read a script unless the film is fully financed.'

In 2011, Dustin Hoffman wanted Finney to play the part of Wilf in *Quartet*, written by Finney's long-time collaborator Ronald Harwood. The film, about a home for retired musicians, would have reunited Finney with his friends Tom Courtenay and Maggie Smith. Sadly, he felt that a long shoot was beyond him. (His part was taken by Billy Connolly.)[6] Courtenay, in particular, was looking forward to working with Finney again. They remained close friends who met often.

Another venture, a possible remake of Sheridan's 1775 comedy *The Rivals*, in which Finney was supposed to appear alongside Imelda Staunton and Joseph Fiennes, fell through because of financing problems. Talk of another series of *Rumpole of the Bailey* (with Finney in the role made famous by Leo McKern) came to nothing.

Later, in 2011, Finney had a comeback of a sort, albeit in a small role, but one that introduced him to a new generation of filmgoers. Sam Mendes cast him as an old gamekeeper in the Bond movie *Skyfall*. The film is named for the Scottish ranch and ancestral home where Bond (Daniel Craig) and M (Judi Dench) take refuge in the film's climax. There they meet a gruff, bearded old rascal who has known Bond since he was a child.

Mendes confirmed that the writers had originally penned the role with Sean Connery in mind:

There was a definite discussion about [Connery playing Kincade] – way, way early on. But I think that's problematic. Because, to me, it becomes too … it would take you out of the movie. Connery is Bond and he's not going to come back as another character. It's like, he's been there. So, it was a very brief flirtation with that thought, but it was never going to happen, because I thought it would distract.

Finney's addition was kept a secret. The story goes that the other actors were reading their parts when Mendes introduced a surprise cast member. It was Finney, making his first ever Bond appearance at the age of 75.

'Welcome to Scotland!' is Kincade's opening salvo as he blasts some villains away. Finney's Kincade, rather hoarse and breathless, is still a formidable foe and adept at putting Bond in his place, having known him since childhood. 'Try and stop me, you jumped up little shit,' he tells him. Finney thought that Daniel Craig, in his third Bond outing 'really fits the jacket snugly and has a nice edge to him'. A bonus was working with Judi Dench for the first time. 'Ridiculous, really. I've been in the business for fifty-odd years and Judi's been in it for some time and we'd never met before. But it was a pleasure. She's a great lady and it was lovely to be in her presence,' said Finney during an on-set interview.

The film was hailed by the critics. The only sniping came from writer Sebastian Faulks. 'The critics said it was one of the greatest Bond films, which is clearly not true. Albert Finney can't do a Scottish accent,' he said, rather ungraciously.[7]

Skyfall was to be Finney's final acting credit. The actor might be 'resting', but discussions about Finney's influence on British acting continue to this day.

REFLECTIONS

He made it possible for the likes of me, my generation, which is one under him, to actually leave the provinces and go to London and make it.

Malcolm McDowell.

Nothing much was heard of Finney after *Skyfall*. But his name was often bandied about in discussions about acting and, in particular, the perennial British obsession with class. In early 2015, the shadow culture minister Chris Bryant said that, although he was delighted by the achievement of people like Eddie Redmayne (who had just won a Golden Globe for playing Stephen Hawking in *The Theory of Everything* and would subsequently win an Oscar) the arts world should hire people from more humble backgrounds.

Bryant's comments came at a time when perceptions were that privileged 'posh' actors like Redmayne, Benedict Cumberbatch, Dominic West and Damian Lewis were too dominant. Julie Walters, Ian McKellen, Christopher Eccleston[1] and Helen Mirren have all voiced similar concerns. 'Where are the Albert Finneys and the Glenda Jacksons?' asked Bryant:

> They came through a meritocratic system. But it wasn't just that. It was also that the writers were writing stuff for them. So is the BBC, ITV, Channel 4, doing that kind of gritty drama, which reflects [the country] more? We can't just have *Downton* programming ad infinitum and think that just because we've got some people in the servants' hall, somehow or other we've done our duty by gritty drama.

To which one could say – consider Danny Dyer or Jason Statham or Ray Winstone, and the endless array of soaps about ordinary people and their problems. And Bryant's view is not unanimously held. Roger Moore, for example, in a *Daily Mail* article in 2010, had noted a different trend:

Commander Bond has to speak the Queen's English – and how I wish more of us would. I have always spoken that way. But if I were a young actor trying to find work today, the way I talk would be a handicap. In fact, my actress daughter, Deborah, who also speaks like me, claims she regularly struggles in auditions because her accent 'isn't regional enough'. For it seems that these days no one wants to speak like Her Majesty, especially on stage and screen. This is a great pity.[2]

Moore, with tongue-in-cheek, went on to blame his friends, Michael Caine and 'Albie' Finney.

James Fox also dismissed the criticism of posh actors like Redmayne:

It's complete balls … it's just classist. I was brought up in a generation that despised upper-class people … I was one of the only actors of my background who made it in my twenties. All the rest were working class: Terry Stamp, Albie Finney, Tom Courtenay, Michael Caine.

Fox implied the rise of 'posh' actors was redressing the balance after decades of success for working-class talent. Celia Imrie agreed and again cited Finney in her comments:

In those days it wasn't fashionable to have a posh voice. It was the era of Albert Finney and northern accents. I read James Blunt's defence of 'posh' in response to Chris Bryant saying there were too many posh people in the arts. I'm on James Blunt's side – you can't help how you were born. Chris Bryant can get stuffed actually.

Prunella Scales also noted the tendency for non-working-class actors to have to hide their origins:

My parents came from a theatre background but I kept schtum about those connections. You were meant to be Albert Finney from a raw working-class family with no theatrical antecedents. It's all right now: my son [Sam West] has two parents, three grandparents and two great-grandparents who have worked in theatre. But there was a feeling then that people who grew up in acting families didn't know about real life. Whereas Albert Finney did.[3]

Finney's friend, Julian Fellowes,[4] who later created *Downton Abbey*, also went through a period where he thought his class went against him: 'There was an assumption that if you came from my background, you couldn't have much to say.'

Yet there is something inaccurate here about Finney. The press were perhaps in danger of confusing Finney's persona in *Saturday Night and Sunday Morning* with the actor. Finney, as we have seen, perhaps more than anyone else, ushered in the new wave of cinema. *Saturday Night and Sunday Morning* was one of the first films set around an authentically working-class character, but the idea that Finney ever *represented* the typical working-class man, or that his name became somehow synonymous with the working class, is a little odd, especially for someone whose background was not all that uncomfortable. Finney has always studiously resented typecasting anyway and has played, very convincingly, 'privileged' parts. For him, Arthur Seaton, groundbreaking though it might have been, was just another role.

The other misconception surrounding Finney goes to the heart of his character. Finney was never really an angry young man. The label was pinned on him because he played Arthur Seaton so well and because the portrayal coincided with a revolution in British cinema. True, Finney might have made a few pronouncements against the middle-class nature of British acting at the time.[5] Yet that did not mean he was angry. On the contrary, everyone who knew, and knows, Finney speaks of his charm and easygoing nature. It was just another label. The press, and perhaps to a lesser extent, the public, like to pigeonhole actors but they got it wrong in Finney's case.

Nicol Williamson might have deserved the label 'angry'; certainly the playwright John Osborne. But Finney? In a sense all young actors who came to fame in the sixties, not only Finney, O'Toole, Harris, Courtenay, Stamp and Caine, but also other leading men like Ian Hendry or Tom Bell, were 'rebels'. But that was only because British cinema of the late fifties was so stuffy and conservative. And although Finney continued to cultivate an image as a bit of an outsider, for example not attending the Oscars, refusing a knighthood and (perhaps jokingly) railing against Caine and Connery for 'letting the side down', this was hardly the stuff of class warfare.

If Finney was groundbreaking it was in his approach to stardom and his (perhaps conscious) rejection of attempts to conceal his background. Finney's northern roots showed through in interviews and even sometimes in his interpretation of roles (we recall Ian McKellen's observation that Finney played Macbeth with a northern accent). So then being a northerner became sexy. Julia Goodman recollects this from her time at the Central School in the mid-sixties: 'Some of the boys even pretended to be from the north and working class. The northern boys were even starting to get the upper hand.' She thinks now that the balance may be too weighted in favour of southern actors but believes that 'a sexy Albert Finney type mark two' would change all that. Perhaps Scottish actors Ewan McGregor or James McAvoy are the nearest modern-day equivalents to Finney in terms of talent, sex appeal, looks and background.

Finney's breakthrough enabled other actors, a few years behind him and from similar backgrounds, to walk tall. Finney and Courtenay became heroes to northerners like Malcolm McDowell and John Thaw. McDowell, in particular, has cited Finney as his favourite actor, 'He made it possible for the likes of me, my generation, which is one under him, to actually leave the provinces and go to London and make it. He made it. He was one of the first to do that.'

And not just big stars are in Finney's debt. Would British television series like *The Likely Lads* have been made without the likes of Finney opening the 'can of peas' first? (Rodney Bewes is another television star who has named Finney as a hero – even more so when Finney turned down a knighthood.)

To jaundiced observers, notably the late Lindsay Anderson, Finney might have kept a rough edge to his accent but he had lost some authenticity along the way:

> Working-class actors can become successful now, but only at the price of making themselves 'respectable' and conforming to bourgeois standards. Albert Finney is a perfect example. He preserves a certain superficial roughness of speech, but has sacrificed his real abrasiveness and any real quality of emotion he had.[6]

But Anderson's comments came before Finney's punchy performances in *Shoot the Moon* and *The Dresser*.

Janet Suzman, speaking in 1997, noted the sea change that the likes of Finney, but *especially* Finney, ushered:

> At the time I went there [to LAMDA in 1959] there'd been a terrific change, there was a new egalitarianism, really. I think the moment people like Albert Finney – which was just pre-me – started hitting drama schools, regional people, vocational training began to change. Because it was with the advent of the Finneys of this world [does regional accent] who talked like that and came from up north, that the whole idea of Received Pronunciation and polite expertise began to devolve.[7]

'Working-class' actors in general, like Ray Winstone and Gary Oldman, also owe a lot to Finney. Not to be forgotten too is that Finney helped to launch the careers of directors like Stephen Frears, Ridley Scott and Mike Leigh.

The real question is whether an actor of Finney's talent and modest background would be able to break through today as Finney did sixty years ago. Jimmy McGovern, creator of *Cracker*, believes not:

I'm constantly looking around for actors who can convincingly portray working-class men. They're getting fewer and fewer because it's only the posh ones
who can afford to go into acting. If you were to cast *Saturday Night and Sunday
Morning* today, who would you get for the Albert Finney role?[8]

Michael Attenborough, on the other hand, who teaches at RADA, makes clear
that Britain's greatest drama school 'never turns down anyone on the grounds of
funding … there's an element of exaggeration in terms of access to the profession and a lot of contemporary TV is not *Downton Abbey*.'

There is no definitive conclusion to all this, especially in such an arbitrary
profession as acting. The debate seems to be ongoing, reignited in January 2016
after the passing of Alan Rickman who grew up in an Acton council house.[9]
Around this time, the director of RADA, Edward Kemp, said that it is not that
they 'train only posh kids' but rather that they 'train kids to be posh' to increase
their chances of finding work.

Connoisseurs of great acting have also noted that Finney is not as well known
nowadays as he should be. It's partly because Finney, although naturally gre-
garious, is also extremely private. He has (mostly) shunned interviews and
chat shows as well as film premieres and award ceremonies. He enjoys a party
but not necessarily those on the 'celebrity circuit'. His reluctance to promote
himself means that he has been surpassed in purely fame stakes not only by the
'obvious suspects' – Caine, Connery, Moore, Harris and Reed – but also by
other peers, the likes of Anthony Hopkins, Ian McKellen, even Derek Jacobi
and Michael Gambon.

He has retained his star quality – the late Susannah York said, 'whether he
[Finney] has got fat or thin, he still has that kind of leading man stature' – without actually being a box office draw. Roger Moore has described his friend's
credo, 'He'll turn up, give a great performance and then go home'. Further
proof of Finney's nonconformist streak is that he doesn't even have an agent,
preferring to negotiate through a lawyer.

Another reason why his name no longer resonates with Joe Public is that,
although he has worked prodigiously, he has been selective. Some of his great
roles are not well known outside theatrical circles. His name lacks an instant
association with an on-screen character. And the public likes to 'categorise' actors.
For example, Caine is Alfie or Carter; Hopkins is Hannibal Lecter; Connery and
Moore are Bond; O'Toole is Lawrence; Finney is … Arthur Seaton, maybe Tom
Jones even more? Perhaps, but it's all too long ago. So was *Lawrence of Arabia*, but
the David Lean classic became an international epic movie.

Finney also lacks that off-screen notoriety – I'm thinking especially of Harris
and Reed – that makes some actors part of the national culture and 'total legends'

to the man, but not necessarily the woman, in the pub (I can't tell you how many times I have heard that phrase about Reed). Finney's chameleon-like transformations mean that his real personality is not as instantly identifiable as, for example, Caine or Connery, both long-standing favourites for impersonators. Who can do a Finney impression? It would be difficult for the most talented mimic. Finney's timbre is unmistakable, but in interviews his accent tends to change. Finney is more likely to mimic *others*. And that gives us the final clue as to how he sees himself. He is a character man, slipping in and out of disguise. 'I'm not the romantic type … I'm a bit like the late, great Peter Sellers, only happy in character roles,' Finney has said, perhaps slightly self-disparagingly.

The result is that, to the ordinary viewing public under the age of 40, he is now relatively unknown. (I once showed a picture of Finney to an educated work colleague. He replied, 'I know him. He was good in *Snatch*.') It's unlikely that Finney would worry about any of this, of course.

It is not just Finney who is under-appreciated. His contemporary Nicol Williamson, for example, has definitely suffered an even worse fate. His death, in 2011, passed virtually unnoticed outside theatrical circles. And, even in 1993, an *Independent* article by Robert Butler noted Williamson's drift into obscurity, 'When I rang a leading producer for a comment on him, the receptionist said, "Sorry, which production is she in?"'.

Steven Berkoff has made a more telling, perhaps sadder point – that even many young aspiring actors do not know as much as they should about the greats of yesteryear. Not only Finney but also Richardson, Guinness, Howard, Gielgud, and even Olivier, leave them cold:

> The young actors today are so ghastly, uninteresting, boring, tedious, they know nothing about their culture, they know nothing about the great legends of the past. You say, what do you think of Gielgud – who's that? What do you think of Trevor Howard? – Oh, I dunno. What do you think of Edmund Kean? – I've never heard of him. They know nothing.[10]

Berkoff claimed, perhaps with some justification, that too many of today's breed chase fame but have no interest in learning their craft on stage.

Brian Cox, in a recent interview, also made a similar point:

> It is important to know the roots of things, where you are from and how acting developed … the passing of people like Peter O'Toole and Alan Bates, people of that generation, they belonged to something which was quite revolutionary, previous to that it was the Oliviers, it was the Gielguds.

Knowledge of yesterday's greats was essential, he said, to establish 'that sense of a continuum, and where these actors broke ground in very different ways. It just needs attention, if nothing else. I think one of the problems of the day is that history started five minutes ago'. Cox also said that some young British actors weren't all that interesting:

> The Benedicts, the Redmaynes are very good. But, I look at a lot of young actors and I don't think they're very good. There's a thing that goes on in acting now where they don't engage, there's a blandness about them, they're homogenised.[11]

Perhaps the comments of Berkoff and Cox just reflect the sometimes misplaced motives of those entering the business.[12] Doubtless, a young professional boxer, aspiring to get to the top, would know about the great fights of Ali, Foreman and Tyson. Acting, however, carries with it the fundamental misconception that anyone can do it. And, in a sense, that is true. But few can act very well. And fewer still can hope to act as well as Finney. Show today's young aspiring actors the great performances of the past and doubtless they would be impressed. But would they bother to investigate them in the first place? (Actor Jeremy Young once told me that many of the drama students he teaches had not even heard of Laurence Olivier.)

Part of the problem also lies in the way our fame-obsessed culture devalues the meaning of words. A bit-part actor in some soap is described as a star in the tabloids. Television soaps, in particular, do not necessarily offer a good training ground for actors. But TV is, as they say, 'where it's at'. A soap star or indeed the star of a regular TV series, and not necessarily a versatile one at that, can become more famous than a leading man like Finney. John Thaw is more famous than Albert Finney and, while I mean no disrespect to the late, great star of *Inspector Morse*, my point is that although Finney was more acclaimed, indeed one of the most lauded actors of his generation and the star of many magnificent international films, TV still makes you more famous.

Such matters will almost certainly not trouble Finney who claimed that he never became an actor to be famous or even rich, although he admitted that wealth was icing on the cake. Finney is, as Maureen Lipman once said, comfortable in his own skin. Similarly, the lack of an Oscar may perturb some of Finney's fans.[13] But it is unlikely to trouble him one iota. All agree that Finney could have been an even bigger star if he so chose. Bernard Hepton, for example, has not seen Finney since 1959 but he says he still thinks about Finney a lot, 'His career could have been very starry. He could have been as big as Caine or Connery but he didn't want it. He has always done what he wanted to do.'

Acting inevitably changes over the years. Ironically, Finney's style, once acclaimed as groundbreaking and revolutionary, has been superseded by – at least on-screen – a great deal of incomprehensible mumbling. A Finney performance, just like one by O'Toole, was a great crowd-drawing event – what's he going to do now? But theatre itself has changed. Certain names *do* attract audiences. Benedict Cumberbatch was the obvious example in 2015. But, in general, a great production is not made or (unmade) by a star turn.

Amanda Waring has also noted the change in acting styles:

Finney had a magnificent aura on stage. He and O'Toole had that slightly maverick quality and an air of danger. You never quite knew what they were going to do next. It was about taking risks. Modern actors have to a certain extent been anaesthetised. Political correctness has come in and, although it has some good aspects to it, it has rubbed out some other qualities. Exorbitant ticket prices don't help. People go in feeling resentful before a show has even started.

Matt Truman wrote an interesting article in response to the furore surrounding Berkoff's comments:

Not only are the spaces often smaller – Olivier never played a seventy-seat studio theatre – but design has taken on more of a role in affecting an audience. Sound, lighting and directorial decisions, even movement direction, all come together to create mood, tone and atmosphere, thereby freeing the actor from bombast. Today's actors can afford to do less, but that requires a different skillset entirely: precision instead of power, subtlety instead of starriness, perhaps even transparency instead of transformation.

Many of Finney's contemporaries may rue that Finney didn't succeed Olivier at the National. He could have had the job if he wanted it. He is a powerful figure who could have drawn many famous names. Perhaps, too, he would have shunned what some saw as an over-intellectualised theatre and brought some fireworks to the South Bank. But the commitment was too much for a person like Finney who liked to go his own way.

These days Finney largely sticks to home turf. He has emphysema, a condition probably linked to his smoking. He's still capable of having a good time, though, and Eileen Atkins remembers Keith Baxter's 80th birthday party in 2013:

Everyone was there, including Maggie and Judi Dench and Albert Finney and the four of us ended up on a table together. I looked at the bunch of us. Judi can't see much, Maggie and I don't hear too well and Albert was drunk. But I thought we all looked rather lovely and we were all roaring with laughter. It was absolutely bloody perfect.

A difficult occasion for Finney was Peter O'Toole's memorial service at the Old Vic on 18 May 2014. Struggling to contain himself as he paid tribute to his old RADA buddy, Finney posed for photographs alongside Benedict Cumberbatch and Kevin Spacey. Annabel Leventon, who had appeared with O'Toole in *Jeffrey Bernard is Unwell*, shared a stage with Finney as they celebrated their mutual friend:

> I'd never met him before and he was utterly charming to me and had no need to be. He had been at RADA with Peter and they adored each other. When Albert got up to give his piece, he broke down a couple of times, but carried on with wonderful presence and humanity.

Finney can look back on a career that has defied typecasting. If there is sadness, it's that he has been unable to continue acting into old age. Finney, like Olivier, loves acting and to lack the stamina for important parts must be frustrating. Yet he leaves behind several truly great performances on film – *Saturday Night and Sunday Morning*, *Murder on the Orient Express*, *The Dresser*, *Miller's Crossing*, *Erin Brockovich* and *The Gathering Storm* readily springing to mind. And all his screen portrayals, if not touched by greatness, are interesting in their own way. On stage, those who were lucky enough to see *Billy Liar*, *Luther* or *Orphans* will never forget them.

Those who accused Finney of 'coasting' in his career have been proven wrong. A tough, challenging role has invariably followed an 'easy' one. In the end, whether he inherited the mantle of Olivier was not really as relevant to Finney as it was to a bunch of esoteric critics. His career, notwithstanding the voluntary 'sabbaticals' that have punctuated it, has had regular highlights.

Living, not art, was more important to Finney. He has managed to live on his own terms. He has got into the skin of all the people he portrays without succumbing to neurosis. In many ways he is an ideal actor. He has created believable characters without suffering unduly for his craft. He has enjoyed life and its pleasures without battering his liver into submission. He has had an exciting life and made it past his 80th birthday. And he still retains a good sense of humour. Roger Moore recently recalled, 'Someone's always asking me to do a eulogy. As Albert Finney, a very funny man, once said to me after he'd done two or three actor memorials, "You'd better get your name down. I'm getting booked up".'

Few actors are seen as being as professional as Finney and fewer still enjoy such respect and popularity among colleagues. Many fellow actors cite Finney as one of their favourite performers. And everyone I interviewed for this book mentioned him with warmth and affection. And for those who declined, if they cited a reason, it was that they were 'very fond of Albert' and did not want to co-operate on an unauthorised biography.

Rather like Harold in *Orphans*, it seems that Finney has given more than a little encouragement to those around him. He has certainly given a meta-phorical tweak of the shoulder to everyone in the profession. A strolling player, sometimes restless, but a mentor for many whose lives he has touched. He might not have been the new Olivier, but many young actors today would be flattered to be called the new Finney.

Not a bad old fellow ...

BIBLIOGRAPHY

Allen, William Rodney, *The Coen Brothers' Interviews* (University Press of Mississippi, 2006)

Anderson, Lindsay, *Lindsay Anderson Diaries* (Methuen Drama, 2006)

Bellingham, Lynda, *There's Something I've Been Dying to Tell You* (Coronet, 2014)

Biskind, Peter, *My Lunches with Orson: Conversations between Henry Jaglom and Orson Welles* (Picador USA, 2014)

Blakemore, Michael, *Stage Blood* (Faber & Faber, 2014)

Bowden, Ken, *Teeing Off* (Triumph Books, 2008)

Bowles, Peter, *Ask Me if I'm Happy: An Actor's Life* (Simon & Schuster, 2011)

Bricusse, Leslie, *The Music Man: The Autobiography of Leslie Bricusse* (Metro Books, London, 2006)

Burton, Tim, *Burton on Burton* (Faber & Faber, 2006)

Caldwell, Zoe, *I will be Cleopatra – An Actress's Journey* (WW Norton & Company, 2002)

Callow, Simon, *Charles Laughton – A Difficult Actor* (Vintage, 2012)

Cardullo, Bert, *Playing to the Camera: Film Actors Discuss their Craft* (Yale University Press, New Haven and London, 2009)

Colby, Paul, *The Bitter End: Hanging Out at America's Nightclub* (Cooper Square Press, 2002)

Coldstream, John, *Ever, Dirk: The Bogarde Letters* (Weidenfeld & Nicolson, 2008)

Courtenay, Tom, *Dear Tom* (Black Swan, 2001)

Curtis, Tony, *American Prince* (Virgin Books, 2009)

Davis, William B., *Where There's Smoke. Musings of a Cigarette-Smoking Man: A Memoir* (ECW Press, 2011)

Douglas, Kirk, *The Ragman's Son* (Simon & Schuster, 1988)

Ewbank, Tim and Stafford Hildred, *Joanna Lumley* (Andre Deutsch Ltd, 2010)

Eyre, Richard, *National Service: Diary of a Decade at the National Theatre* (Bloomsbury Publishing PLC, 2004)

Falk, Quentin, *Albert Finney in Character* (1992, Robson Books)

Ferguson, Alex, *Managing My Life: My Autobiography* (Hodder Paperbacks, 2000)

Ford, Peter, *Glenn Ford: A Life* (University of Wisconsin Press, 2011)

Gielgud, John, *Gielgud's Letters: John Gielgud in His Own Words.* (Weidenfeld & Nicolson, 2004)

Gussow, Mel, *Michael Gambon: A Life in Acting* (Nick Hern Books, 2005)

Hall, Peter, *Making an Exhibition of Myself* (Oberon Books, 2000)

Hudd, Roy, *A Fart in a Colander* (Michael O'Mara, 2010)

Imrie, Celia, *The Happy Hoofer* (Hodder Paperbacks, 2011)

Jacobi, Derek, *As Luck Would Have It* (HarperCollins, 2013)

Johnston, Sue, *Things I Couldn't Tell my Mother* (Ebury Press, 2012)

King, Denis, *Key Changes: A Musical Memoir* (CreateSpace Independent Publishing Platform, 2015)

Lowenstein, Stephen, *My First Movie* (Faber & Faber, 2000)

Mackintosh, Iain, *Architecture, Actor & Audience* (Routledge, 1993)

MacNeice, Louis, Selected *Letters of Louis MacNeice* by (Faber & Faber, 2010)

Mason, Marsha, *Journey: A Personal Odyssey* (Simon & Schuster, 2000)

Maxwell, Roy. *From Poorhouse to Penthouse and Back* (Lulu.com, 2010)

McCabe, Bob, *Ronnie Barker* (BBC Books, 2005)

Miller, Gabriel, *The Films of Martin Ritt: Fanfare for the Common Man* (University Press of Mississippi, 2000)

Müller, Jürgen, *Movies of the 1980s* (Taschen GmbH, 2002)

O'Mara, Kate, *Vamp Until Ready: A Life Laid Bare* (Robson Books Ltd, 2003)

Olivier, Tarquin, *My Father Laurence Olivier* (Headline Book Publishing, 1993)

Osborne, John, *Almost a Gentleman* (Faber & Faber, 2004)

Parkinson, Michael, *Parky: My Autobiography* (Hodder Paperbacks, 2009)

Purcell, Hugh, *The Nine Lives of John Freeman* (Biteback Publishing, 2015)

Roisman Cooper, Barbara, *Great Britons of Stage and Screen: In Conversation* by Barbara Roisman Cooper (Rowman & Littlefield Publishers, 2015)

Sassoon, Vidal, *Vidal: The Autobiography* (Macmillan, 2010)

Sellers, Robert, *Peter O'Toole: The Definitive Biography* (Sidgwick & Jackson Ltd, 2015)

Sellers, Robert, *What Fresh Lunacy Is This? A Biography of Oliver Reed* (Constable, 2013)

Shepherd Jack and Keith Dewhurst, *Impossible Plays: Adventures with the Cottesloe Company* (Methuen Drama, 2007)

Sherman, Eddie, *Frank, Sammy, Marlon & Me: Adventures in Paradise with the Celebrity Set* (Watermark Publishing, 2006)

Spada, James, *Julia: Her Life* (St Martin's Press, 2007)

Stierer, Jack, 'Serving Albert Finney', http://jackstierer.com/

Suchet, David, *Poirot and Me* (Headline, 2014)

Welsh, James M. and John C. Tibbetts, *The Cinema of Tony Richardson: Essays and Interviews* (State University of New York Press, 1999)

White, Carol, *Carol Comes Home* (New English Library Ltd, 1982)

Wilder, Gene, *Kiss Me Like A Stranger: My Search for Love and Art* (HarperCollins Entertainment, 2011)

Williams, Chris, (ed.), *The Richard Burton Diaries* (Yale University Press, 2013)

Winstone, Ray, *Young Winstone* (Canongate Books, 2015)

Winters, Shelley, *Shelley 2: The Middle of My Century* (Simon & Schuster, 1989)

Zucker, Carole, *In the Company of Actors: Reflections on the Craft of Acting* (Methuen Drama, 1999)

NOTES

Prologue

1   *Where There's Smoke. Musings of a Cigarette-Smoking Man: A Memoir* by William B. Davis.
2   A phrase originally used by Sir Ben Kingsley to describe Sir Richard Attenborough. But Michael Attenborough believes it applies equally to Finney.

Chapter 1

1   Finney's Salford, at least when he moved to Weaste, was a more comfortable and upmarket version than that depicted in Delaney's *A Taste of Honey*.
2   Robert Powell (born 1946) has said that Finney was always a great hero to him, 'Just down the road from me, as I grew up, was Albert Finney. He was a little bit older, but if ever I needed someone to look up to, follow and admire, then it would be Albert. My mother and his mother used to share the same hairdresser, and would swap notes about us, which was quite funny.'
3   An examination administered to some students in their last year of primary education, governing admission to various types of secondary school.
4   Finney and Harold Riley helped to set up the Eric Simm Award in 1978 in memory of their old headmaster who gained a reputation for encouraging young people in the dramatic and visual arts. Although Finney was never an academic high flyer, he was awarded an honorary degree by the University of Salford in 1979.
5   The Royal Academy of Dramatic Art was founded by Sir Herbert Beerbohm Tree (1852–1917) in 1904. His grandson was the actor Oliver Reed.
6   Richard Briers (1934–2013).
7   Bryan Pringle (1935–2002).
8   Virginia Maskell committed suicide in 1968.
9   *From Poorhouse to Penthouse and Back* by Roy Maxwell.
10 *In the Company of Actors: Reflections on the Craft of Acting* by Carole Zucker.
11 Interview with Sheridan Morley in *The Times*, February 1974.
12 *Ask Me if I'm Happy – An Actor's Life* by Peter Bowles (born 1936).
13 Brian Bedford (1935–2016) interview in *The Toronto Star* – 26 May 2007.
14 *Daily Mail*, 22 June 2008.
15 Interview with Frank Finlay (1926–2016) quoted in the *Sydney Morning Herald*, 9 November 1988.
16 *Dear Tom* by Tom Courtenay (born 1937).

17 The importance of this presentation, as a showcase of RADA talent, cannot be overstated. So much so that one student, Roy Maxwell, who was excluded from the final show after a disagreement with Fernald, believed that it hindered him: 'Fernald, the bastard, overruled the decisions of his tutorial staff, and maliciously excluded me from performing in the Public Show. I have no doubt that the cost to me, career-wise, was inestimable.' Richard Briers, on the other hand, always admired Fernald, and described him as the first person who saw potential in him.

18 *Playing to the Camera: Film Actors Discuss their Craft* by Bert Cardullo.

Chapter 2

1 In 1963, Finney came to Birmingham to see Derek Jacobi in *Henry VIII*. According to Jacobi, 'Afterwards Winnie Banks invited him and the cast back to the house. All of us sat round while this energetic young actor talked and talked about theatre and his life. It was so inspiring for he had all the coherence of successful talent. He had it all made and he was mesmeric.'

2 June Brown (born 1927) also saw Finney's Macbeth at the National Theatre in 1978, twenty years after their Birmingham production: 'I was thinking to myself, well, I don't know, Albie. Parts of it I liked better when you were 21.'

3 Interview with Mark Kingston (1934–2011) for British Library Theatre Archive Project, 31 March 2006.

4 Interview with Colin George (born 1929) for British Library Theatre Archive Project, 21 November 2005.

5 Pamela Howard interview with Kate Harris for Theatre Archive Project, 9 November 2005.

6 Laughton played Bligh so well that some naïve souls seemed a bit confused. My mother, a London tour guide, once pointed out Bligh's gravestone at St Mary's, Lambeth, to some American tourists. An elderly sightseer turned to his wife and said, in all seriousness, 'Ethel, that's where Charles Laughton is buried'. Nobody flinched.

Chapter 3

1 *Charles Laughton – A Difficult Actor* by Simon Callow.

2 Robeson, who had been accused of being a Communist and had had his passport seized by the authorities, had travelled to Russia in August 1959 – performing in Moscow to enthusiastic crowds – after his travel ban was revoked.

3 *I will be Cleopatra – An Actress's Journey* by Zoe Caldwell.

4 Peter Hall had already directed several plays at Stratford, including *Love's Labour's Lost* in 1956 and *Cymbeline* in 1957.

5 Priscilla Morgan, interview with the author, 28 January 2016.

6 Albert Finney in conversation with Clive Goodwin, 4 March 1962.

7 Albert Finney interview with *The Rockmart Journal*, 10 June 1992.

8 *In the Company of Actors – Reflections on the Art of Acting* by Eileen Atkins.

9 *My Father Laurence Olivier* by Tarquin Olivier.

10 Interview with Elijah Moshinsky in *The Saturday Paper*, 18 July 2015.

11 Sue Johnston – interview in the *Coventry Evening Telegraph*, 2001.

12 Understudies can indeed steal the show. The story goes that when Anthony Hopkins stepped in for Olivier in *Dance of Death* he was so good that Olivier, panicking that his own performance was being surpassed, forced himself out of bed.

13 *Letters of Louis MacNeice* by Louis MacNeice.

Chapter 4

1 Woodfall Films was a film production company set up by Tony Richardson, John Osborne and Harry Saltzman in the late fifties. Among its most famous films were *Look Back in Anger, Saturday Night and Sunday Morning, A Taste of Honey, Tom Jones* and *Kes.*

2 Albert Finney in a 1982 interview with Michael Billington.

3 The late Pete Postlethwaite (1946–2011), for example, said of Finney and Shirley Anne Field in the film, 'I realised, watching them, that you didn't have to be poncey to be an actor'.

4 Everyone agrees that *Saturday Night and Sunday Morning*, and Finney, were instrumental in the enormous sea change that followed. Take British actor Patrick Mower: 'I think Finney was responsible, along with the character Jimmy Porter in Osborne's *Look Back in Anger* at the Royal Court, for the change in style and approach of all British actors from that day to this.' From *Patrick Mower: My Story.*

5 Quoted in the *Nottingham Post*, 31 October 2012.

Chapter 5

1 Brian Viner recalled this anecdote in a letter to the *Independent* after Keith Waterhouse's death in 2009.

2 *Daily Mail*, 7 August 2009.

3 This was way off the mark. Jack Hawkins played Allenby and Omar Sharif played Ali.

4 Keith Waterhouse, writing in 2009, recalled the two actors' different approaches to the role. 'Albert Finney played the part for nine months before Tom Courtenay took over. It was fascinating to contrast their performances – Finney's extrovert "I am a star" Billy, Tom's introvert "I wish I were a star" Billy. Both interpretations were equally correct, for locked in Billy Fisher's tangled psyche are both characters, star and nonentity, battling it out.'

5 Finney and Courtenay's portrayal of Billy Fisher impressed not only British actors. Australian actor Terence Donovan (father of Jason) who subsequently played the part, remembered the play's impact: 'Finney and Tom Courtenay – they played it and I just adored what they did and I went to everything I could see for them because they were just measures of excellence, you know. And, of course, they came from a real working-class background and our business was not always like that. You always had to have a very polished voice, you know, or something like this, [Terence puts on a posh accent] and that's really bullshit [Terence laughs] and those guys came from working-class backgrounds and they were just blokes on the street showing they could cut the mustard and that's fantastic.' Interview with Terence Donovan, 2006.

6   *Almost a Gentleman* by John Osborne.
7   Quoted in *The Cinema of Tony Richardson: Essays and Interviews* by James M. Welsh and John C. Tibbetts.
8   *Parky:My Autobiography* by Michael Parkinson.

Chapter 6

1   Hugh Purcell in *The Nine Lives of John Freeman*: 'There were two weak interviews, with the actor Albert Finney and the playwright John Osborne. Freeman seemed unprepared and, for the first time, lacked drive and persistence. As a result the interviews fell flat.' Later, Freeman reportedly conceded that his new post as editor of *The New Statesman* had made him soften his adversarial approach. Ironically, Freeman was just as publicity shy as Finney. Purcell wrote to him asking for his co-operation in writing a biography, but Freeman politely refused. 'I wish everybody would forget I was alive,' he said, shortly before his death, aged 99, in 2014.
2   This was long before video cameras and mobile phones made life even harder for actors. And Finney's outburst seems restrained compared to, for example, George C. Scott, who once jumped off the stage and ran up the aisle to seize a camera off a theatregoer.
3   Actor Rodney Bewes puts Finney's dissatisfaction more crudely. He claims that Finney described the film, while making it, as nothing more than 'Richardson wanking through Dorset'.
4   Film versions were made in 1970 and 2003, starring Mick Jagger and Heath Ledger respectively.
5   Hard-drinking diminutive actor Michael Dunn (1934–73) won an Oscar nomination for *Ship of Fools*. He died in London while filming *The Abdication* with Peter Finch.
6   Coincidentally, Finney would also have been in New York, performing in *A Day in the Death of Joe Egg*, when Martin Luther King was assassinated on 6 June 1968.
7   *Shelley 2: The Middle of My Century* by Shelley Winters.
8   Interview with the *Daily Mail*, 29 December 2002.
9   *Glenn Ford: A Life* by Peter Ford.

Chapter 7

1   *New York Times* interview, 26 July 1981.
2   *Frank, Sammy, Marlon & Me: Adventures in Paradise with the Celebrity Set* by Eddie Sherman.
3   Annette Nancarrow, American painter (1907–92).
4   *The Films of Martin Ritt: Fanfare for the Common Man* by Gabriel Miller. The director of *The Molly Maguires*, Martin Ritt, had wanted Finney for the role of McParlan and Sean Connery for the part of Kehoe. Finney, however, declined. He said the film 'was full of promise' but he was 'unsure of what he wanted to do in the future'.
5   Early in 1964, Finney apparently sent his London agent Philip Pearman a postcard from Fiji in which he cited all the parts he had been offered and marked 'no' beside them all. Pearman, the husband of actress Coral Browne,

died in October of that year. Finney's subsequent agent was Laurence Evans (1912–2002) who also managed, among (many) others, Laurence Olivier, John Mills, Ralph Richardson, John Gielgud and Alec Guinness. Evans, speaking in 1990, said, 'Of all my clients, Albert is in the most demand. He gets one or two offers a week. Only Olivier surpassed this.' When Evans retired in 1993, Finney gave him a valedictory send-off at the Ivy restaurant.

6   *As Luck Would Have It* by Derek Jacobi.

7   *Where There's Smoke. Musings of a Cigarette-Smoking Man: A Memoir* by William B. Davis.

8   Gordon Smythe (1926–2004) saddled Charlottown, the winner of the 1966 Derby at Epsom, in his first season as a trainer.

9   Peter Shaffer (1926–2016). Finney, Simon Callow and Patrick Stewart were among the stars taking part in Chichester Festival Theatre's celebrations in 2014, to mark its long association with the playwright.

10 When Hopkins was interviewed on LBC radio, just before *Silence of the Lambs*, a caller rang in to say that she had once met the actor's parents. Hopkins replied, instantly, and with a note of contemptuous dismissal in his voice, 'Small world!'

11 *Playboy* interview with Laurence Grobel, 1994.

12 Charon subsequently directed a film version in 1968 with Rex Harrison and Rachel Roberts.

13 *Vidal: The Autobiography* by Vidal Sassoon.

Chapter 8

1   *American Prince* by Tony Curtis.

2   Quoted in *The Times*, 13 June 2015.

3   *The Bitter End: Hanging Out at America's Nightclub* by Paul Colby.

Chapter 9

1   Clive Goodwin (1932–78).

2   Billie Whitelaw (1932–2014) interview in the *Independent*, 2 June 1997.

3   George Best (1946–2005) interview with Sean O'Hagan in *The Observer*, 21 July 2002.

4   Blakely was a fine, underrated actor, and modest with it. I went backstage to see him during the run of *A Chorus of Disapproval* in the summer of 1986. He was already ill with leukemia. It was subsequently revealed that he was in such pain he had trouble standing. But he forced himself to run up and down the theatre aisle in character as the manic director Dafydd Ap Llewellyn in this hilarious play within a play. He died in May 1987.

5   *Vamp Until Ready: A Life Laid Bare* by Kate O'Mara.

6   *New York Times* interview, 26 July 1981.

7   Mike Leigh, a fellow Salfordian, wrote, 'Occasionally Finney turned up in his Range Rover with his stunt double bodyguard and tied up the location payphone making calls to his bookie. One day he brought his new wife. "This is Mrs Finney." It was Anouk Aimée. "Call her nookie," he said.'

8   Director Peter Medak said that Finney was the first choice for the film but did not want to play it again. He thought that Finney had been 'brilliant' in the play. Peter Nichols, interviewed in 2011 in the *Herald*, judged that Finney was

'too big' in performance terms for the part. He thought that Clive Owen, who
played Bri in 2001, was 'quite fantastic'.

9   Harold Clurman, *New York Magazine*, 29 April 1968.
10 *The Observer*, 1 May 2000.
11 Author's interview with Robert Sallin, 12 February 2016.
12 Douglas Hayward (1934–2008) was a tailor who dressed many famous stars in
    the sixties, including Peter Sellers, Terence Stamp and Richard Burton.

Chapter 10

1   Director Ronald Neame's version is lightly different, however: 'We were going
    to have Richard Harris. He was going to play the lead. And he had to go and
    make a film in Israel, I think. Something went wrong with it and he had to
    take it over, and he had to direct it. So we couldn't get him. The company
    who were financing the film said, well, if you can't get him, there are only
    two or three other names that are acceptable to us. One of those names was
    Finney – who turned it down. He said, "I don't want to make a film just now."
    So we thought, Rex, Rex Harrison. Rex could sort of play Scrooge. So we
    gave the script to Rex and he liked it very much and we cast him. But there
    was a problem. Because he was at the end of a play which he was working on
    in London. He had three weeks more to play. We had to start in two weeks,
    because of weather conditions, summer and winter scenes. So this three weeks
    was really a nuisance, but we had to face it. And then we decided we would
    pay the theatre off. We'd pay for the three weeks, and we'd get Rex earlier. And
    then one day, we had a phone call from Alby Finney, who said, on the phone,
    I have just read your screenplay, in my office, because my partner is playing a
    small part, and [he said] you know, I would love to play it. And we said, Oh,
    Alby, oh goodness me! We've cast Rex Harrison. And he said, Oh well, it's my
    fault, but I would have loved it. And we did a terrible thing. Slightly ashamed
    to tell you. We told Rex that we hadn't got the money to pay off the theatre,
    but we had to start shooting the following Monday. Rex didn't mind very
    much. And Alby played the part.'
2   *The Music Man: The Autobiography of Leslie Bricusse.*
3   Annabel Leventon interview with the author, 29 December 2015.
4   *My First Movie* by Stephen Lowenstein.
5   Maureen Lipman, interview with the author, 4 December 2015.
6   Carolyn Seymour interview with the author, 3 December 2015.

Chapter 11

1   Finney was filming *Looker* in California when he heard of Rachel Roberts's
    death. 'I was at the Bel Air Hotel, when I heard – David Lewin woke me with
    the news. I was appalled and shocked. If he hadn't indicated there was a strong
    possibility of suicide, I'd have suspected it was murder.'
2   Stephen Rea in the *Irish Times*, 2 October 2015.
3   *Poirot and Me* by David Suchet.
4   *Albert Finney in Character* by Quentin Falk.
5   Sidney Lumet interview in *The Times*, 19 March 1974.
6   *The Times* interview, 19 January 1974.

7   *Lindsay Anderson Diaries* by Lindsay Anderson (1923–94).
8   *Albert Finney in Character* by Quentin Falk.

Chapter 12

1   In a 1996 interview Finney appeared not to regret his decision to take over the stewardship of the National, noting that it was now impossible for an actor to run the place because of 'all those bloody meetings … like the National Health Service there are more people running these places than there used to be'.
2   Peter Hall diary entry from 2 July 1974, 'Albert Finney came to the Barbican flat this morning. An excellent meeting. He said he now felt ready to take on the big parts. He wants to try to examine a rougher, more instinctive form of classical acting. He would like to do *Tamburlaine* and *Hamlet*. It is five years too late for *Hamlet* but he wants to try. I think he must. *Tamburlaine* is perfect for him, and *Hamlet* must assuredly be entertaining.'
3   Quote from *Stage Blood* by Michael Blakemore.
4   *The Times* obituary of Nicol Williamson, 26 January 2012.
5   Jill Townsend, interview with the author, 12 December 2015.
6   According to Robert Gore-Langton, 'After "how all occasions do inform against me", he [Finney] would go off and have a Guinness, a smoke and a snooze before coming back on for the Gravedigger.' *Daily Telegraph*, 28 September 2010.
7   *Kiss Me Like A Stranger* by Gene Wilder.
8   *Carol Comes Home* by Carol White (1943–91).
9   Kenneth Hurren (1920–1993). This kind of acidic review with its false humility '… my modest requirement is …', a haymaker delivered by a velvet glove, does make one sit back and appreciate the resilience of actors like Finney who put themselves in the front line.
10   Many years later, Bernard Levin was one of Maurice Allington's – alias Finney's – guests in the BBC adaptation of Kingsley Amis's *The Green Man*.
11   *Gielgud's Letters*, John Gielgud in his own words.
12   Interview in the *New York Times*, 26 July 1981.
13   Quoted in *The Stage*, 30 April 2015.
14   *Young Winstone* by Ray Winstone.
15   Peter Hall diary entry from 19 January 1976.
16   *Making an Exhibition of Myself* by Peter Hall.
17   Brian Cox remembered the production as 'horrendous', if only because of the eight-month rehearsal period during which the opening of the Olivier Theatre was constantly being put back.
18   Hill Place. Interview with Cristina Raines, 2014.
19   *Key Changes: A Musical Memoir* by Denis King.
20   Interview with Albert Finney in *Times News, NC*, 4 August 1977.

Chapter 13

1   Tony Richardson, interviewed in 1977, thought that in Britain 'there's a ludicrous desire to see other people fail. Look at the treatment the press have recently given the National Theatre.'

2   Now renamed the Dorfman Theatre after philanthropist Lloyd Dorfman.

3   *Impossible Plays: Adventures with the Cottesloe Company* by Jack Shepherd and Keith Dewhurst.

4   Actress Susan Littler (1947–82) was just 34 when she died of cancer. On 24 October 1982, Finney hosted a special programme in Littler's memory at the National Theatre. Proceeds were donated to cancer research.

5   Amanda Waring – interview with the author, 8 January 2016.

6   Tom Bell obituary in the *Guardian*, 6 October 2006.

7   Letter to Polish-born photographer, Slawek, 25 May 1977.

8   Albert Finney in conversation with Peter Lewis. Quoted in *Architecture, Actor & Audience* by Iain Mackintosh.

9   1988 was Peter Hall's final year as Director of the National Theatre. His successors were Richard Eyre (1988–97), Trevor Nunn (1997–2003), Nicholas Hytner (2003–15) and Rufus Norris (2015–).

10   Review by Simon Callow of Michael Blakemore's *Stage Blood*.

11   Rivette made the same film twenty-seven years later with Emmanuelle Béart and Jerzy Radziwiłowicz.

Chapter 14

1   Interview in the *New York Times*, 26 July 1981.

2   Don Shewey interview with Gregory Hines in 1986.

3   Author's interview with John Quested, 8 January 2016.

Chapter 15

1   *Albert Finney in Character* by Quentin Falk.

2   Albert Finney interview, *Photoplay*, August 1982.

3   Alan Parker interview in *Photoplay*, August 1982.

4   Albert Finney interview, *Photoplay*, August 1982.

5   Quoted in the *New York Post*, 5 December 2010.

6   *Serving Albert Finney* by Jack Stierer, Executive Chef.

Chapter 16

1   *New York Times* interview, 26 July 1981.

2   'This Might Possibly be Albert Finney' – *Rolling Stone* profile by David Rosenthal, 24 June 1982.

3   Author's interview with Peter Allis, 4 January 2016.

4   *Teeing Off* by Ken Bowden.

5   Great actors are always astute observers and Finney is no exception. He once said in a 1964 interview, 'If somebody told me my best friend had died, a part of me would feel the pain. But the actor part of me would be watching and taking notes and saying, "So that's how it feels! Remember! You can use that in a performance".'

6   *Daily Mail*, 10 July 2012.

7   *Peter O'Toole: The Definitive Biography* by Robert Sellers.

8   Ronald Harwood Screenwriters' Lecture, 1990.

9   Peter Yates quoted in *Photoplay*, April 1984.

10 McKellen's Norman was slightly less prissy than Courtenay's. Hopkins could not quite convey the mental confusion that made Finney's portrayal so compelling.

11 *New York Times*, 4 December 1983.

12 Many actors interviewed for this book also cited Finney's performance in *The Dresser* as his greatest.

13 *Great Britons of Stage and Screen: In Conversation* by Barbara Roisman Cooper.

14 Peter Yates quoted in the *New York Times*, 4 December 1983.

15 Henry Jaglom reported these comments from Orson Welles when *The Dresser* was released, 'I have no intention of seeing it. I know it'll be good, and I know Finney will be great in it. That's why I won't see it. Why should I make myself sick? If I had any hope that it was bad, I'd go.' From *My Lunches with Orson: Conversations between Henry Jaglom and Orson Welles* by Peter Biskind.

16 'The Outrageous Confessions of an Upper-Class Lolita' – the *Daily Mail*, 12 March 2013.

17 Perhaps much of Pope John Paul's appeal can be attributed to his voice. When he visited London in 1982, I remember his voice resounding around Westminster when he gave an address outside the cathedral. Finney managed to capture the timbre perfectly.

Chapter 17

1 Malcolm Lowry (1909–57).

2 L.S. Lowry (1887–1976). One of Salford's most famous sons.

3 Richard Burton's diaries contain several references to *Under the Volcano*. For example, 1 December 1971, 'What I must really get after is *Under the Volcano*. That, if any film can be considered so, is an important piece.' *The Richard Burton Diaries*, edited by Chris Williams.

4 Quoted in *The Times*, 5 October 1983.

5 One of the funniest (presumably straight-faced) commentaries on Finney's performance is in the book *Movies of the 1980s* by Jürgen Müller. It says, 'For his depiction of the alcoholic Geoffrey Firmin in *Under the Volcano*, Finney spent a period of time drinking excessively, in order to register the physical and mental changes brought about by addiction.'

6 Jeannine Dominy interview with the author, 23 October 2015.

7 *The Times*, 5 October 1983.

8 Some people might have thought that Villiers was better placed to play the consul but I couldn't possibly comment. The funniest story involving Finney and Villiers is in Peter Bowles's autobiography. The occasion was Brook Williams's 21st birthday in 1959. A car containing various actors, including Villiers, Bowles, Williams, O'Toole and Finney, was pulled over by the police in London after some dodgy manoeuvres. Villiers explained the cause of the erratic driving to the policeman. 'We are very sorry, officer, but the fact of the matter is that whilst travelling in an easterly direction, Mr Albert Finney broke wind and, in the ensuing panic, which as you can imagine was quite considerable in such a confined space, Mr Brook Williams, in his endeavour to open a window, lost control immediately and struck an Austin.'

I once saw Villiers in a tube train at Victoria Station. I looked into the tube and saw him sitting by a window. He seemed pale, gaunt and lined. I was about to board the train when the doors closed. This was in 1997. He died several months later.

9 *Ever, Dirk: The Bogarde Letters*, edited by John Coldstream.

10 Michael Fitzgerald, quoted in the *New York Times*, 10 June 1984.

Chapter 18

1 This reminds me of Kirk Douglas's story, perhaps apocryphal, noted in his autobiography, *The Ragman's Son*, on casting for the movie *The Defiant Ones*, about two chained escaped prisoners, one white, the other black. According to Douglas, Robert Mitchum refused to act with a black guy and Marlon Brando would only agree IF he played the black man.

2 Lord Attenborough's 1965 letter to Finney, offering him the part of Gandhi, was one of many items auctioned by Bonham's in 2015.

3 Jon Blair interview with the author, 19 October 2015.

4 Finney has little record of political involvement. But, in 1975, he had led a delegation, which included Peggy Ashcroft and Clement Freud, to Downing Street to launch a petition against the imposition of VAT on theatre tickets. Labour Chancellor Denis Healey met them outside the door to Number 11.

In October 1976, Finney protested outside the South African Embassy, alongside Sheila Hancock, Eileen Atkins, Robert Morley, Kenneth Haigh and Kenneth Williams, to demand the release of Winston Ntshona and John Kani, two black South African actors known for their work in Britain, who had been detained in South Africa after their appearance in Athol Fugard's *Sizwe Banzi is Dead*. Equity, the actors' union, sent a telegram to John Vorster, the South African Prime Minister, asking him to order the immediate release of Kani and Ntshona, who were both Equity members. The two actors were subsequently released. (Ntshona and Kani later played roles in *The Wild Geese*.)

Fugard subsequently wrote to *The Times* to praise London's theatrical community. 'I do not have the slightest doubt that these protests secured the release of my two friends,' he said.

Chapter 19

1 Thirty years on and Hampstead Theatre has been revamped and has capacity for at least 400 theatregoers.

2 Author's interview with Michael Attenborough, 30 March 2016.

3 Lyle Kessler interview with the author, 22 October 2015.

4 Kevin Rigdon interview with the author, November 2015.

5 Nan Cibula-Jenkins interview with the author, 31 October 2015.

6 The movie version of *Orphans* did not rival the play's commercial success. It is described by *Brewer's Cinema* as 'one of Hollywood's worst ever flops, comparing budget to box office'.

7 Graham Benson interview with the author, 24 October 2015.

Chapter 20

1   The only other possible contender for the part, after Wilson's death, was actor Richard Jenkins. As Jenkins tells it, 'I auditioned for *Miller's Crossing*, and my agent called me up and said, "I've got great news, it's between you and Albert Finney." I said, "Oh really, that's great. Who would you choose?" And of course, Albert was wonderful in it.'

2   *The Coen Brothers' Interviews*, edited by William Rodney Allen.

3   Alex Simon interview with Gabriel Byrne in 2009.

4   Interview with Dennis Haskins on *Daily Actor*, 20 October 2009.

5   *Journey: A Personal Odyssey* by Marsha Mason.

6   Laurence Olivier once told Derek Jacobi, 'You've got to learn how to take the call as you gain a lot by doing a wonderful curtain call.'

Chapter 21

1   *Albert Finney in Character* by Quentin Falk.

2   Quote from theatregoer Dean Atkinson: 'When I was a student we went to see him [Finney] in *Reflected Glory*. We waited at the stage door for him and he spent so much time with us chatting and signing autographs.'

3   *A Patriot For Us* – John Heilpern's biography of John Osborne.

4   Osborne was known for his invective; by his standards this was a mild mauling.

5   Carolyn Seymour, interview with the author, 3 December 2015.

6   *LA Times* profile, 28 February 1993.

7   Mike Figgis, interview with the author, 1 October 2015.

8   Quoted in *The Ridley Scott Encyclopedia* by Laurence Raw.

Chapter 22

1   Suri Krishnamma, interview with the author, 16 December 2015.

2   *Just Representations* by Robert Gardner.

3   This was for *Nostromo*. But the series did not actually air until January 1997.

Chapter 23

1   *A Fart in a Colander: The Autobiography*, Roy Hudd.

2   The *Independent* profile of Finney by Terry Coleman, 26 January 1997.

3   Agnieszka Holland, interview with the author, 5 November 2015.

Chapter 24

1   The first choice to play Yvan was Michael Gambon but producer David Pugh said that Christopher Hampton, who adapted the play into English from the original French, took so long to finish – eighteen months in total – that they lost Gambon to a Broadway play.

British actors, to judge from the behind-the-scenes shenanigans that characterised the Broadway staging of *Art*, are still more down-to-earth and amenable. American producers wanted some starry players, at least ones to rival Finney and Courtenay, when the play opened in New York in 1998. Lengthy discussions revolved around the possibility of 'the big three' – Robert De Niro, Al Pacino and Harvey Keitel – leading the run. But, according to producer David Pugh, 'They wanted cars from the theatre. They'd only do six performances a week. They wanted seat prices to go to $100.' Compare this to Finney and Courtenay, who made no fancy demands and always insisted that Stott be paid the same as them, a relatively humble £3,000 a week. In the end, the Broadway production of *Art* opened with Alan Alda, Victor Garber and Alfred Molina.

2   Ken Stott interview in the *Guardian*, 9 February 1999.

3   *National Service: Diary of a Decade at the National Theatre* by Richard Eyre.

4   *Managing My Life: My Autobiography* by Alex Ferguson.

5   From Ken Wilson's blog, 14 August 2010.

6   Ken Wilson bumped into Finney again a couple of years later while walking in central London, 'And he recognised me from the night backstage and asked me what I was doing. (I was waiting for a co-author before a meeting at Macmillan's London office.) He asked what kind of writing and I explained about ELT course books. Albert was with two other people and they were clearly late for an appointment of some kind, but we talked for about five minutes – about writing books for English learners!!! Albert seemed really interested, and reluctant to stop talking (which he did the third time one of his colleagues said they had to go).

   'Maybe Albert is just polite (and a good actor) but what I like to think this conversation demonstrated is what many people have said before – Albert is a very down to earth, ordinary guy who isn't the least bit theatrical and precious about acting. He works hard at his job, tries to improve with every stage performance and film, but doesn't make a song and dance about it. Very Salford, in fact ...'

7   Finney first expressed his distaste for long runs on his *Face to Face* interview with John Freeman. He believed they were 'bad for an actor'. I was reminded of Richard Todd who starred in *The Business of Murder* for eight years in the eighties at London's Mayfair Theatre. Michael Aspel intercepted Todd on stage for *This is Your Life*, just post-performance. And Todd grimaced to the crowd in an expression just like the character he was portraying. It may, or may not, have been intentional, but for a moment it seemed that the actor had a confused identity.

8   *Joanna Lumley* by Tim Ewbank and Stafford Hildred.

Chapter 25

1   *Julia: Her Life* by James Spada.

2   Michael Harney interview with Joel Keller, A.V. Club, 22 June 2015.

3   The *Daily Telegraph* was wrong on both counts. Judi Dench lost to Marcia Gay Harden, Finney's co-star in *Miller's Crossing*, for her role in *Pollock*.

4   Significantly, Richard Burton, Peter O'Toole and Finney, probably in most people's Top 10 of great British actors, never won an Oscar despite having twenty nominations between them. (O'Toole, however, was given an honorary Oscar in 2003.)

5   *Michael Gambon: A Life in Acting* by Mel Gussow.

6   Soderbergh once made a pithy appraisal of *Tom Jones*, '*Tom Jones* is pleasurable every time you see it, but always in the same way. You have this historical film with crazy helicopter shots, speeded-up action, freeze-frame and actors looking at the camera.'

7   Finney attended the wedding in 2000 of Michael Douglas and Catherine
    Zeta-Jones. Guests were asked to make a donation to a new charitable
    foundation. Finney, who appeared with Douglas in *Traffic*, donated £1,057,
    according to documents from the US Internal Revenue Service. Michael
    Douglas said, 'Two of my favourite actors are Michael Caine and Albert
    Finney. They're two Brits who have mellowed like a fine wine and they are
    inspirational to me.'
8   *What Fresh Lunacy Is This? A biography of Oliver Reed* by Robert Sellers.
9   *Things I Couldn't Tell my Mother* by Sue Johnston.

Chapter 26

1   But Gambon would *not* disrobe for the part. Speaking of Finney's performance,
    he said, 'I remember Albert taking his clothes off and lying in the bath.
    I thought, I don't want to do that. Oh no.'
2   *Ronnie Barker* by Bob McCabe.
3   *The Happy Hoofer* by Celia Imrie.
4   *Radio 4 Today*, 4 November 2011.
5   *Burton on Burton* by Tim Burton.
6   Albert Finney interview with Paul Fischer.

Chapter 27

1   Interview with Ridley Scott in *IndieLondon*.
2   John Newton (1725–1807).
3   *There's Something I've Been Dying to Tell You* by Lynda Bellingham.
4   Finney was at Birmingham Rep on the day of the disaster, 6 February 1958.
5   Albert Finney interview in *The Times*, 5 February 2008.
6   At the premiere of *Quartet* in Toronto in 2012, Connolly, a keen football fan,
    joked about his attitude to the part. He then made a gaffe, 'I saw I found myself
    replacing Tom Finney and [bleeped] myself.'
7   *Daily Telegraph*, 25 January 2013.

Chapter 28

1   The Salford-born former star of *Doctor Who*. Eccleston has said of his
    background, 'There were lots of jokes about Albert Finney. He's my hero. I saw
    him once at an event and a journalist asked if I'd like to meet him, and I said,
    "Oh no." I was too overawed. Then later that day, I was pretty drunk and got
    a tap on my shoulder. It was Albert Finney, who joked I was from the posh
    part of Salford [Langworthy] and was lovely to me.' Perhaps it's no coincidence
    that Eccleston has a son named Albert. Eccleston has also said, in an interview
    with the *Salford Star*, 'Sir Ben Kingsley is doing a very unSalfordian thing at
    the moment by insisting people call him "Sir" ... Albert Finney famously
    turned down a knighthood and said "I would never call anyone 'Sir' myself and
    I certainly never expect anyone to call me 'Sir'"... and then you've got Ben
    Kingsley doing that ... very odd ... I'll have to check his Salford credentials.'
2   *Daily Mail*, 5 July 2010.
3   *The Guardian*, 30 June 2014.

4   Julian Fellowes recalls a conversation with Albert Finney, 'In the early eighties, I lived in Hollywood for a while and one night I went out for dinner and Albert Finney was there. At one stage, he turned to me and said, "I know your sort – you're the sort who has never been given a chance to show what you can do" … And he went on: "But if you've got it, they always find you." I left the restaurant absolutely haunted because I thought, he's quite right and what if that chance never comes?'

5   The most striking dates back to his time at Birmingham Rep when Finney attacked the Alexandra Theatre as 'middle-aged, musty and middle-class'.

6   Letter from Lindsay Anderson to Slavek, 21 September 1977.

7   *In the Company of Actors: Reflections on the Craft of Acting* by Carole Zucker.

8   *The Guardian*, 24 February 2015.

9   For example, read the article by Janice Turner in *The Times*, 16 January 2016.

10   Steven Berkoff in the *Daily Telegraph*, 21 October 2015.

11   Brian Cox interviews in *The Stage* and *Calibre* magazine, 2015.

12   In a BBC interview, in early 2016, Michael Caine noted the tendency for young actors to say they wanted to be 'rich and famous' whereas, according to Caine, he entered the business to be the best actor he could be.

13   In 2006, coinciding with Finney's 70th birthday, a London-based chain called Sausage and Mash Café set up a petition to get Finney awarded a lifetime achievement Oscar. Obviously it did not succeed. (Unlike the Academy Awards, on which Academy members vote as a whole, the honorary award is chosen by the Academy's board of governors.)

INDEX